very good book

DR. Safi ullah (M.D)
07-19-94.

MONEY
AND MIND

MONEY AND MIND

Edited by

Sheila Klebanow
and
Eugene L. Lowenkopf

PLENUM PRESS • NEW YORK AND LONDON

HG
222.3
M66
1991

ISBN 0-306-43915-8

© 1991 Plenum Press, New York
A Division of Plenum Publishing Corporation
233 Spring Street, New York, N.Y. 10013

Printed in the United States of America

For Marianne Horney Eckardt, M.D.
whose dedication to psychoanalysis,
academic freedom and scientific inquiry
has been an inspiration.

PREFACE

Money, like sex, has been essential to the rise and development of civilization. The first known writings were records of simple business transactions and later on money came to be used as a common denominator for all goods. Current dealings with money have become infinitely more complicated than at the beginning of recorded history but its basic meaning is the same, a medium underlying all goods and services, in which comparative values are measured and by which they are acquired.

Certainly, money is a vital and essential part of our everyday life. It is hard, if not impossible, to conceive of any of us going through a single day's series of experiences without using it or one of its symbolic equivalents: checks, credit cards, letters of credit, IOU's, scrip, food stamps or what have you.

Both of us have had a longstanding interest in money, in what it could and could not buy, in investing, spending and allocating. Our personal interest in money antedated our professional training and our career pathways for we were people first before we became people who were therapists. When we got together socially as friends and colleagues going back to medical school days, we often found that we discussed money matters in addition to other issues to which we had established strong commitments such as our families, our patients, politics and the arts. Perhaps it was because we were friends of such long duration that we could be so open about such an intimate topic as money.

When, three years ago, we started to organize a day-long symposium for the American Academy of Psychoanalysis examining various psychological aspects of money, we planned to review the literature on the subject. We expected to come across at least dozens of papers but found first to our relief and then to our dismay that our task was both much easier and much more difficult than we had anticipated. The relief was because there was so little library work to be done. Considering its importance, it is startling that money has gone almost unnoticed by psychoanalysts. Just as homo sapiens' existence and sexuality may be measured in terms of hundreds of thousands of years compared to money's appearance in only the last 5000 years or so, there have probably been thousands of psychoanalytic papers treating of sexuality in contrast to a bare handful on money. Our dismay was due to the realization that we were in the position of trailblazers investigating a major area of human behavior that had hardly been addressed by psychoanalytic writers.

We were at a loss to explain such a conspiracy of silence and found that any explanations for this silence that we could come up with were incomplete. Was money equivalent to feces, and interest in it (at this point, our faces were very red, indeed) indicative of a fixation at the anal level? Was it that we, as psychoanalysts, were too genteel to stoop to such mundane considerations? Or was psychoanalysis too ethereal and abstract to be bothered with something so concrete and substantial? Could it be the psychoanalysts shared with society a reluctance to talk about something that revealed too many hidden personal hopes and fears?

No one answer was fully satisfying, and we were tempted to fall into line with our psychoanalytic predecessors and drop the matter as unsuitable for examination. Yet, we really could not ignore it since virtually every one of our patients referred to it at some point in treatment, and some dwelt on it at great length. They were not all anal personalities, and their interest and involvement could not be dismissed as a mere fixation. These were real people dealing with real problems in their lives even when their personalities contributed to their problems with money. And, at this point, we realized yet another cause contributing to the neglect of money in psychoanalysis; it was no easy matter to separate out people's real problems with money from their neurotic distortions in relation to it, and there certainly were a full panoply of neurotic distortions.

Our one day meeting, in which eleven of the papers presented here were read, proved a great success but it left us feeling dissatisfied since too much had had to be omitted. We decided that a subject so important had to be gone into in greater depth, and that led us to the conclusion that we should expand those eleven papers into a book that would be more comprehensive and could explore more facets of the subject. Our hope was that we could persuade a group of distinguished authors to examine the issue of money in life and in therapy, and report how things stand today; how money affects people, how they deal with it and how it appears in psychotherapy.

Our instruction to our contributors was to examine some particular aspect of the money-mind relationship that appealed to them. We made no request that they follow the lines of any particular psychoanalytic approach. Indeed, in some instances, they departed from psychoanalysis altogether and dealt more in a psychodynamic mode or even in a general psychological or sociological examination of the topic. Since so little had been previously written, each author was in the position of staking out new territory.

As we reviewed the papers, we realized that they very naturally fit into two separate sections. The first we have chosen to call "Money and Life". Here the importance of money to the psyche is traced from childhood to old age, with consideration given to certain nodal points along this progression. For the most part, these papers do not treat of severe psychopathology but show how money is understood and used as people develop, mature, age and die. However, at times, money has truly pathological significance and the substance itself comes to have an exaggerated meaning to people. Here, its value exceeds anything that might be considered part of normal development and usage, although such distinctions remain always hard to define.

And the second section focusses on "Money in Therapy", how money appears and re-appears during treatment, and how it influences what goes on in the consultation room on both sides of the desk. This section also touches on money in the history of psychoanalysis and on the significance of changing patterns of payment on psychotherapeutic practice and technique.

We must confess that we feel there is yet more to be said about money and mind. It was our hope that, by presenting a collection of thought-provoking articles under one cover, we would stimulate interest in money as a psychological entity. This, we trusted, would lead to further thinking and further examination of this important psychological phenomenon. We are pleased with the high quality of all the papers, and we are also pleased that some of our contributors are continuing to delve into money from a psychological and psychodynamic standpoint. We hope that this book will encourage yet others to think about and publish further in this area. This introduction would not be complete without an expression of our very sincere appreciation of the efforts of Joan Breitenbucher and Ramona Otero, who worked far beyond the call of duty to help us get this book into presentable form. We also wish to note that all cases discussed throughout the book have been disguised in such a way as to make identification of patients impossible.

Sheila Klebanow, M.D.
Eugene L. Lowenkopf, M.D.

CONTRIBUTORS

Paul Chodoff, M.D. is Clinical Professor of Psychiatry, George Washington University, and Past President of the American Academy of Psychoanalysis.

Lawrence Cuzzi, D.S.W. is Director of the Department of Social Work Services at Elmhurst Hospital, Queens, N.Y. and Instructor at the Mt. Sinai School of Medicine.

Marvin G. Drellich, M.D. is Clinical Professor of Psychiatry at New York Medical College and is on the Faculty of the Division of Psychoanalytic Training there.

Richard C. Friedman, M.D. is Clinical Associate Professor of Psychiatry at the College of Physicians and Surgeons of Columbia University, Associate Attending at St. Luke's-Roosevelt Hospital Center and is on Faculty at the Columbia Psychoanalytic Clinic.

Robert E. Gould, M.D. is Clinical Professor of Psychiatry at New York Medical College, Attending at Metropolitan Hospital, Senior Psychiatric Consultant for the New York City Board of Education and Director of the New York Office of the National Coalition on Television Violence.

William J. Grace, Jr. is Vice President, Merrill Lynch in Washington, D.C.

Edward M. Hallowell, M.D. is Instructor in Psychiatry at Harvard Medical School and Director of Training in Child Psychiatry at the Massachusetts Mental Health Center.

Althea J. Horner, Ph.D. is Associate Clinical Professor of Psychology at U.C.L.A., Scientific Associate of the American Academy of Psychoanalysis and the author of *Object Relations and the Developing Ego in Therapy*.

Leonard I. Jacobson, Ph.D. is Professor of Psychology and Pediatrics at the University of Miami, Coral Gables, Florida.

xi

Sheila Klebanow, M.D. is Associate Clinical Professor of Psychiatry, and Training and Supervising Analyst in the Division of Psychoanalytic Training of New York Medical College.

Naomi Leiter, M.D. is Director of Medical Training at the Queens Children's Psychiatric Center, Assistant Clinical Professor of Psychiatry at the College of Physicians and Surgeons, and a Graduate Analyst of the William Alanson White Institute.

Joyce A. Lerner, C.S.W. is Director, Faculty Member and Supervisor at the Metropolitan Institue for Training in Psychoanalytic Psychotherapy, and is on the Faculty of the American Institute for Psychoanalysis, and Supervisor at the Karen Horney Clinic.

Eugene L. Lowenkopf, M.D. is Assistant Clinical Professor of Psychiatry, Mt. Sinai Medical School and Chief of the Mental Hygiene Clinic at Elmhurst Hospital, Queens, New York.

Mario Rendon, M.D. is Director, Department of Psychiatry, Lincoln Medical and Mental Health Center, Professor of Clinical Psychiatry at New York Medical College, Editor of The American Journal of Psychoanalysis, and Training and Supervising Analyst at the American Institute for Psychoanalysis.

Arnold Rothstein, M.D. is a member of the New York Psychoanalytic Society, Chairman of the Program Committee of the American Psychoanalytic Association, Founding Editor of the Workshop Series of the American Psychoanalytic Association and author of *The Narcissistic Pursuit of Perfection*.

Natalie Shainess, M.D. is on the Faculty of the Long Island Institute of Psychoanalysis, Fellow and former Trustee of the American Academy of Psychoanalysis, Fellow of the New York Academy of Medicine and author of *Sweet Suffering: Woman as Victim*.

Marianne L. Sussman, J.D. is Counsel to Marcus Rippa and Gould, White Plains, New York and currently is President of the Westchester Women's Bar Association.

Ann Ruth Turkel, M.D. is Assistant Clinical Professor of Psychiatry at Columbia University College of Physicians and Surgeons, Supervising Analyst and Psychotherapy Supervisor at the William Alanson White Institute, and Attending Psychiatrist at Roosevelt and St. Luke's Hospitals.

Silas L. Warner, M.D. recently retired. He was formerly Dean of the Philadelphia Academy of Psychoanalysis and Senior Psychiatrist at the Institute of Pennsylvania Hospital, as well as Psychiatric Consultant to Swarthmore and Haverford Colleges.

Josef Weissberg, M.D. is Associate Clinical Professor of Psychiatry at Columbia University, a Faculty Member of the Columbia University Psychoanalytic Center, and a Faculty Member of the New York Medical College Division of Psychoanalytic Education.

Miltiades L. Zaphiropoulos, M.D. is Director of Training, and Training and Supervising Analyst at the William Alanson White Psychoanalytic Institute, and Special Lecturer in Psychiatry at the College of Physicians and Surgeons of Columbia University.

CONTENTS

Part I - Money in Life

xv

Part I

MONEY IN LIFE

CHAPTER 1

HOW MUCH IS ENOUGH?
A PSYCHOLOGICAL OVERVIEW OF
MONEY AND THE MIDDLE CLASS

Sheila Klebanow M.D.

Tolstoy in one of his short stories posed the question, "How much land is enough for a man?" This issue is of great relevance for people in all economic strata in terms of assessing for each individual what is a sufficient amount of money to maintain a desired standard of living. Tolstoy answered his own question: "land enough in which to be buried". While philosophically this may be the ultimate answer, it does not address the issue of the importance of money in all parts of the life cycle and of what amount people would consider to be sufficient for the here and now and in trying to provide for the future.

Over the course of life, there are many times when an individual must ask "How much is enough?" These occur at normative phases of the life cycle – marriage, raising children, home ownership, retirement, etc., as well as during catastrophic events, such as major illness and accidents and loss of a job. These are issues which confront all people.

Often, when such matters come up during the course of psychotherapy, they are insufficiently addressed. Frequently, a therapist states that these are "reality" issues rather than "intrapsychic" and, as such, are not an appropriate topic for psychodynamic exploration. The therapist's own insufficiently understood and unanalyzed concerns about money may serve as a deterrent to an open discussion. How an individual decides to spend his or her financial resources has many determinants. Such decisions involve every fiber of the personality structure, self esteem, one's personal history, and ethical and moral values. They all impact upon any allocation of personal economic resources. Often old conflicts and issues will be reactivated and require a working through before the person is able to make an appropriate and non-neurotic choice.

Most people in the United States, when asked to identify themselves by economic position, place themselves in the middle class. In financial terms, this may translate into an income ranging from perhaps $25,000 for an individual to a joint income of $80,000 for a family. Being in the middle class should, but does not always, presuppose certain conditions: the ability to provide decent housing, food and clothing for oneself and one's family, the capacity to help finance a college education for one's children, the ability to

Money and Mind, Edited by S. Klebanow and
E.L. Lowenkopf, Plenum Press, New York, 1991

save some money for future use, including retirement, and to have some disposable income left over for a variety of recreational activities.

In reality, many people in the middle class live in what has been described as "hand to mouth prosperity". While many are able to maintain a comfortable lifestyle for themselves, they have minimal financial resources to cover an emergency situation. The saving rate in this country is very low compared to past saving rates and compared to current savings in Japan. Perhaps this reflects not so much a heightened consumerism, but the reality that it is costly to maintain all the parameters of a middle class lifestyle. Many people in the middle class live from paycheck to paycheck.

People react differently to the awareness that they will be all right financially only provided that they continue to work. Many accept this understanding with equanimity. For others, it is a cause for constant preoccupation and anxiety about money. It is a reality that for most, the loss of a job, prolonged unemployment, or a catastrophic illness can destroy financial and/or emotional well being.

It is important to differentiate between normative and catastrophic issues regarding the use of money. Catastrophic events include prolonged unemployment, the loss of expected investments and pension, business failure, loss of health insurance, and major accidents and chronic illness. All these can have a devastating emotional and financial impact upon an individual and his or her family. The loss of a job or a major illness can result in financial wipeout.

By contrast, there are normative, non-catastrophic events during the life cycle when people must confront the issue of how much is enough. There are always a myriad of intrapsychic and financial factors which come into play when an individual or a family decides how much is enough. These involve decisions where a person must consider needs and aspirations and temper them with the reality of what economic resources are at hand and how far they should or should not be stretched. There are many emotional factors which influence an individual to conclude how much money he or she needs for a particular life event, how much money he or she will strive for to attain that particular goal or series of goals and to what ends to go to achieve that goal.

Among the nodal events during the life cycle when an individual must confront the issue of how much is enough are the following:

> Getting married
> Saving for the home
> Having children
> Higher education
> Retirement
> Dealing with the other generation(s)

The financial impact of these nodal events is felt strongly by the middle class. People whose financial resources enable them to make choices about spending and savings may have a different perception about their economic decisions than do those who are either very wealthy or very poor. For example, those who are affluent may not be obliged to make either-or choices regarding money in the sense that financing their children's education will not be at the expense of their own vacations or of future retirement plans. By contrast, for many who live below the poverty line, home ownership, college education for their children or planning for an economically secure old age are elusive, never-to-be-realized goals.

GETTING MARRIED

Getting married is not only about love, sex, procreation and companionship. It is also about money. A variety of issues concerning money arise during courtship. Financial attitudes and aspirations may play a prominent role as a couple decides whether or not they want to try to spend the rest of their lives together.

Financial compatibility or incompatibility impacts upon the viability of a marriage. People with complementary financial styles agree more than they differ about how to spend and save. They are likely to be more harmonious than couples who are unable to concur. A variety of adaptations are complementary. For example, one couple may agree to handle money as co-equals. Another couple designates one spouse as the main financial decision maker. Yet other pairs may take turns paying bills and writing checks. When a couple has similar values about spending and saving money, their money styles are complementary.

When money styles clash, conflicts are greater. If one spouse is frugal and the other extravagant, or one financially sophisticated and the other uninformed, the stage is set for financial misunderstanding.

Many questions regarding money should be raised during courtship, both individually and jointly. One basic question concerns the belief that each party has enough money and the expectation that the person and his or her future spouse have the potential to earn an adequate amount of money. The answer to "how much is enough" is always individual and unique.

This query has many ramifications. If one spouse has a higher earning potential than the other, will that create difficulties for either? Will the spouse who earns more resent contributing more to the household or be unwilling to share financial decision making? Will the spouse with the smaller earnings be jealous, resentful or competitive?

How a couple agrees to share and allocate money has far ranging implications. Both parties may have widely disparate views about what constitutes sharing and mutuality. One may conclude, "What's mine is mine; what's yours is mine; what's ours is mine". The other thinks, "I earn so I can spend, you earn so I can spend; we earn so I can spend". Unless these beliefs are resolved, there can be endless quarrels about money and its power in the relationship.

Under optimal situations, each should understand his or her and the future spouse's spending and saving philosophy before they get married. Making the actual arrangements for the wedding affords the opportunity to many couples to examine, clarify and work through many of these issues.

If the pair is able to agree on the financial plans for the wedding, a major hurdle is overcome. Currently many couples make their own weddings, rather than have their parents pay. People are marrying somewhat later than earlier generations did. Many young women have significantly higher paying jobs than in previous years. Thus, many couples have the wherewithal to pay for their own weddings and prefer to exercise greater choice in making their own decisions.

The couple need to concur on important matters: how much to spend and how much each will contribute. If they disagree, how will they settle their differences? Perhaps one wants a lavish wedding and the other prefers to save for a down-payment on a home. One may be willing to go into debt to pay for a large wedding and the other wants a less costly reception and to remain debt free. How a couple achieve a compromise on these matters has prognostic importance for the future of their marriage.

If, in keeping with a more traditional pattern, the parents pay for the wedding, there are many decisions to be made. A basic one is whether the parents will make the wedding to please themselves or the bridal couple. There are many variants on this theme. One couple requests a small wedding and a cash gift towards a down-payment on a home. The parents prefer to impress relatives and friends with a lavish affair. In another variation, the parents prefer to give cash, but the couple requests a large wedding. The family of one prospective spouse may pressure for a large wedding and the family of the other for a small one. Both sets of parents may disagree about the costs that each is willing to bear. In some forms of intergenerational conflict, the bridal couple may believe that one or both sets of parents are stingy and uncaring and should provide a more costly wedding and/or a larger cash gift as a proof of their love.

SAVING FOR THE HOME

Perhaps no financial issue in the life cycle is more emotionally charged than home purchase. It has been a given of American middle class society that people prefer to own their residence rather than rent. For many, home ownership connotes solidity, stability, self-esteem, putting down roots, and making a commitment to oneself, or to marriage and family. Often it represents psychological enfranchisement and being an adult.

Buying the first house is of especial concern both to individuals and to couples in their 20's and 30's. Historically, home ownership previously was an issue only for married couples, but in contemporary society, many single people, as well, have the goal of owning. Apart from psychological factors, it generally makes good financial sense to own, so as to build up equity and to derive favorable tax consequences. It is everyone's favorite investment.

Many couples enter marriage with the stated agenda of saving up to buy a home. But the problems may begin there, as well. There may be a hidden agenda that is not put on the table. Optimally, both parties agree on the mutually desired goal and on the spending and saving philosophy designed to implement that goal.

Often, one spouse has a stronger commitment to the agenda. While the home traditionally has been seen as the woman's domain, the enhanced status and prestige of owning a residence seems to accrue more to the man, even among dual income couples.

Discordant agendas may present with variety of forms. Although both spouses presumably agree on the goal of home ownership and to a schedule of savings toward that goal, one spouse may have reservations. This may take the form of complaining that too little money is allocated for current activities such as more frequent vacations, dining out often or buying more clothes.

Perhaps the complaint may come from a wife who earns less than her husband. She may be envious of his greater earning power and she ambivalently shares the husband's belief that, since he makes more money, he is entitled to make the financial decisions unilaterally. In another variant, one spouse may want to save for a $150,000 house while the other wants a residence costing $200,000 or more. They may have very different answers to "how much is enough", to how much they are willing to sacrifice and save based on different considerations of power, status and prestige.

When a couple has difficulties in agreeing on the desirability of buying and saving, this may signal ambivalence about the viability of the marriage on the part of one or both partners. Perhaps there is an underlying assumption that the couple who pays together stays together. Thus one spouse may doubt the future of the relationship and is unwilling to make the financial sacrifice entailed in home purchase. The other may push to buy as a way of binding the mate or may hope that owning a home together will help them to work out their marital problems.

One spouse may see the house or condo as a burden inflicted by the other. For example, a woman who does not feel ready to have children and who views home ownership as the last step before starting a family, may procrastinate about buying. Similarly, a man who is equally ambivalent about having children may want to defer home ownership. Such a dynamic may tie in with issues of how much money to spend. If home ownership can be deferred and made more costly, decisions about having children can be put on hold.

Since home ownership is so expensive, many young individuals and couples cannot afford to buy unless they receive financial assistance for the down-payment from their parents. This raises a myriad of dilemmas. How much will the parents be able to control as the *quid pro quo* of their contribution? In the case of a couple, what if only one set of parents is willing or able to contribute? How will each spouse react to such a situation? Frequently, the spouse with the parents who contributed will denigrate the other set of parents and the hapless mate as well. When the couple quarrels, one may accuse the other of not caring enough about the marriage, otherwise he or she would have persuaded the other set of parents to contribute. Often this allegation contradicts financial reality.

Chronic marital and individual discord may develop when people are unable to agree on the goal of home ownership or to achieve that aspiration. If a couple concurs, but are unable to realize their goal, each spouse is likely to accuse the other of not living up to their contract, of being a poor provider, of being insensitive to the other's needs, of lacking the financial "smarts" to buy, rather than wasting so much money for so many years in renting rather than in owning.

The inability to buy rather than rent may become the focus of all individual and marital difficulties. It may represent all the broken dreams and promises that have gone awry during the life cycle.

STARTING A FAMILY

At some point, before or after home purchase, couples may consider starting a family. This decision has many financial ramifications. Often, it entails a decision for the wife to stop working, at least temporarily, while the children are very young. It generally involves the decision to live on one salary, instead of two, for a varying length of time.

A couple often will take a hard look at what changes they are willing to make in their lifestyle for the sake of having children. Invariably, for the middle class, having children will require financial adjustments. Frequently, the home or condo is acquired first, since many young middle class couples view it as more financially feasible to start a family after the hurdle of home purchase has been completed. Many think that, if they have children first, home ownership will be an impossible goal.

How soon the mother will return to the workplace is problematic. Many women would not return to work until their children are well along in school if they and their husbands believed that they could live on only one salary. Another equally difficult solution is for the man to take on a second or third job so that his wife can remain at home to care for their children.

So the financial conundrum continues: a dual income couple requires both salaries to maintain themselves and their children. They have to make a variety of childcare arrangements, work full-time, maintain a home and raise their children all at the same time. Both parents have two full jobs – the salaried one and the task of looking after children and home.

Many planning a family take into consideration how many children – one, two, three or more – they think that they will be able to afford to send to college.

HIGHER EDUCATION

Being in the middle class presupposes the expectation that one's children will go to college with parental financial assistance. This is frequently more easily said than done. For many families, providing the children with a higher education is difficult and anxiety-provoking. Unless people have been foresighted and fortunate enough to have started saving for education while their children were infants, the approach of the college years can be full of dread.

For many it is a major financial sacrifice to send children not only to a costly private university but to a low-cost state college as well.

There are many "creative" solutions, all of which can be draining both financially and emotionally. One parent or both may work a second job and may attempt to find other sources of aid. These might take the form of loans or gifts from grandparents, uncles, aunts, friends, unions, and employers. The children might apply for scholarships, grants and other financial assistance.

All of these courses have many ramifications both for parents and their children. For many to be beholden to relatives, friends, employers, etc., may leave them open to unwelcome influence and criticism. Someone who has borrowed from an employer may be locked into an uncomfortable work situation until the debt is paid.

The factors that go into the decision about money for education are almost endless. Should parents opt for an expensive and prestigious college, for example? They would increase their own (and their children's) indebtedness with the expectation that such an education would provide greater career and social opportunities. Will all the children be accorded the same educational opportunity? Will the oldest, or the sons, or the brightest receive the more prestigious education while the youngest, or the daughters or the less bright be offered only a state or municipal college?

How much debt can parents emotionally tolerate for themselves and for their children? Often parents need to temper their own needs with those of their children. Should they finance a more modest college education for their children so as to enable themselves to retire from work earlier rather than later and with a larger nest egg? If they finance a less costly education now would they be able to leave a larger inheritance later on? Should they send their children only to "The Best" (most expensive) schools at all cost with the belief that this is the real key to future success? These are all dilemmas which must be confronted.

The impact on the children is equally significant. In a family where education has been provided unequally there are many ramifications. The sibling who has received the more prestigious or costly education may suffer from a form of survivor guilt. He or she may believe that this so-called superior education has been at the expense of the siblings, while the brothers and sisters may be resentful of the favored one. The parents may be recipients of much anger that they did not "sacrifice" enough to provide better or more equitably for their children.

Many young people are in debt when they complete college or graduate/professional training. It is a burden, both financially and emotionally to embark on a career while being from $10,000 to $50,000 or more in debt. Such a person may believe that he or she is a less desirable marriage partner on account of the debt. The spouse or future spouse (especially if he or she is lucky enough not to have outstanding loans) may resent the other's allocation of earnings to pay off education loans rather than for joint expenses and goals.

Often, the presence of outstanding education loans will affect the decision to purchase a home or to have children and such decisions will be deferred. It is even more difficult to finance a home purchase and to start a family when there are still college loans to pay off. To be simultaneously paying off one's own educational loans and starting early savings for one's children's college is commonplace. It can feel like an economic treadmill, an emotional never-never land.

RETIREMENT

There is always an admixture of psychological and financial factors which influence planning for retirement. For many, retirement is a well-deserved and hard-earned reward for years of productivity in the workplace. It is a time to enjoy new found leisure, to seek new and interesting activities. It is a time for hobbies, to travel, perhaps a time to take on a second career. For others, it represents a time to endure: it is full of dread, of inevitable loss and of a constriction of interests and activities. For still others, retirement represents something in-between.

How an individual plans for retirement generally correlates with how he or she views that stage in life. Someone who looks forward to retirement rather than dreading it is apt to make more proactive and constructive plans. Financial considerations are enormous factors. A person, for example, who has been able to save for retirement, who has a pension which will enable him or her to maintain a comparable standard of living past retirement may have considerably less apprehension and anxiety than one who is less well off.

Many issues of self-esteem and psychological self-worth must be confronted in retirement planning. So much of one's identity is interwoven with the work that one does. This is a time when many reflect upon what kind of person he or she is apart from work and upon one's identity outside of work.

There are psychological factors which interfere with the ability to learn to live one's retirement in a realistic manner. Many people have a lifelong preoccupation with not having enough money for old age. That concern may become a guiding principle throughout the life cycle. Decisions and behaviors hinge on this concern: a need to save always, to defer current expense and enjoyment if these cost money, an impulse to calculate frequently what one's pension, social security and investments are worth currently or at the projected time of retirement.

Such people always ask, "How much is enough?" Earlier in life, they may have bought a less costly house or sent their children to less expensive colleges. They are likely to grow more frugal as they age. Having enough money becomes a defense against the inevitability of death: "if I have enough money, I won't die." This becomes their *leitmotif.*

Many in middle-class America are fortunate enough to retire with enough money to maintain a comfortable lifestyle. Others make adaptations which contradict their financial reality. There is a wide spectrum of maladaptive behavior. This ranges from minor inconveniences such as shopping only where a senior citizen discount is offered, to a man refusing to buy a needed new car or a woman depriving herself the luxury of a new coat. In its most extreme form, this concern will have a deleterious effect on the quality of life.

Frequently an older individual faces wrenching decisions about health care for one's self or spouse. It is problematic when an individual with a *substantial* income will forgo much needed private duty nurses after surgery out of the desire to continue to save for old age. Or a spouse who is guaranteed a pension for life, and who has other assets as well, will elect to place the other – and ailing – spouse in a nursing home rather than pay for home care because the latter costs too much money. These dilemmas represent core issues about love of self, others and money.

In contrast to such individuals are the agonizing quandaries of those who, having worked all their lives, find that in retirement they do not have the means to provide for themselves should a health catastrophe and/or inflation overtake them. Their options are limited. They can try to make further economies in their standard of living. Often they eat an inadequate diet, buy no necessary clothing, and forgo needed medical care. If their adult offspring are able to provide financial assistance, they are more fortunate. Otherwise they can go on welfare. All these options are accompanied by a loss in self-esteem.

A related dilemma in retirement involves the need to weigh one's current and future financial requirements vis-a-vis the current needs of a sick spouse. If the couple spends all their savings on the medical and nursing care of the sick or dying spouse, what resources will be available to the surviving spouse?

The timing of retirement has many antecedents. For example, a workaholic may dread the loss of structure, prestige and power associated with work. Apart from the loss of income, he or she may fear the prospect of finding other constructive and interesting things to do. A spouse who wants to continue to work may resent the other's decision to retire. A non-working spouse may worry that the spouse who is about to retire will make inordinate demands to spend time with the other. The couple may disagree about what represents adequate retirement income.

A significant number of people opt for early retirement. Frequently they conclude that no matter how much they enjoy work, it no longer makes financial sense to do so. For example, an individual whose pension pays 80-90% of current salary, may decide that it is time to retire. He or she concludes that it is possible either to live on less money or to work part-time to make up the difference. Often such people are optimistic, have strong interests outside of work and have an emotionally supportive spouse, family and circle of friends.

On the other end of the spectrum are people who choose to continue to work or resume work after they retire. Many enjoy work too much to stop whether or not they can afford to. Some find that they cannot manage on their pension and social security alone. Others realize that working part-time gives an added zest and structure to life as well as providing a supplemental income.

DEALING WITH THE OTHER GENERATION(S)

As life expectancy has increased, it is ironic that many people nearing retirement or who are actually retired must confront the issue of caring for an elderly parent. Perhaps the parent or parents have been able to live independently before but now require constant care, either at home or in a nursing home. Who is going to pay? And at what psychological cost?

If the second generation offspring, now perhaps in their fifties or sixties, have to spend savings on the parent, will enough money be left over for their own old age? The person may have looked forward during all his or her working years to the pursuit of leisure activities during retirement.

How will (generally) a daughter or a daughter-in-law, rather than a son or son-in-law, feel about tending to the parent? Invariably, her own children are grown, educated, out of the home and settled down. Such a woman is likely to resent the physical drudgery of nurturing her original (or her husband's) nurturers. Both the woman and her husband will feel weighed down by the financial burden and psychological resentment of caring for the parents.

How does one balance one's needs with those of one's elderly parents? If the elderly require costly medical and nursing care, how will this be financed? Do they have sufficient funds to cover their own expenses? Will they need to go on welfare? Will they continue to live in their own homes, with an offspring, or in a nursing home?

Invariably, such situations will revive old, perhaps long dormant, conflicts between parents and the now middle-aged offspring. Old issues of separation, individuation, nurturance, rivalry, ambivalence, or putting one's needs before others, or other's needs before one's own, will come up and have to be reexamined by the person in terms of the realities of the here and now.

The second generation is forced to deal with issues of financial security and the meaning of inheritance. If the elderly go through all their assets, the second generation will lose their anticipated inheritance. Perhaps in the past for estate planning purposes the elderly had given away some of their assets to their offspring. Does it follow that the offspring have an obligation to spend their parents' money and then live with the guilt over declining to pay for appropriate care? Some rationalize that their parents intended for them to have the money in the first place. Others use massive denial for withholding the necessary money for appropriate care. For example, an elderly man, hitherto self-sufficient, has Alzheimer's disease and can no longer live alone. His offspring are broken-hearted, but convince themselves that he is still able to manage. This way they can try to preserve his assets for their own use.

Analogously, the second generation must confront its feelings about passing on money to children and grandchildren. Generally speaking, in the middle class, there is only a limited amount of money to be passed on. If more is spent during one's lifetime, there is less to bequeath to others.

People hold differing attitudes about inheritance. Some believe that, having toiled all their lives, money is meant to be spent and enjoyed by themselves without regard to the wishes and needs of the succeeding generation. The bumper sticker which proclaims: "I'm spending my kids' inheritance" expresses this idea. Perhaps such people have put their offspring through college and have seen them settle down. Now they feel is the time to put their own needs first; perhaps to travel, to move to a warmer climate or to enjoy expensive hobbies. If there is anything left over to leave to their children, it is great, but it is not their primary goal.

On the other end of the spectrum are individuals who believe that their money has no value unless it is passed on in its entirety to their heirs. Such people, as they age, may be extremely self-denying. Immortality is equated with leaving everything to their beneficiaries. This way they will live on by providing for the material needs of children and grandchildren. In its most extreme form, such people forego better food, new clothes and deny themselves recreational activities. This is done, not so much out of the fear that they will run out of money in old age, but out of the desire to live on through their money.

Still other people have a more balanced perspective. They weigh their own needs to spend and to enjoy the money that they have worked for all their lives and temper these needs with their desire to assist the younger generation. Considerations of self-esteem influence these decisions. An individual genuinely must like himself or herself in order to find an appropriate balance of the needs of self and others.

The issue of how to allocate assets to one's heirs can be thorny. Should all the children and grandchildren be treated equally? That has many ramifications. If one offspring is considerably wealthier, should he or she receive less of the estate than the less well-to-do siblings? One child may have a chronic disease or disability with anticipated large medical expenses. Another offspring may have five or six children, while the others have one or two each. Should these differences be taken into account when one is dividing up an estate?

Decisions regarding the use of money during the life cycle are complex and multi-determined. Many factors – psychological and realistic – influence the choices that must be made at critical points. Perhaps, ultimately, there are more questions than answers.

CHAPTER 2

MONEY STYLES

Edward M. Hallowell, M.D.
and
William J. Grace, Jr.

What little has been written in the psychiatric and psychoanalytic literature on dealings with money has tended to focus either on obsessive-compulsive dynamics, where money becomes a tool of control, or on extreme pathology, as seen in ruinous overspending during periods of mania or pathological gambling. Relatively little has been written about the styles we all have in dealing with money, and how these styles reflect our psychic makeup in general. That a topic of such everyday emotional importance should receive so little attention suggests that it may be as taboo as sexual topics were decades ago. Indeed, in most consulting rooms today, the details of a sexual history are easily elicited while the patient remains testily guarded around financial affairs.

In this chapter, we will offer an overview of various money styles in an effort to illustrate what a wide range of psychodynamics they encompass. Our classification is, by no means, exhaustive; rather, it attempts to present a way of thinking about money in clinical terms that can be amended according to one's experience.

We begin with the premise that money has emotional meaning. It has a psychic currency, so to speak, that varies from person to person according to temperament and life experience. Most people surround their feelings about money with so much anxiety that they are unable to focus on the topic long enough and calmly enough to discover its various disguised meanings. Instead, they dismiss serious consideration with a humorous, albeit simplistic, remark like, "I wish I had more."

The meaning of money is by no means static or readily apparent, and certainly cannot automatically be linked to any one developmental period. Rather, it is a meaning in dynamic flux, evolving over a lifetime. The emotional meaning of money to any one person may have roots that twist and turn through the past and the unconscious as circuitously and mysteriously as any other deeply felt issue, and getting at those roots may require abundant

Money and Mind, Edited by S. Klebanow and
E.L. Lowenkopf, Plenum Press, New York, 1991

patience and imagination. Most people have a rich and complex set of associations to money, full of displaced meaning, rife with the most intense affects, and guarded by a host of dogged defenses.

In gaining access to this vein of psychic material, there is much fool's gold along the way, because, to put it bluntly, we all lie about money. However, if we observe behavior over time, we can usually see a pattern emerge, a characteristic style of dealing with money that reflects the emotional meaning(s) money has to the individual. This money style, once identified, can become a most profitable source for further investigation.

As dynamic and changeable as these styles may be, as surrounded by subterfuge and confounded by contradiction and ambivalence, certain trends persist in most people's lives sufficiently so to be gathered into a system of classification. The system we have developed is based upon the predominant emotional meaning(s) of money to the individual, and how these meanings translate into behavior. The system was developed for a popular audience and therefore the terminology, in the main, skirts the nomenclature of psychiatric diagnosis. We speak of a hustler, rather than a phallic personality, for example, or an Icarus rather than a narcissist, or a dodger rather than an hysteric. The links to more formal terminology should be clear, however.

OVERVIEW OF MONEY STYLES

	Style	Meanings of Money
The Enthusiasts:	The Jock The Hustler The Icarus	Power, Freedom Self-esteem
The Spenders:	The Gambler The Optimist The Manic The Overspender	Action, Freedom
The Underinvolved:	The Victim The Dodger The Depressive	Anxiety, Dependency
The Skeptics:	The Pessimist The Worrier The Miser	Security, Control

THE ENTHUSIASTS

The enthusiasts are the least ambivalent in their love of money, the most aggressive in getting it, and the least guilty in having it. The predominant meanings of money to this group are power, freedom, and self-esteem. For them, money is the ultimate scorecard and the final court of appeals.

The jock, as his name implies, applies the values of team sports to his dealings with money. He gets "up" for the game, each day starting with a psyche session where he whips himself into the proper frame of mind for the day's game. He works for himself, but also with a team. He loves the camaraderie of the group effort, and he gives his all to put points—dollars—on the board. The role of his coach is crucial. This figure—it may be his boss or an internalized gung-ho figure from his past—drives him on to ever greater scores. Emblemized by the late Green Bay Packer coach, Vince Lombardi, the coach dogs the jock at every turn to score more, make more, for the greater glory of the team. The jock lives to please the coach, and he is terrified of letting him down. This daily psychological drama can last a lifetime. It really has nothing to do with money, anymore than football has to do with points, but a great many dollars spew out of the collisions along the way. Always mindful of the coach and of the team, the jock will work until he drops.

Meeting these people in everyday life one is often surprised at how little they enjoy or use their money. They often own modest homes, take short vacations, and have simple habits. Their families often feel neglected. This is because enjoying the money is not the goal. Spending money for pleasure is like taking points off the scoreboard. The goal is running up the score forevermore.

The hustler is similar to the jock except that he is a lone ranger. He does not care about the team. He prefers to go it on his own. Independent and entrepreneurial, the hustler wants to make it for himself, not for some coach on the sidelines. In extreme forms, the hustler can become an Icarus. Like the figure from Greek mythology who flew too close to the sun, the Icarus is not content with flying above the rest. He wants to prove there are no limits to his power. Like Ivan Boesky, he disregards caution, breaks the rules, and, often, falls. Although this drama can be played on many stages, the financial stage is a favorite. Since money is countable, the Icarus can know just how high to fly to be the best. Like the jock, he uses money not to make tangible purchases, but to purchase self-esteem

The enthusiasts' hard-driving money style usually profits in the capitalist system. Dissatisfactions in their lives usually result not from financial frustrations, but from the inevitable interpersonal difficulties such a money style creates. This is because the enthusiasts often displace their need for intimate human contact onto the drive to profit, to make more money. The sphere of the marketplace, with its approval of aggression and competition, allows for the restriction of one's softer side.

In their most adaptive forms, the enthusiasts' money styles are rugged, hardy, and very much in the American grain. Problems arise when the drive for money crowds out everything else.

THE SPENDERS

The spenders, who include all of us at one time or another, comprise the most fun-loving money styles. The predominant meanings money takes on for the spenders are action and freedom. Action, a term taken from the gambler's lexicon, refers to the heady feeling of having a bet down, a deal in the making, a stock in flux. It is all nerves and tingles, not any single emotion, but rather a surge of pre-emotion created by the autonomic nervous system. While spenders may be enjoying the freedom money seems to provide as one spends it, they also may be seeking action as a means of avoiding certain other more painful states.

The Optimist: This most adaptive style of the spenders' group treats money with buoyant positivism. Not in need of action, the optimist simply wants, and expects, that there will always be enough. His optimism allows him to invest aggressively, take risks, and weather bad periods without despair. Whether his optimism is the result of genetic temperament, good parenting, or good luck, it is durable and usually adaptive. Problems arise when the optimism includes too much denial. Some people, when it comes to money, simply will not hear any bad news. Good money may be thrown after bad until it is all thrown away. The optimist believes his will alone can reverse fortune, and as often as this may be true, sometimes it is not. If the optimist cannot hear of problems, if he simply cannot bear financial dysphoria but must instantly reverse it through denial, he sets himself up for disaster. Sometimes the magical thinking of the extreme optimist (or pessimist, for that matter) defends against helpless feelings. Sometimes it is a learned behavior, like a superstition. Sometimes it may be the prodrome of a more severe problem, such as mania.

When not rooted solely in denial, the optimist's money style can ride the wings of positive thinking past the inhibiting anxiety money creates in so many of us.

The Overspender: We are a country of overspenders, taught from an early age that living with debt is not only possible, but necessary. Although most people spend more than they have at times, the overspender does so chronically. He bounces back and forth between the euphoric state of I-do-have-enough, where he makes most of his purchases, and the dysphoric state of I-do-not-have-enough, where he attempts to curb his spending behavior. It is a cyclical pattern. The overspender, in the despondent state of deprivation, turns to the quick fix of spending, made easy by credit. In this new state, money is spent, which induces the guilt and fear that sends the overspender back to the dysphoric state. Mood states are regulating money, rather than reason.

To some degree, this cycle describes the money style of virtually every American, and it explains in part why saving is so difficult for most people. We are treating feelings, often, when we spend rather than save. We are assuaging old pains or deprivations by spending, rather than bolstering a sense of security by saving. Put differently, it can be argued that the overspender is recreating in his financial life a mild, chronic sense of loss or failure he feels in his emotional life. How common it is to treat depression through spending, only to discover that the depression becomes accentuated. The pattern is so common that it practically defines our national money style, with the opposing poles of the cycle represented by "liberal" and "conservative" economists.

In its adaptive form, the overspender's money style takes advantage of the opportunities created by credit. But in its more self-destructive form, this money style, the financial hallmark of the baby-boom generation, postpones independence, and in its search for freedom, creates a kind of financial slavery and dependence upon financial institutions. And, at a national level, we are currently seeing such potential slavery and dependence.

The Gambler: The money style of the gambler covers a spectrum from the adaptive to the pathological. The unifying theme is the emotional meaning of money as action. In the adaptive form the gambler can tolerate action in order to profit; in the pathological form the gambler must have action seemingly in order to survive.

Action itself is one of the most intriguing emotional meanings of money. Action may be described as those moments of uncertainty between placing some sort of wager and learning of the result. The wager may be of any sort, from a real estate deal to a stock purchase to a lottery ticket. The moments of uncertainty may span years, as in real estate, or seconds, as in the casino. In general, the intensity of the action is inversely proportional to the duration of the action. The longer the wait, the less intense, although by no means the less pleasurable, is the action. Adaptive gamblers tend to go for mild action. They enjoy the risk, the uncertainty, up to a point, but they protect themselves in the process. They do not like to lose. Pathological gamblers do not really care whether they win or lose. They simply want the action, as if it were a drug. Repeated losses, which would have an aversive effect on an adaptive gambler, either have no effect on the pathological gambler, or, paradoxically, they intensify his desire to gamble. Action here is functioning as a euphoric or an anaesthetic. During those moments while the bet is down, the gambler is transported. He forgets everything else. All attention focuses on the play. When the play is over, there is an immediate reflex to get back to the action, not necessarily to double the gains or make up the losses, but to get back to the emotionally protective cocoon the action provides.

Most pathological gamblers are using money, and the action it provides, to escape some dysphoric mood state. It may be clinical depression, or just the boredom of everyday life. Such gambling may mask a host of psychiatric disorders, most commonly affective disorders, either unipolar or bipolar, narcissistic disorders, and the adult version of attention deficit disorder. It is also commonly associated with substance abuse.

In any case, the action has an emotional purpose, and if that can be understood, the behavior can better be treated or controlled.

The Manic: The manic shares much with the pathological gambler in that he is using money as a means of flight. Of all the money styles discussed here, these two are the most potentially disastrous and in need of prompt professional intervention. During periods of mania, people can go through a life's savings in a month or even in an afternoon. Money becomes a means toward a grandiose goal. Unfortunately, limits are often set only after much damage has been done. Beginning with an understanding of mania as a biologically driven high, a flight from all that is mundane, restricted, sad, or even slow, it is not hard to see how money should fit so well into the symptomatology. What better way to change one's self instantly than by buying a new one? Money is quick, accessible, and produces tangible results. A new suit of clothes, some new jewelry, a new car, and a trip around the world. It can all be done in an afternoon, and most people these days have the credit cards to do it. Most of us have had the experience of treating a bad mood by buying something. That same process, multiplied many times over, produces the spending of mania. That money should be so easily associated with grandiosity is summed up in our culture's popular question, "What are you worth?" The question does not refer to the number of good deeds you have done, but the number of dollars you have.

During periods of mania money thus becomes a ticket to another place, a new you. Although more money could help us all, the manic unfortunately spends with blatant disregard for what he actually has.

THE UNDERINVOLVED

Unlike the spenders and the enthusiasts, who have an active, albeit not always convivial relationship with money, the group of people discussed here tend, for one reason or another, to sidestep the issue. This is because money makes these people so anxious. It is hard to get at what money really means to them in emotional terms because, above all else, it appears to mean anxiety.

The Dodger: The paradigm of this group we call the dodger. Typically this person is competent, even highly successful in most aspects of life, a professional person perhaps, or an artist or a professor. He or she is intelligent, well-educated and in most respects responsible and creative. However, around the topic of money the dodger falls to his or her cerebral knees. "I just can't be bothered with it." "I know it's important, but I just can't seem to take the time to manage it well." "I'm no good with figures." "I'm drowning in free advice, and I still don't know whom to ask or what to do." The dodger's predominant emotional response to money is anxiety or its cousin, boredom. So, with a vague feeling of discomfort and/or guilt, money management is postponed, finessed, avoided, and in general just plain flubbed.

It is extraordinary how common this type is, particularly among the educated. It is not restricted to artists and humanists, "liberal arts" types, although it abounds there. Doctors and scientists, well-trained in quantitative disciplines, typically fiddle and diddle their money away without any sound planning. Their anxiety makes them susceptible to get-rich schemes, which they impulsively invest in without research, just as their boredom sets them up for years of avoidance of the subject. Over time, money becomes a bedeviling factor in the dodger's life. Never quite in control, always putting off taking charge, the dodger puts more effort into avoiding the topic than it would take to master it. Akin to resistance in psychotherapy which may take years of concentrated effort to overcome, the dodger's resistance to coming to terms with money can last a lifetime. The problem is clearly not intellectual. Most dodgers are manifestly smart enough to understand the rudiments of finance. Indeed, many are smart enough to teach the subject if they put their minds to it. But they put their minds elsewhere as money problems silently ensnare their lives.

The problem is, of course, emotional. There is a host of ways in which money can become toxified, so to speak, so that by adulthood it becomes too hot to touch. Few families are without some traumatic story involving money. If all the emotion involved gets displaced onto money, then money becomes a symbol for trouble, for division, for rancor.

Short of trauma, in many families money is simply not discussed reasonably, but rather feverishly or irrationally, so that one can come to associate dealing with money with dealing with tension, distemper, or confusion.

Short of that, one may become a dodger simply out of ignorance. Many families do not take up the topic in an informative way at all. Certainly, schools do not cover money management. Just as one's sex education may be based on rumor and fanciful misinformation, so can one's money education be rooted more in fable than in fact. One reaches an age where it becomes embarrassing to admit ignorance about money. Hence, the feelings of helplessness and anxiety lead to avoidance, and one becomes a dodger. Whether it grows out of emotional trauma or lack of education, the dodger's anxiety is only intensified by the demands of everyday adult life, where financial decisions must be made daily. Left on his or her own, the dodger makes those decisions based on expedience and impulse, hunch and hearsay. What the dodger needs is a guide, whether it be a therapist or advisor or friend, to detoxify the topic and provide the rudimentary information that can lead past the anxiety toward mastery.

The Victim: The victim is a variation on the theme of the dodger. Like the dodger, he has trouble taking control of his financial life, usually letting it run him instead of the other way around. However, while the dodger usually finds a way of muddling through, albeit less than ideally, the victim stumbles repeatedly. He always seems to be in money trouble, ostensibly not of his own making. Unlike the gambler or the manic, who flagrantly and often flamboyantly mastermind their own disasters, the victim simply cannot avoid his. His every financial move goes sour, and he chronically bemoans his bad luck.

If one looks more closely at most victims, one usually finds that the emotional meaning of money centers around dependency and independence. The victim wants to be taken care of, he seeks to preserve the dependent position, and he covertly avoids gaining his own independence. Money management becomes an arena for this conflict. Unconsciously, the victim sets up his own financial demise in the hope that he will be saved. The price he pays, literally is high. And so is the figurative price: humiliation, shame, embarrassment. However, such are his fears of independence that it feels worth any price.

The Depressive: The most ɯninvolved of the underinvolved, the depressive deals with money the way he deals with everything else: as little as possible. To the depressive, money becomes another demand, another burden, another irksome piece of reality to be coped with. To the extent that depression involves a global loss of interest, motivation, and energy, the depressive neglects the concerns of everyday life. Since money is chief among those concerns for most people, the depressive is at financial risk.

In addition to clinical depressives, who lose interest in everything, including money, there are those people who are depressive specifically around money. Similar in behavior to the victim and the pessimist, whom we shall discuss shortly, the financial depressive knows no good news. But unlike the victim, he does not set up failure, and, unlike the pessimist, he does not make plans based on superstition. Rather, he carries with him a listless defeatist attitude about money. He tends to be uninvolved out of a feeling of, "Why bother?" His stance is often a defense against rage. He fends off feelings of bitterness, injustice, and injury around money by, consciously or unconsciously, adapting an attitude of passive negativism. No plan will work, so why undertake it. The deck is stacked, so why play the game. You can't win, so why bother?

If the depressive can get past the defeatism to the anger it may conceal, he can activate a lot of energy. More than a few fortunes have been made on energy derived from narcissistic injury, class anger or indignation.

THE SKEPTICS

The skeptics are the most cautious group in our classification. They look at people's dealings with money with mistrust and doubt, and they favor a generally conservative approach. The predominant emotional meanings of money to this group are security and control. Risk feels toxic to this group. Often their cautious dealings with money parallel excessive caution and control with their emotions. Their need for control and quest for illusive security inhibits spontaneity in their lives. Their dealings with money symbolically reflects an underlying restricted emotional style.

The Pessimist: There is a genus of sports fan that defines the pessimist. It is a genus located largely in the Northeast, but there are outposts all over the world. It is called the Red Sox fan. The Red Sox have not won a World Series since the First World War, yet they have often come close, close enough to spark hope. But the minute a Red Sox fan feels hope sparked, he tells himself, no, that cannot be. So begins the cycle. He has long conversations with himself about why the team cannot win. At the same time, deep within him, in a pure and innocent part of his heart, hope is rising. At some point, usually in September, sometimes in August, rarely in October (it is a day more variable than Easter, but equally certain to come), hope and skepticism collide, as hope dolefully retreats amid catcalls. Some say the Red Sox will never win because Fenway Park is too small, or the left field wall is too high, or because the management is racist and will not sign the best black and Latin players, or because the team lacks speed, or because the atmosphere is too country club, or because the owners are too poor and George Steinbrenner is too rich, or because the team has always lacked a killer instinct, or because God wills it. None of these reasons, however plausible, is true.

The real reason the Red Sox will never win the World Series is that the Red Sox fans do not want them to. Why did the team trade Babe Ruth? Why did Johnny Pesky hold the ball? Why did Darrell Johnson pinch-hit for Jim Willoughby? Why did the ball go through Bill Buckner's legs? Because, quite simply, the fans wanted it. The fans so fill the team with their own gloom that the team can never win. And the fans' world view can remain intact.

So it is with the pessimist and money. No matter how positive the outcome, there will always be bad news. Even as hope leads him to invest, reason will find a downside. No matter how good things seem, or how much money is simply rolling in, the pessimist will fretfully look both ways as he crosses the one-way street. Ever a champion of Murphy's law, after the last thing that can go wrong has gone wrong, he starts looking for things that can't go wrong to go wrong. When the pessimist gets a raise, he wonders if the company can afford to pay it. When the value of his house rises, he wonders if it is artificially inflated. If he wins a little money in the lottery, he worries about having used up his supply of good luck. Consciously, the pessimist tells money, "Come what may, you will let me down." His consistent expectation of the worst conceals an unconscious agreement with money that says, "If I doubt you persistently, you will be true to me." The pessimist believes he purchases pleasure with pain. According to this superstitious agreement, it is bad luck ever to proclaim that things will be all right, that the money will be there. So the pessimist continues to mutter gloom and doom, like magic imprecators over a cauldron of money.

The Worrier: Although most people worry about money, some people worry about it incessantly. They live in a constant state of near-panic, fretting over the financial consequences of their every action. Money comes to mean not only control and security, but psychic integrity. The balance sheet reflects emotional, as well as financial, equilibrium. Through the mechanism of displacement, worries from every corner of life end up on the spread sheet. Conflicts at work, conflicts at home, conflicts with a shopkeeper or conflicts in traffic all transmogrify into money worries. The worrier may be rich or poor. His worrying is independent of his net worth. No matter how much he has, it is not enough. Just as the hypochondriac displaces general human vulnerability onto the human body, so the worrier becomes a sort of fiscal hypochondriac, displacing all manner of concerns onto the checkbook. His list of symptoms rivals the hypochondriac's, and his inability to be reassured can make him equally exasperating. However, with patience and insight, he may be able to ferret out the true causes of his obsessive worrying.

The Miser: The miser looks to money for control. He begins with a basic need always to be in control, and he tries to meet this need through money. He holds onto money as he holds onto control. Indeed, the term "holdings" well describes the miser's money. For him, to part with money is to part with more than dollars. It is to part with something far more valuable, his basic sense of security and control. He is usually as withholding of his emotions as of his money, as the parallelism between finance and feelings persists.

SUMMARY

Each person has a characteristic style of dealing with money, a style that is representative of that person's general psychology. While most people are oblivious to their money style, saying simply that their style is that they want more, a close look will reveal a host of feelings centering around money. By beginning to understand the individual's money style, one can begin to resolve the conflicts that surround it.

CHAPTER 3

MATERIAL INCENTIVES IN CHILDHOOD AND ADOLESCENCE

Leonard I. Jacobson, Ph.D.

The role of money and material incentives in childhood and adolescence is complex just as it is in adulthood. The process of growing up is one of socialization and acculturation, of learning how to be a successful child and adult. The definition of a successful child and adult, communicated both verbally and nonverbally, is taught and interpreted to the child, first by his parents and immediate relatives, and later by school and peers.

We would expect the role of money, the child's socioeconomic milieu, and tangible material rewards to change from earliest childhood as the child progresses towards adolescence. The assumption is that the child increasingly comes to understand the role and value of material incentives as they operate in the adult world as mediated and interpreted to him by parents, by observation of how they operate in other families, by the school, and by peers.

There is not a simple 1:1 relationship between material incentives and behavior, given the complexity of the human psyche. For example, an adolescent in rebellion may *choose* to smash the personal property of his parents as a way of getting even with them and punishing them.

In early childhood, prior to age six, money has little direct significance. There is some direct value to it. A child may see that his parents are unable to afford something that another family can purchase. The child may ask his parents why he cannot have a particular toy like that of his friend. His parents may answer with: "They have more money than we do." The child is learning that money is significant and that it may control whether he will be given something he wishes.

A basic issue concerning the learning of attitudes about money involved whether the parents will use money and financial incentives to train the child in autonomous development and toward the acquisition of pro-social

Money and Mind, Edited by S. Klebanow and
E.L. Lowenkopf, Plenum Press, New York, 1991

conduct or as a tool to manipulate the child more directly towards their wishes. This is an important issue, but sometimes in early childhood it is not always possible to delineate between the two clearly in any specific situation. When a parent says to a seventeen-year-old boy: "If you continue to see that girl, I won't buy you a car" it is clear that money is used as a manipulative tool in order to control. When a ten-year-old is given a dollar to mow the grass, it is not necessarily clear whether this is a controlling tactic or an effort to build autonomy and pro-social conduct in the child.

It is the overall intent and game plan of the parents, conscious or unconscious, that is of importance. Indeed, it is necessary to evaluate the general strategy of the parents actually being implemented in order to shape the child's attitudes towards money and work and not to consider specific acts in isolation.

Let us begin with the ideal manner in which a parent would train a child. It is desirable for parents to use material incentives as tools to enable the child to learn to behave in a prosocial manner, maintain and enhance age-appropriate behavior, and facilitate the acquisition of new behavior that is in the child's interest. Independence training is critical particularly in highly competitive, achievement-oriented cultures such as that in North America.

Within this context, material incentives are simply another socially reinforcing stimulus that a parent has at his or her disposal. In addition, the parent at each appropriate age can train the child with regard to an understanding of the value of money and its importance in the acquisition of more mature behavior.

A parent can have a child open a bank account in the first grade and deposit an allowance of a dollar per week into this account. When the child has sufficient funds, he may be allowed to purchase some desired object. The child would be responsible for making the deposit, monitoring the size of the account, and selecting appropriate purchases with parental guidance.

The child would learn the value of a savings account, of saving regularly, the importance of delay of gratification, and the ultimate utilitarian value of the funds. Since the final decision concerning the purchase would be a collaborative effort of parents and child, a further lesson in democratic planning is included. The child learns also that his or her wishes are important and respected by the parents. This is collaborative, guided, independence training.

Parents frequently resort to other mechanisms. A parent may use material rewards to threaten a child. The parent may say, "If you don't cut the grass, you won't go to the movies!" In this case the parent is trying to associate a failure to perform a desired act with later punishment. The parent demonstrates control in a direct way to the child.

Such an approach as a general strategy is a negative one. It is generally more desirable to teach children to perform positive acts that are subsequently rewarded than to threaten them with the consequences of negative actions. When parents teach a child to associate a failure to comply with their instructions with punishment, they are not helping the child to acquire motivation to perform actions.

Parents frequently resort to blatant bribery. "If you do X, I'll give you Y." The child learns that he is performing a prosocial response for his parents' benefit rather than his own. It would be far more desirable for the parent to teach the child a sequence of activity that would directly aid the child's own interests and result in what behavioral psychologists refer to as natural rewards or reinforcers.

Motivating a child to do homework to obtain good grades is a form of teaching that generates tangible, positive consequences. Instruction that results in praise, social success, and personal accomplishment is the most effective way to encourage positive behavior. At first the actions occur because of their utilitarian effects and later as ends in themselves. This process is referred to as functional autonomy (Allport, 1961).

In order to look specifically at the role of material incentives in childhood and adolescence, I will use a developmental framework that uses concepts derived from Erik Erikson, Erich Fromm, object relations theory, contemporary family therapy, and social learning theorists.

1. INFANCY AND THE EARLY CHILDHOOD

In infancy the material situation influences the child indirectly. The parents' socioeconomic status and their attitudes toward money and property influence the manner in which the child is treated. The child does not directly perceive the material situation apart from how it is mediated by parents and environmental contingencies.

If the parents are poor and both work, the child may be left alone for relatively long periods of time. Problems may develop with regard to the development of basic trust vs. mistrust and basic security vs. insecurity (Erikson, 1963). The child will feel intuitively, on a nonverbal level, that he or she is not being well cared for and is not truly wanted, and that something is fundamentally wrong with the care administered.

The child is not able to understand the system of interdependent relations and economic conditions that create this milieu. During infancy material variables operate but are of indirect, rather that of immediate relevance, and the child does not comprehend clearly the system of relations in which he or she functions and develops. What the child learns is mediated largely through the environment created by the parents. The basic learning that occurs is unconscious, emotional learning related to basic survival and security functions.

2. CHILDHOOD (PLAY AGE)

By age four the child is well able to differentiate from the environment so as to appreciate the differences between self and other objects. The range of movements has been extended, the use of language refined, and the ability to manipulate objects as independent entities has occurred. At this point, the child begins to emulate others more directly.

At this stage, the importance of the material environment becomes greater. The child watches the way his parents, other members of the family, and members of other families use money and objects and the way they employ these to influence their own lives and the lives of others.

For most children, toys are purchased at this age. If the parents are prosperous, they may lavish toys on their child; if the parents are of modest means, the child will have fewer toys. In wealthier homes, toys are frequently bestowed in such quantity as to demonstrate that their purchase and provision has little meaning for the parents. Toys may come to have little value for the child.

Parents may or may not punish the child for the breaking of toys. Parents who express little concern whether children break or misuse toys usually communicate the following: a) material possessions are always there and new ones will come; b) the possession of material objects is a right to be taken for granted and not something to be earned; c) the child need not act as if toys are a custodial trust; and d) the child may do whatever he or she pleases with them with impunity.

Parents can provide more positive orientations if they teach the child that toys do have value, are limited in quantity, must be cared for, and require a sense of responsibility. Additionally, the child may take pride in exercising this custodial function satisfactorily. Finally, by having a more finite quantity of toys the child may learn to appreciate each of them more.

3. CHILDHOOD (SCHOOL AGE)

During this stage the basic ego strength developed is that of competence. Erikson has defined competence as "the free exercise of dexterity and intelligence in the completion of tasks, unimpaired by infantile inferiority" (Erikson, 1964, p 124). During this period, the child attends school, and for the first time, has to confront external demands imposed by school authorities and, at the same time, must find a place within a peer culture.

This stage is quite important. For the first time, the child is able to materially compare the economic situation of his family with that of other families, particularly if the child attends a public school situation where children may vary significantly in familial socioeconomic background.

Parental resources and attitudes are important here. If the child comes from a poor family, does the child have sufficient money each day to purchase lunch? If the parents are wealthier, do they give the child a ten-dollar bill, in order to purchase a three dollar lunch and not ask about the change?

Clothing becomes important particularly if the child is not in a parochial school where uniforms are worn. Children do observe keenly who is wearing the latest style designer jeans or other apparel, and it can make a difference in their status hierarchies. As children progress through school, they frequently learn to judge each other in part on the basis of socioeconomic status and by age-related symbols of conspicuous consumption.

The attitudes of the parents here are important. Do the parents demonstrate more concern with the child's achievement than with the clothes they wear? Do they encourage their children to develop friends based on the personal characteristics of these peers or based on their socioeconomic and social status? Do they teach the child to separate clearly what the child is from what he or she has? To paraphrase Fromm (1976): do the parents train the child to function in a Being mode or a Having mode? Does the child learn "I am who I am" or "I am what I have"?

The care of personal property is also important during this developmental epic. Do the parents continue to lavish gifts of clothing, watches and other objects on the child without requiring anything in return? Or do they instruct them on how to care for property? Do they teach the child that property has value, and that sometimes effort and sacrifice may be necessary in order to attain and preserve it.

It becomes clear that many parents begin to substitute the giving of material possessions for sincere interest, time spent, nurturance, and love. They substitute material giving for affection and shared activities, and children become aware and draw their own conclusions.

On a more positive note, this period of development is an excellent time for parents to develop meaningful interactions with their children and share a goodly portion of their lives. It is a propitious moment for parents to reinforce the values of industry and achievement within a context of close, warm and loving relations. Whether parents choose to attempt to buy their children's love by material means or to relate to them in an affectively meaningful form is one of the most critical issues in parent-child relations in childhood. The road the parents take will shape significantly the growing and developing sense of self-esteem and self-worth. Failure to provide adequate affection and nurturing may teach the child that he or she has little real value to the parents. Many conclude that if their parents do not love or care for them, who can?

Unfortunately, current child-rearing practices frequently cross the border of inattention into outright neglect. In the majority of homes in North America, both parents work and pursue independent careers and frequently do not return home until 6:00 or 7:00 P.M. At this point both parents are tired and yet must begin the ritual of feeding the family. By the end of feeding, cleaning, and opening the morning mail, many parents find little time to interact with their children, help them with their homework, or respond to them in a meaningful way. Interactions are frequently limited to chastising the children for problems that occurred in school that have been silently and bureaucratically communicated to the parents by teachers in the form of disciplinary notes.

Family interactions under these circumstances are often negative and frequently are limited to verbal criticisms of the children for their assorted failings – not doing well in class, not studying, not cleaning their rooms, not doing assigned chores, not having their friends call on the children's line, spending too much time on the phone, not answering when spoken to, etc.

Parents frequently justify this sad situation by pointing out that both parents work long hours so as to generate income, in order to "give the children more." That is, the parents' way of life is said by them to be organized so as to be in the best interests of the child. Such an attitude may result from economic necessity. However, it may also serve as a pretext for parents to pursue *their* own personal and material goals apart from the children's welfare. Still other parents have not learned that children have needs other than material ones and many of the developmental problems in childhood and adolescence require parental assistance, emotional support, time and genuine interest.

The problem of two working parents is a new one for middle-class, although not for lower class society where it has been common for generations as a result of economic exigency. Middle class parents do not work for basic survival, although it is frequently couched in such terms. That is, two, three, and four cars in a family are desirable, but not a survival issue. Designer jeans are nice, but standard blue jeans are quite serviceable.

We are far from speaking of the privations that have led lower class mothers and single parents to work. Increasingly, economic necessities are secondary to the "personal fulfillment" and growth that is involved in mothers working during their children's growing-up years.

We would hope that if the mother is spending less time with the family, the father would spend more time in child-rearing tasks. This would be an improvement over the traditional maternal-dominated household, which was never desirable from a psychological viewpoint. Unfortunately, this rarely occurs.

Children are best served when they have two parents, both of whom actively participate in child-rearing. Other arrangements do not necessarily lead to negative outcomes, but they clearly are not as desirable when compared with the two-parent option. Currently, other forms of family arrangement are frequent as a result of separation, divorce, and death. Rarely do individuals strive to create one parent homes – although this trend appears to be increasing in recent years as well.

An increasing trend is to two-parent homes in which *neither* parent takes an active role in raising the children, particularly when they reach high school age. The absence of the mother from the household has not generally been replaced by a more active father taking primary responsibility for child care. *Kramer v. Kramer* remains more the exception than the rule.

Children in many one-parent homes now receive more attention from a single parent than millions do in two-parent homes. As a result of divorce and remarriage, the author has seen many four-parent families where none of the four pays attention to the children. The children are frequently shuffled from house to house in the hope that someone will take the time to do some genuine parenting.

If the American family is to reorganize itself on more productive lines, it will be necessary for both parents to take a more active role in family affairs. Fathers will have to learn that their children vitally need them and that working is not a sufficient expression of the male familial role; similarly, many mothers will have to relearn that they do have responsibilities in their homes and not simply to themselves, their careers, and their self-actualization.

As child and family therapists can attest, egotistical children frequently reflect the values transmitted to them by their egotistical parents. Scratch a narcissistic child and you find narcissistic parents living out fantasies through the child or acting out projections of unresolved residual conflicts from their own childhoods. Frequently, the child has modeled himself after a parent who sees in his children only an extension of himself and a further source of personal gratification. The child as a separate entity simply does not exist for these parents. However, proper child-rearing *does* require that parents invest themselves in their children and strive to meet *their* needs as developing and, with increasing age, more autonomous beings.

4. EARLY ADOLESCENCE (12-16)

It is during adolescence that children begin to take on more adult-like characteristics. In school, they begin to develop preferences concerning the particular types of subject matter that they find of particular interest. Some are influenced by teachers. They begin to develop more significant interactions with peers and frequently become members of a specific social group. They begin to attend parties and develop both strong same-sex peer relations as well as burgeoning interests in the opposite sex.

This is a period in which the development of competence becomes of increasing importance in school, athletics, and social achievement. The child begins to get a taste of what some of the themes of adult life are about. During this period the role of money becomes more significant. The child becomes more aware of the type of neighborhood he lives in, whether he is going to the "right" school or not, and of the material position of his family. VCRs, CD players, computers, and other teenage status symbols become of increasing importance. For many children, particularly boys, the main goal is to get a flashy car when they are of age.

During this period it becomes clear whether the child is more oriented towards building a basic repertoire of skills related to personal competence or associating with status groups and/or possessions. It is important during this developmental epic that parents encourage their children to take the competence route. Even the most achievement-oriented of children require some reinforcement of this value system during this time where peer pressure is of enormous significance.

The ethical values of the parents and the examples they set are of significance. Do they emphasize the development of competence and autonomy or do they emphasize material acquisition and knowing the "right" people? Do they emphasize the importance of fair play and of doing things the "right" way or do they emphasize winning at any price?

Do the parents behave in their own right and in their own lives so as to set moral, productive, and loving models for their children? Do they spend time communicating and sharing experiences with the children so that they learn the importance of these values and skills? What kind of marital relationship do children observe in their own homes? Will they know how to be good spouses and parents based on their own parents' examples?

An illustration may suffice. Assume two fifteen-year-old boys very much want cars of their own when they are eighteen. One boy is required by his parents to hold a part-time job between fifteen and eighteen and to contribute a portion of each check towards the purchase of the car. During these years, his parents take an active interest in how the part-time job is going and commiserate with the boy about how dumb some supervisors can be at work and how greasy you get flipping hamburgers. They counsel the boy on how to deal with the supervisor and other fellow-workers. At age eighteen the boy goes with his parents to find a car that he likes and that is acceptable to his parents. They then buy the car.

The second boy does nothing for his car other than turn eighteen. His parents never discussed the matter with him although they listened continually with one ear to his complaints about how life is not worth living without a car, how he will lose all of his friends if he does not get the car soon, how it will be completely his parents' fault if this happens, and how badly they will appear in the eyes of the other parents. Furthermore, no girl worth having would date him or consider him worthy of attention, love, or sex if he does not have a new Corvette or similar appendage of his fantasized, symbolic self.

When the boy turns eighteen, the Vette suddenly appears in the driveway thanks to his magnanimous parents who surprise him with it for his birthday. The question: which boy had the type of social learning experience that would best prepare him for adulthood?

Another important issue is the relationship between parental behavior and child development. It is a truism that children frequently turn out like their parents, both in ways they consciously seek to emulate and in more subtle patterns that are communicated unconsciously. However, we tend to overestimate the importance of modeled behavior, such as gestures, and patterns of speech in which children appear similar to their parents and to underemphasize communicated and learned emotional patterns that are transmitted intergenerationally.

Clinicians frequently find in therapy that their patients have acquired the same types of emotional problems, patterns and conflicts that were possessed by their parents or grandparents and that have been absorbed in the familial womb through observations and modeling. These emotional patterns have been passed from generation to generation with such exquisite subtlety that their very existence remains largely unknown to family members themselves. Indeed, much within contemporary family therapy, particularly that area influenced by modern object relations theory (Bowen, 1971,1978; Singleton, 1982) has given considerable attention to the importance of how emotional patterns are transmitted from generation to generation and how the next generation tends to act out the emotional problems of the former and even of generations still before.

Marital, family, behavioral, and non-analytic therapists generally are currently gaining an appreciation of the importance of historical variables but not as traditionally conceived by analysts. It is now common in family therapy, an area that always has emphasized the here-and-now, to trace how emotional patterns are transmitted over the generations (Satir, 1982). Similarly, analysts have learned that the first five years of life are but a part of a larger transmission process of intergenerational psychic and social communication patterns.

Attitudes toward money, material possessions, the values that motivate and energize our lives are important aspects of this intergenerational transmission process. Parental insecurities concerning the family finances tend naturally to be related to other personal insecurities, problems, and conflicts. All of these are easily learned by the children, converted into their own feelings of insecurity and grafted onto previously developed insecurities and mistrusts. The extent to which parents value possessions over friends, status over achievement, winning over competition, material objects over emotional honesty and genuineness, as well as the simple degree to which parents allow financial considerations to dominate their lives are of critical importance in the intergenerational transmission process.

Parents have an opportunity to create highly salutary conditions for their children's development by emphasizing the importance of emotional expression, open communication, ethical dealings with others, and helping one's fellow-man as opposed to exploitative and marketing orientations (Fromm, 1947), in which individuals base their lives on selling themselves and moving ahead at the expense of others. Indeed, much of what is called success and "getting ahead" in contemporary society is based on the central importance of individuals acquiring these orientations. Parents frequently do not state these objectives directly. The example of the parents as they lead their lives in accord with their values and reinforce selectively behavioral patterns in their children is quite sufficient to communicate clearly the nature of these values and promote their acquisition.

Let us return to the theme of the parents who try to buy their children's love and respect by material gifts. These parents frequently come to a family therapy consultation session after their child has committed some anti-social act, such as stealing, cheating at high school sports, or using or selling drugs, and complain that they have given the child "everything" and the child has let them down.

These parents fail to view their children as developing and autonomous persons nor do they comprehend that it was part of their responsibility to foster this process. This fact is demonstrated by these parents' direct concern with the immediate social consequences of the act for themselves, rather than as an indication that something is wrong with their children's values and life styles.

Such parents frequently begin a first family consultation with a litany such as: "Doctor I have given this kid everything and look what he has done to me! Don't you think my child is completely ungrateful?" In the course of treatment, the thoughtful therapist must attempt to communicate to the parents something of the following:

"No, I don't think that you have done everything; certainly not everything you needed to do or should have done. You didn't give the child the love and affection that was necessary; certainly you didn't spend the time with the child that he or she needed so as to provide a good example of a decent, functioning and successful person who really cares.

Instead, you tried to buy your child with clothes, VCR's, and a hundred other objects. I know that you meant these to be expressions of your love, but this is part of your problem, you have been unable to separate the giving of property from love and they are not the same. Really, your giving has not even convinced your child that you really care. Quite the contrary, your gifts are viewed as consolation prizes because your child believes you are unwilling or unable to express love and affection. In fact, your child believes that you really don't care, certainly not enough to spend a minimal amount of time getting to know him or her. Your child doesn't share thoughts and feelings with you because he or she feels you wouldn't understand or want to understand.

You may not feel that these statements are fair, but they do represent the impressions that your child has drawn from watching you for the past sixteen years, and as such the burden is on you. Why does someone so close to you so misunderstand your motives and see you so differently than you see yourself? Perhaps your child is seeing a part of you that is all too real and which you have been unable to admit to yourself or see in this way? Perhaps it's time for you to begin to serve as a better role model for your child and to examine your own life and values? That is, although you have a right to expect your child to change, you need to begin also by changing yourself."

SOME CONCLUSIONS AND FINAL THOUGHTS

Attitudes and examples of the parents are highly important in shaping the thought, affect, and motivation of children towards material incentives and rewards. Money can be used to motivate a child to develop as an autonomous and productive individual with constructive life goals based on well-grounded ethical and moral principles. Conversely, money can be used as a method of bribing children to perform activities for the benefit of the parents or to demonstrate the control the parents have over their offspring. Parents can guide the children towards becoming fully functioning persons or toward identifying with possessions and social groups as an alternative to personal effort and achievement.

Studies of the multigenerational transmission process (Singleton, 1982) suggest that problems not resolved in one generation will become more severe in the next as each subsequent generation moves toward a lower level of differentiation. That is, parents tend to reproduce in their own lives the problems previously demonstrated by their own parents and antecedents. Unless resolution is sought and attained these emotional and behavioral patterns are perpetuated with greater severity in each new generation.

It is of particular importance that we begin the task of reconstructing the modern family unit on a sounder basis. The role of material incentives and financial rewards can be seen as a significant aspect of a larger set of psychodynamic, psychosocial, and intergenerational change processes currently playing themselves out within the context of a rapidly changing society. Whether the resolution of these developments holds future promise or disaster will depend on our capacity to assess these problems and our motivation to solve them.

ACKNOWLEDGMENT

The author wishes to thank David E. Rubin for his stimulating ideas concerning the subject matter of this paper and Karen M. Jefferson for her general assistance.

REFERENCES

Allport, G. (1961). Patterns and growth in personality. New York: Holt, Rinehart and Winston.

Bowen, M. (1976). Theory in the practice of psychotherapy. In P.J. Guerin (Ed.), Family therapy: Theory and Practice (pp. 42-90). New York: Gardner Press.

Bowen, M. (1978). Family therapy in clinical practice. New York: Jason Aronson.

Erikson, E.H. (1963). Childhood and society (2nd ed.). New York: Norton.

Erikson, E.H. (1964). Insight and responsibility. New York: Norton.

Fromm, E. (1944). Individual and social origins of neurosis. American Sociological Review, 9, 380-384.

Fromm, E. (1944). Man for himself. Greenwich, CT: Fawcett Books.

Fromm, E. (1976). To have or to be? New York: Harper & Row.

Satir, V. (1982). The therapist and family therapy: Process model, in A.M. Horne & M.M. Ohlsen (Eds.), Family counseling and therapy (pp. 12-42). Itasca, IL: F.E. Peacock.

Singleton, G. (1982). Bowen family systems theory. In A.M. Horne & M.M. Ohlsen (Eds.), Family counseling and therapy (pp. 75-111). Itasca, IL: F.E. Peacock.

CHAPTER 4

POVERTY AND PSYCHOPATHOLOGY

Eugene L. Lowenkopf, M.D.

The absence (or shortage) of money is a condition which affects large numbers of people across the globe. That poverty has psychological consequences is a certainty although just how and in what ways it produces specific psychological damages, character traits and personality styles is much less clear. Since large numbers of poor people do not all have the same personality, the effects are obviously not uniform. Rather, poverty is only one among many influences, often being overshadowed by other considerations. In examining the interrelationship between poverty and psychopathology, I will present some conclusions and questions based on my own clinical experiences working with poor people.

Inseparable from poverty itself, although distinguishable in their effects, are such fellow travelers as inadequate nutrition, poor housing and insufficient medical care, as well as a host of social disruptions and problems. The inadequate nutrition resulting from poverty begins its malignant influence even before birth with the mother often being unable to provide an adequate intrauterine environment. This, as does severe nutritional deficiency at any age, may lead to death, but our interest here is the psychological outcome in the living. First and foremost is some compromise in brain development resulting in more or less dysfunction. This may be manifested as a degree of intellectual deficiency, a disability in one or several specific areas, problems in coping, rigidity in personality or greater than average irritability. Intrauterine nutrition may be adequate, but deficiencies arising later in the child's life may similarly produce brain damage and result in compromised brain functioning. Even when normal brain development does take place, there may eventuate physical defects such as rickets which can severely handicap the individual's physical appearance and competence, resulting in poor self-esteem and feelings of inferiority.

Inadequate nutrition resulting from poverty may occur at any age, but the later it appears, the less likely it is to produce brain damage and impair intellectual functioning. Instead, it is more likely to result in personality

Money and Mind, Edited by S. Klebanow and
E.L. Lowenkopf, Plenum Press, New York, 1991

41

dysfunction, social maladjustment and unhappiness. One example is that poor people often eat large quantities of "junk food" which can result in a state of vitamin-and protein-deficient obesity. Such obesity may, in its own right, produce a variety of physical illnesses and severe problems in self-image and adjustment to life.

Although inadequate housing may not seem at first glance to have direct psychological sequelae, dirt, roaches, rats, nonfunctional plumbing and insufficient heat expose the child to many infections and disorders. Housing poor in construction and location also entails greater exposure to a host of toxins, from lead paint on the walls to radioactive wastes. The child of poverty has less access to good medical treatment when illnesses due to poverty strike. Poorer medical care also tends to increase the number of long-term complications, among which there may well be psychological ones.

Social problems of many sorts are more prevalent in impoverished families whether they are causal of the poverty or its result. I am thinking of such entities as alcoholism, drug abuse, exposure to crime and violence, child abuse and prostitution. Overexposure to the darker side of human experience not only contributes to a wider prevalence of these problems in the next generation, but also seriously slants the child's view of the world. In the face of grim realities, it is harder to believe in fairy tales and Santa Claus, and poor children miss out on whatever benefit these fantastic accompaniments of a protected childhood provide. Instead, grim experiences lead to a more concrete and more cynical approach to life. We often say that such children have "street smarts", acknowledging their loss of naivete and their absence of optimism. It would be difficult to measure how much early disillusionment they have gone through and how destructive to their adult potential this is.

Often enough, children of poverty come from broken families with absent fathers. The male role model is denied them and even the mother, in her struggle to support her children, is often away; as a result, there may be a want of suitable parenting and guidance, as well as inconsistency and lack of direction. In any case, the stable, supportive environment which is necessary for mental health may be absent in spite of very considerable conscious positive efforts on the family's part. Both inadequate mothering and early exposure to the criminal way of life have been associated with the development of a psychopathic life style.

Schools do not compensate for any of these social or familial deficiencies. Rather, the schooling available to the poor child is almost invariably inadequate. Over the years, there have been innumerable reports demonstrating that reading skills in poor neighborhoods are way below standard, as are other measures of education. In addition, the child is exposed to the same deleterious social influences within the school walls that were prevalent outside in the street. Since so much time in school must be given over to managing behavior problems and providing the bare rudiments of education, there is considerable reduction in intellectual stimulation, compounding the prior absence of fairy tales and Santa Claus. Exactly how this inadequate intellectual stimulation translates into psychopathology on a specific cause and effect basis is not clear. Nevertheless, someone with inferior educational and creative skills is at a disadvantage in a competitive world; it is hard, if not impossible, to catch up with and reverse such serious gaps in education at a later time.

Compounding the sense of hopelessness that may arise from unhappy homes and inappropriate schooling is the awareness of diminished opportunity for changes in the future. The welfare system, created to fend off starvation and direst want, is often blamed for promoting a way of life in which generation after generation comes and goes, knowing no other means of support than the public dole. A great deal of imagination may be funneled into dealing with the "system" in order to obtain maximum financial allowances, but this creativity and imagination have all too often no other outlet and only go to waste. Important from the viewpoint of psychopathology is the depression that arises from such pathological dependency and stunted growth.

The poor child obviously has many psychological strikes against him or her, and it cannot be ignored that a disproportionate number of the poor are members of minority groups who are often victims of racism as well. While it may be impossible to separate out completely the emotional consequence of racism from those of poverty, I want to concentrate only on those that are distinctly tied in with insufficiency of money. To repeat what I have already noted in this overview, the child of poverty is at greater risk for organic brain disease and for social deviance, intellectual stultification, pessimism and hopelessness. A caveat must be introduced that these conclusions are derived from my experiences in American society and while such complications as organicity may be seen worldwide, the other characteristics may be limited to my purview.

What, for example, are the emotional consequences of poverty in a totally poor society such as exists in many a third world country? What occurs when poverty is an unpleasant but accepted fact of life? What happens when poor people have little idea of what it means to be wealthy as demonstrated by living examples, by television and by movies? How much does one's perception that one is poor, deprived and excluded from the mainstream, influence the psychological outcome? Or what transpires when upward social mobility is not a regular aspect of a particular society? Certainly, it is not easy to compare in the abstract the mental health of a rural Bangladeshi child with that of an American inner city minority one.

Returning to a consideration of the psychological consequences of poverty in our society, I would like to examine a variety of traits said to characterize those who grow up poor. The reasoning is that the absence or shortage of money implants in these people special feelings which are either experienced directly or reacted against, producing a defensive negation. Needless to say, not all of these occur in every poor person, and indeed none may actually show up in any one individual. And some may very well appear in people who have been wealthy all their lives and never known want.

Perhaps the least remarkable trait from a pathological viewpoint is a deep and healthy respect for money and an awareness of the suffering that goes along with having too little. People with this trait are usually extremely cautious in their dealings with money, measure every expense and place a great premium on saving against a "rainy day." While they may appear tightfisted to family and friends, their careful management of funds really represents a super-prudence based on hard experience.

Growing up without money in a society that highly values it and what it can buy places one in a socially inferior position. As a result, someone with an impoverished background may feel at a social disadvantage later on in life. This may be evidenced as a feeling of inferiority with doubts about acceptability. Such a person may show this as discomfort in society with protective withdrawal into semi-isolation. Another possible outcome of such a feeling is the building up of buttresses to insulate against it. This might include great sensitivity to signs and symbols of prestige and achievement, with such individuals becoming barometers of the latest expensive fashions in cars, clothing, restaurants, night clubs and travel destinations. One example of such wretched excess was portrayed by Strauss and von Hoffmansthal in their opera *Ariadne auf Naxos*. The nouveau riche host provides his guests with not one, but two simultaneous entertainments which clash with each other with humorous results. Poor people also may engage in flash and splash to conceal their financial limitations from others.

At other times, there is a reaction against the importance of money in life and a passionate aversion to even reasonable goods that money might purchase. People who do this often appear highly ascetic, and seem to ascribe to "higher" spiritual values instead of enjoying mere materiality. I have seen reactions of material snobbery and material renunciation in poor people who are still poor and in poor people who have gone on to become wealthy.

Other poor people make a virtue of their poverty in the sense that they assume the posture of the "little guys". Not for them the show, but instead they pride themselves on the modesty and sincerity of their lives. In them rest the real values of home and warmth while the rich have traded in such essentials of the good life for shallowness and superficiality. One sees a similar phenomenon in minority racial groups who feel that only they are open, honest and frank while the majority has sold its soul.

A further extension of the denial of money's value is to disprize those who have it and mock what they do with it. The vigor with which these positions are advanced and the severity of the scorn heaped on the wealthy and their doings suggest that they arise not from sober estimation, but from envy and frustration. For those to whom money is an impossible goal, criticism is one way to handle the ensuing resentment, expressed outright or through bitter humor.

To the poor person, abundant money is a dream rather than something that one can work towards and attain. Yet the fantasy is a delightful one and promotes the success of easily available gambling among poor people. Numbers playing has long been the special province of poor neighborhoods, and lotto, off-track betting, wagering at the track, sports betting and so forth are probably more prevalent among the poor than among the wealthier classes. This is not to say that compulsive gambling is more common among the poor; for one thing, the criteria for that diagnosis insist that there be disruption in one's personal life, and poor people never get to the point that they ruin their credit since they don't have any. However, I doubt that pathological gambling is more frequent in poor people. Rather, their need for the fantasy of large amounts of money is greater and there is consequently more widespread indulgence. I sometimes wonder whether the spectacular success of state lotto games relates to the creeping impoverishment of the middle class in our country; as making a lot of money becomes more and more difficult, the recourse to fantasies moves up from the lowest economic classes to the middle range.

Should the poor person suddenly come into a sum of money, it is perhaps inaccurately believed that it would be dealt with in a manner substantially different from what would take place with a wealthier person. Supposedly it would be squandered on meaningless purchases and treats in an "easy come, easy go" fashion with little appreciation of its real value. Perhaps this is so when the amount is relatively small and promises little change in a lifelong pattern of poverty. Indeed, a brief fling may be more appropriate than caution. However, squandering does not necessarily occur when the sum is significant and can produce a permanent alteration of life style.

Worthy of consideration by those who are interested in the psychopathology resulting from poverty is the suggestion that poor people lack the capacity to assess and utilize money correctly. I have not indeed observed this, and I wonder if this is not another of the misconceptions of other classes found in each social class, in this case the distortion residing in the middle class viewpoint.

Similarly, it has been suggested that poor people are more altruistic than wealthy ones, having greater sympathy with others of limited means. The accuracy of this belief is supported by even a short trip on the New York City subway system. As the itinerant beggars go from car to car making their appeals, it is the poor who respond rather than those who have more disposable money.

Living with an absence of money may inculcate in the victim a desperate urge to obtain money by whatever means possible, fair or foul. Fair includes working longer hours, putting more effort into one's work, constant preoccupation with the issue of money and a workaholic adjustment to life; much creativity arises from an individual's wish to separate himself or herself from impoverished surroundings. Foul means of obtaining funds range from aggressive business practices through sharp dealings to criminal ventures.

Without a doubt, stealing is more prevalent in poor people; psychopathy is related to certain kinds of inadequate mothering and there is a hunger for money deriving from constant neediness and short supply. Frustration in day to day life may also make one more prone to impulsive taking from others. Additional evidence for this assertion derives from the overrepresentation of poor people in criminal courts and prisons. Yet there certainly is a great deal of stealing, although of a different sort, in populations that have not been poor all their lives – witness white collar crime and the outrageous manipulations of recent memory in the stock market. Kleptomania, as one specialized form of stealing, exists across the social range although what one steals has some relationship to economic level. A rich woman is unlikely to steal meat from a supermarket to feed her children, but may lift a silk blouse or cosmetics, items which have a different psychodynamic significance.

It has become commonplace for money to be used as a tranquilizer, the act of purchasing luxuries serving to make one forget one's troubles and to enhance one's self-esteem. Getting away from it all to a beautiful Caribbean island is something only the wealthy can afford. Such "therapy" not being available, the poor must make do with staying at home locked up with their problems. Since food, shelter, and other basics are at stake, poor people live at a higher level of pressure and irritability and may be more prone to erupt in impulsive outbursts. Both the pressure and the outbursts may be self-treated with drugs or with alcohol. But, again, substance abuse is not limited to the poor.

Anger at the larger society which imposed poverty and its unhappiness on one may occur, but this requires that the victim view issues from a more societal and less individual perspective and subscribe to a particular political stance. This may occasionally lead to outbursts of violence directed against the "oppressors", but more frequently, the negative emotion exists as a persistent low-grade bitterness.

From the diversity of characteristics presented, it is clear that poverty does influence personality in a variety of ways. Even when specific traits may be doubted as being pure products of poverty because they appear elsewhere as well, a picture does emerge. This picture, written large, may be applied to whole segments of society which function under the shadow of grinding, severe impoverishment. A culture of poverty develops in which the primary goal is to survive from one day to the next; other values become subordinated and people in this culture may have little to do with the larger circumambient society and its values. Indeed, it has been suggested that poverty cultures in such diverse areas of the world as Mexico City, Calcutta, San Juan, Cairo and so forth have more in common with each other than with other subcultures in their own countries. From the standpoint of the psychopathology of poverty, an outside observer must be able to recognize which traits represent successful and necessary adaptations to poverty and which are aberrations; this is a task that is often difficult for the unsophisticated observer to accomplish. Prejudices supervene as, for example, when a group of American tourists finds it "disgusting" to observe the clamorous stridency of Egyptian beggars.

Indeed, this sort of misapprehension of values from one group to another has often influenced the diagnoses applied to poor people and has even extended into the treatment they receive. Studies of diagnoses assigned to poor people reveal considerably higher rates of schizophrenia and psychopathy and lower rates of depression, mania and personality disorders. While the statistics for psychopathy are supported by criminal records, it has been argued that a lack of understanding of the values of the lower class (often black) culture by the middle class (often white) diagnostician has resulted in classifying confusing symptoms, signs and complaints as indications of psychosis. When this type of diagnosing prevails, there may be less sensitivity to feelings such as depression or to patterns of adjustment, and they are underestimated and underreported. Concerning mania, one rarely sees poor people giving away one hundred dollar bills or running up huge debts on their non-existent credit cards, so that this diagnosis is less often made.

Statistics concerning diagnosis are also complicated by the downward social drift of severely disturbed people. They may start out in the middle or upper class but because they cannot work and because their health care is so expensive, they wind up in the lowest economic class, tending to increase the prevalence of schizophrenia in the poor.

Care given to the mentally ill poor is also different, with a whole alternate structure of medical and therapeutic services provided for them. Wealthier people have private therapists or clinics and as a rule go to private hospitals if they need inpatient treatment. The poor must use government institutions with their emphases on the briefest and cheapest methods of treatment. Woe unto the poor person who needs psychotherapy; it is virtually unattainable unless one happens to run into a particularly kind-hearted and altruistic therapist. Even the advent of third party payers, while it has altered the previously established patterns and has brought the two systems closer together, has not bridged the gap.

Electroconvulsive therapy (ECT) has had a history which reflects this disparity in access to treatment. At first it was a modality available only to the wealthy, but then psychotherapy came more and more to the fore in the 50's and 60's, becoming the preferred treatment for depression for the wealthy. ECT simultaneously became a popular approach in public hospitals where large shock units were established. Resistance soon arose in government and in the press to the widespread, sometimes indiscriminate, use of ECT which was seen as a brain destroying treatment; recall the book and film *One Flew Over the Cuckoo's Nest*. Public institutions then began to give up this rather frightening treatment at the same time that serious studies were revealing that it was truly the best method for handling certain kinds of depression. Its use in private hospitals became much more frequent, it now being a treatment primarily available to the haves and not the have-nots.

Another example of finances dictating treatment struck me about twenty years ago when I vacationed in a third-world country newly emerging from colonial status. I visited the psychiatric hospital there and was told that the two most popular treatments were ECT and prefrontal lobotomy, this at a time when medication was in and lobotomy out in American psychiatry. I expressed my surprise but was informed that lobotomy required no more than a sterilized needle inserted into the brain through the supraorbital fossa, a simple office procedure, and ECT required no more than a few milliseconds of electricity. Both were cheap, while medication cost a great deal of money which the government could ill afford.

A few words about psychotherapy are in order as I come to the close of this article. Many of the psychological consequences of poverty are not treatable in a therapist's office except in a supportive way. Brain damage and psychopathy are all but irreversible with current treatment modalities and can only be prevented through public health measures applied early on. However, when a therapist is confronted with a poor or a formerly poor person, he or she should be on the lookout for characteristic approaches to life which reflect early poverty and which are maladjustive in the patient's current day life. The good news is that these can be dealt with and treated in the same ways and with the same success as other psychological problems that the patient may present.

SUGGESTED READINGS:

1.   Allen, VL, ed, Psychological Factors in Poverty, Chicago, Markham, 1970.
2.   Harrington, M, The New American Poverty, New York, Holt, Rinehart and Winston,   1984.
3.   Langner, TS and Michael, ST, Life Stress and Mental Health, The Midtown   Manhattan Study, New York, Free Press of Glencoe, 1963.
4.   Lewis, O. The Children of Sancez, New York, Random House, 1961.
5.   Lewis, I. La Vida, New York, Random House, 1966.

CHAPTER 5

POWER, GENDER AND MONEY

Sheila Klebanow, M.D.

Money makes the world go round. There are many concrete reasons why people want and need to acquire money. In our society people have to earn money so as to make a living. Money is a vehicle necessary to provide for the means of existence—to support oneself and one's family—to pay the rent or the mortgage on the apartment or house, to purchase food and clothing, to send one's children to school, to invest and increase one's wealth, to save for retirement and old age, to provide for a wide spectrum of recreational activities, hobbies and fun as one's income allows, and, of course, to pay taxes.

Besides these material considerations, money has many psychological meanings. Most importantly, it represents an avenue to autonomy and self-esteem. A man or woman who works and earns money to support himself or herself and loved ones, will feel better for so doing. It is self-enhancing to rely on oneself and not on parents, children, friends or the welfare system to provide for one's basic economic needs. The corollary is also true: it is damaging to self-esteem not to be able to look after oneself.

Money is also the currency both of work and love which Freud postulated to be the two cornerstones which give life meaning. People work to obtain money necessary to live. This gives a structure to life and facilitates finding satisfaction through interacting with other people. People love one another for similar reasons. No one can live in an emotional or financial vacuum. In loving another — whether spouse, child, parent or friend — emotional structure and a reason for being are added to life. Often money is equated with love. The giving to another of money or the goods that money can buy is widely and perhaps universally perceived as being synonymous with loving that person.

The many adages that describe money such as "money talks", "money

An earlier version of this chapter appeared in the Journal of the American Academy of Psychoanalysis, 1989, _17_(2), pp.321-328.

Money and Mind, Edited by S. Klebanow and
E.L. Lowenkopf, Plenum Press, New York, 1991

makes the world go round", and "money is the root of all evil" all point to the relationship between money and power. Money is power. He or she who possesses money has power as well.

Money is a vehicle for power both effective and abusive. In dyadic relationships, the person who has more money is likely to be the dominant partner – be he or she parent, child, lover or boss. How both parties relate to each other regarding money has enormous consequences for the relationship. Is all decision-making about the spending, saving and allocation of money dictated by the dominant, money-earning partner? Are there collaborative, informed discussions between the pair? Does the financially more sophisticated partner endeavor to share some of this knowledge with the other, as for example, a husband with a non-working wife, or a parent with a child? Does either partner deceive, coerce or manipulate the other with money as the focus? These issues have major consequences in all human relationships.

Since money is so vital a constituent in human interactions, it is astounding that scant attention has been paid in the mental health literature to the role of money. The reasons for this are manifold. Currently, few subscribe to the classical psychoanalytic notion that money equals feces and is, therefore, unclean. But the old concept has many consequences. It is easier to talk about sex than money. Money is too private, too intimate, its personal details far too revealing.

As therapists, many of us may not be quite comfortable talking about money with our patients not only as money applies to treatment, but in a wide variety of life situations. Perhaps either we are mesmerized by the power of money or, in reaction formation, we try to ignore its importance.

Our tradition is that of "the impossible profession". Our function is, against all odds, to help alleviate human suffering. Perhaps there is a basic contradiction. As professionals, we are expected to earn a comfortable living but, as healers, we are presumed to temper the pursuit of our economic interests with a leaven of altruism.

Perhaps this contradiction has been reinforced during the arduous years of professional training. Salaries and stipends during this phase are relatively low. During residency and psychoanalytic training, most supervision is directed to therapy with low-fee clinic patients. The realities of money, both in treatment and outside, are insufficiently addressed. The young therapist embarking upon a private practice often has to learn what supervisors did not teach adequately – that money matters – not only to himself or herself, but to patients as well.

The power which derives from money varies over a wide economic spectrum. At one end, its absence and scarcity reflect poverty and living at a subsistence level. Hard-core poverty represents powerlessness. It brings in its wake despair, crime, limited aspirations and a perpetuation of the poverty chain. Then there is a wide middle range in which people have sufficient resources to have effective autonomy and to provide for both necessities and some variable, discretionary spending. At the other end of the spectrum lies great wealth and the possibility of power naked and unalloyed.

MEN, WOMEN AND MONEY

Neither sex has a monopoly on problems about money. Both men and women suffer from the lack of it, struggle to attain it and may or may not be able to enjoy the benefits of money. In both sexes, the presence and absence of money lend themselves to endless uses, abuses and inhibitions. The pursuit and non-pursuit of money represent a wide variety of dynamic issues.

Many psychological factors interfere with a person's ability to earn money sufficient to provide for autonomy and effective power. Neurotic inhibitions – the fear of success or failure, the fear of reaching or outstripping the oedipal rival, the excessive wish to be taken care of are prevalent. Greed, compulsive gambling, miserliness, extravagance and intentional naivete about money all represent maladaptive behaviors which derive from intrapsychic conflicts about money.

Inhibitions of success – financial and otherwise – are ubiquitous. How often do we see people who are unable to work and earn money up to their potential? They are afraid of success, and unable to be their own power source. Making money can symbolize true adulthood. Not looking after one's finances to an adequate degree means that one is only a kid and does not have to be taken seriously. This dynamic has oedipal roots. Autonomy associated with financial success is equated with being grownup and one's own power source. An altruistic surrender of one's financial interest in favor of another can serve as a magical defense to ward off the doom of annihilation from the oedipal rival (or his or her substitute, the boss).

For example, men who are successful while working for someone else may fail or sabotage themselves if they go into business for themselves. One's boss variously can be seen as a benevolent father who is providing all the goodies, knowledge and savvy or as the rival to be feared and not surpassed. In one situation, a man who was very successful as a salesman finally went into business for himself at his wife's urging. She believed him to be a capable businessman able to earn far more money and to receive the recognition associated with having his own business. He did poorly on account of self-sabotaging maneuvers and earned only a fraction of his former income. Exploration of his dynamics revealed his wish to be provided for and nurtured by a dominant other who would take care of him as his father had not done. His wife, who has her own career, helped to finance his business. He tried in vain to turn his wife into his boss by attributing to her vast technical knowledge of his field which was very different from her area of expertise. She steadfastly refused to fill this role. While he worked for someone else, he could maintain the fantasy that his boss was providing for all his needs rather than accept responsibility for his own success.

Another inhibition regarding money involves the inability to look after one's personal finances adequately despite being financially competent and responsible in the work situation. An individual who at work scrupulously maintains financial records, controls budgets, etc. may not balance his or her own checkbook or may not collect on his or her debts while rigorously paying off all obligations owed to others. Such individuals believe that another's needs matter more than their own. Their low self-esteem precludes looking after their own financial affairs capably.

A woman who served as secretary to a top executive at a Fortune 500 company kept careful track of corporate finances as well as her boss's personal investments. She always had at her fingertips all the details of his dealings, yet she was indifferent to making any investment for herself or even to balancing her own checkbook. Her inner conviction was that she was worthless and, therefore, she did not owe herself an obligation to look after her own finances. She felt valuable only insofar as she was connected to a powerful mogul of a man.

Many factors influence vocational and career choices. Educational opportunities, social class, personal contacts, family relationships, personality and individual abilities and inclinations all play a role. Generally it takes money to obtain the necessary training for a given career. One ghetto youngster might not see the advantages of going to school and training for a good job with a higher earning potential. Another might. Identification with family, peers and social groups are major determinants in all social strata.

An individual may strive to earn a great deal of money or very little money or something in between for many reasons. Identification or disidentification with one's parents, competitive strivings with the oedipal rival, its absence, or its intensity are of paramount importance.

One brilliant student chose to pursue a prestigious academic, but relatively low paying, career out of identification with his father whom he saw as a caring and altruistic man who was active in his labor union. Earning a lot of money did not seem as important as contributing to the good of humanity until, in mid-life, he was faced with the prospect of sending three children to college. Another, student, equally brilliant, differently perceived the struggles of his hard-working father to provide for his family. He, like Scarlett O'Hara, resolved never to go hungry again and deliberately chose to enter a high-paying field.

The wish to have more money or the same or less than one's parents is of universal importance. It can be fraught with guilt and anxiety leading to maladaptive behavior if equated with the belief that it is an act of disloyalty to make more money than one's parents. Alternately, it can be seen as an act of love, something to validate the correctness of the parents' love for their offspring, something to make the parents proud.

Power and money are intimately connected in all aspects of life. Insider trading scandals on Wall Street have focussed public attention on the abuse of money and power in the service of greed. We have witnessed the spectacle of individuals who earn millions of dollars a year who resort to insider trading to add to their enormous wealth. To outsiders it appears that they have all the money they need to provide for countless luxuries, prestige and recognition, let alone necessities. Some have described this as an addiction to money, but this does not explain adequately the underlying reason for the compulsive acquisition of wealth. To others it represents the search for vast undiluted power, the power being more significant than any commodity that money can buy.

Many have noted the relative youth of financial moguls who earn $300,000 or $400,000 in their twenties or thirties and the lack of ethical and moral standards by which they operate. The deals that they make, the vast commissions and bonuses which they generate, have not been tempered either by direct experience of lean times in high finance or by the maturity and wisdom which the middle years may bring. Finance is the "in" profession, the lodestar for young M.B.A.'s and lawyers, the new glamour field which currently attracts many competitive and talented people. In the "me generation" both the quest for power and money and the rewards for competition are intense. The inner sense of personal value is confirmed only by beating the competition.

In the press various reasons for such abuses have been advanced. Thus, Martin Siegel's insider trading has been attributed to the trauma of seeing his father go bankrupt and to his desire to have as much wealth as his mentor Ivan Boesky. Why should someone settle for perhaps a $2,000,000 house and a cabin cruiser when another has an ocean-going yacht and a $5,000,000 mansion? Thus, wealth is a focus for invulnerability, for regulation of self-esteem and for the acquisition of power. In this dynamic, an individual attains immortality through the ability to wield power. He has bested his oedipal rival and all other competitors. He believes that he will beat death because he is too powerful to die. The equation becomes: money = power = immortality.

THE POWER SOURCE:
DIFFERENCES BETWEEN MEN AND WOMEN

It is striking that only men and no women have been implicated in the Wall Street Scandals. This cannot be explained solely on the basis that there are more men than women in financial inner circles, or the relative absence of an Old Girl network or the lack of mentors for women. It cannot be explained on the basis that women hold higher ethical standards than men. Perhaps differing perceptions about money and power come into play.

In general, in white collar crimes, men embezzle large sums of money for personal aggrandizement while women steal relatively smaller amounts, perhaps to pay the rent or to buy necessities for their families. The big scams that make headlines invariably are pulled off by men.

Despite the work of the women's movement and the strides that women have made in achieving economic and power parity with men, some major differences remain. In my work with many young women who have impressive careers and high professional and personal aspirations, I have encountered some fascinating differences. Many of these differences center about seeing oneself or another as one's power source.

Traditionally, in our society, little boys have been reared with the expectation that they would grow up to be the breadwinner, the mainstay of their families. By contrast, little girls ultimately expected to grow up to be wives and mothers with only an ancillary duty to bring in wages after marriage. One implication of this has been (at least in middle class culture) that a girl would go from being financially dependent upon her father to a phase of perhaps several years duration when she would work and earn her own money and then to marriage and financial dependence upon her husband. If a woman worked after marriage, it was expected that her earnings would be less than her husband's. If a woman never married, it was presumed that she would never earn as much as a man. In some marriages, women would manage the household finances. In other families, the bulk of financial assets would be placed in the wife's name for estate purposes on account of women's greater longevity. In the emotional relationship between the couple, no one lost sight of the fact that it was the man who invariably brought in the money and thereby had the major decision-making power in its allocation. Insofar as men made the money, men held the power. Part of the male persona, the sense of autonomy stemming from the ability to earn a living involves the perception of oneself as a power source.

Perhaps in this sense men may have less neurotic conflict than women about the equation: money = power. They also may have less conflict about the abuse of money as the insider trading scandals may suggest. If men understand more effectively the use of money as power, they may understand more effectively how to *abuse* that power.

In order to abuse power effectively, it is necessary to understand effectively the nature and meaning of power. Insofar as men and women have differing perceptions about money and power, they may have differing abilities to abuse power. Both sexes, of course, have moral and ethical values about the abuse of power. Moral and ethical considerations aside – and they should never be put aside –it is easier for an individual who views himself or herself as his or her own power source to abuse power than it is for someone who sees another, and not the self, as the source of power.

Women may have greater difficulty in understanding this equation of money and power. Despite impressive professional and vocational attainments, many women expect their money and power to derive from their relationships with a man rather than as a result of their own labor.

In one dramatic example of this paradigm, an extremely talented young woman told me that she and her husband intended to sell their house and buy a costlier one. She commanded a large salary from her work. Nevertheless, she was very vague and became visibly anxious when I inquired how they planned to finance their transactions. She did not understand the details. Despite two large salaries, this affluent young couple lacked the cash for the downpayment on the opulent new home. When I asked if they planned to take out a bridge loan, she exclaimed, "You think like a man!" Exploration of that transaction was crucial in her analysis. No matter what recognition she received for her work, no matter what salary she brought home, it was "unfeminine" to grasp the uses of money. It was her husband's role, as previously it had been her father's to provide her with a showcase home, elegant clothes and jewels and extravagant vacations. She selectively tuned out her own considerable contributions to the family's finances. If she overspent it was because her husband gave her carte blanche to do so. As a woman she had no responsibility to be involved in any joint financial planning. That was the sphere of her husband and his (male) financial advisers.

Subsequent analytic work enabled her to take her own work and the money which she brought home more seriously. Money and power for her had always come from a man. She was being disloyal to father because she earned more than he. Equally important, she was disloyal to mother by renouncing her identification with her as a woman who could only be given to financially in favor of a new identification as a feminine, although financially responsible and powerful woman.

Problems about seeing oneself as an effective power source can have many ramifications. In dyadic relationships it can lead to endless jockeying not only for power but for powerlessness. When either partner has difficulty in acknowledging his or her own effectiveness and competency, money matters are likely to suffer. A woman executive who efficiently manages her own department will leave major financial decisions at home to her husband. This is not done because she recognizes him to be an abler financial manager, but rather in the service of being "helpless" and therefore needing care from her husband. The underlying fear is of being abandoned if one is competent.

In other situations, I have been impressed by a number of young, sophisticated career women who, when they divorce, suspend their financial judgment in working out a divorce settlement. They give away far more of their assets than is legally required.

In exploring this issue in treatment several dynamics emerge. Frequently, there is the guilt at the breakup of the marriage. At times a woman on a fast career track may believe that she has the greater current income or earning potential than her soon-to-be ex-spouse. So the decision to give more than is legally required may be generous, altruistic, masochistic or an atonement.

Often yet another dynamic is involved. It has to do with not quite being comfortable about earning money when one is a woman. In one situation, a young woman executive who was responsible for the budget of the firm where she worked agreed to her husband's request during the negotiations for divorce that he keep their car and all their household goods even though she had paid for most of their purchases. She had to borrow money to set up housekeeping again while he remained financially solvent and bought a new luxury car. She entered treatment after all these financial arrangements were made. In addition to her considerable guilt and masochism, what emerged was her peculiar inability to integrate the financial knowledge which she constantly utilized in her job into her private and inner life. For this woman as for many women the power to have money as a result of one's own labor rather than through a relationship with a man is a concept not fully integrated.

This data suggests to me that men and women frequently have differing perceptions of the uses and abuses of money. Insofar as a man is effective and autonomous, he is likely to see himself as his own power source. Insofar as a woman is effective and autonomous, she may come to the same conclusion about herself. Just as likely, however, she may deny that conclusion and attribute the power source to another—to the man whom she expects to take care of her —even though she really may be taking care of herself.

Perhaps some part of this issue is transitional in nature. As the next generation of women works in increasingly responsible careers, more women will learn something that perhaps some men understand better: that money is power, that it is neither "feminine" nor "masculine" to seek to be one's own effective power source but merely human.

CHAPTER 6

MEN, MONEY AND MASCULINITY

Robert E. Gould, M.D.

In our culture money equals success. Is it also connected to a man's sense of his masculinity? Yes, to the extent that men are often judged and measured by their money, what they are "worth." Unfortunately, a man's worth as a human being is too nebulous for accurate evaluation, but, more pointedly, our cultural climate tends to put more value on a man's income, what he is able to earn, how much he can command on the "open market" than on his human and social values.

Everyone agrees that sexual behavior is an area that must be explored in therapy. Arguably, one's attitude and behavior concerning money is equally important. Just as sex was a taboo subject in another era, many find talking openly and honestly about money to be extraordinarily difficult. It is easier to speak of premature ejaculation than of one's cheapness, pettiness, shop-lifting, stealing from friends, greed – to name just a few money-related patterns of behavior and attitudes which cause shame, embarrassment and/or guilt.

In my years of psychiatric practice I have seen a number of male patients, of all ages, who equated moneymaking with a sense of masculinity.

Peter G. was a 23-year-old, very inhibited and socially inept man who had had very little contact with girls and virtually no dating experience until his second year of college. He had been brought up in a strict and religious home where money was equated with security. He was sure that no woman would find him attractive unless he was making good money. In therapy it became evident that he was painfully insecure and unsure of his abilities in *any* area. Money was his "cover"; if he flashed a roll of bills, no one would see how little else there was to him. He needed "a beautiful girl with big boobs." His idea that women were essentially passive and looking to be taken care of by a big, strong male demanded that he "make" good money before he could "make" the woman of his dreams.

This kind of thinking is often found in both men and women who have been culturally conditioned to endow a money-making man with sexiness and

Money and Mind, Edited by S. Klebanow and
E.L. Lowenkopf, Plenum Press, New York, 1991

virility, and is based on man's dominance, strength, and ability to provide and care for "his" woman. The more insecure a man is in relation to women, the more he needs to behave in a dominant, superior way. What gives him this leverage is often money. If he makes it and she does not, he gets to call the shots. He can behave in a bullying, sexist fashion and if she is without means to earn a living, she is powerless and is often forced to stay in a marriage she would otherwise leave.

Women often play a significant role in reinforcing the pattern of a male self-image based on money-making power. Brainwashed by the same cultural teachings as men are, a traditional woman who happens to be earning more than her man may lose respect for him and think of him as inadequate, failing to fulfill his masculine role.

The cultural models of masculinity have been portrayed most unrealistically in the Hollywood movie, the purveyor and conveyer of much of our concept of how life is or should be lived. The John Wayne-style cowboy, the tough laconic private eye, the war hero, and lone adventurer – all "he-men" (a phrase that in its redundancy seems to protest too much) who use physical strength, courage, and masculine prowess to conquer their worlds, their villainous rivals, and their women. In these film genres, *money* rarely has anything to do with masculinity.

But in real, rather than reel, life in the late 1980's, few women have much concern about men like that. They do not really exist. After all, there are few frontiers left to conquer or international spy rings to crack or glorious wars to wage. All that is left to show strength, power, dominance, mastery for the real-life, middle-class man is the battle for the bulging wallet.

This measure of one's "masculinity quotient" becomes a convenient fallback to those who have a weak sense of self and who doubt their innate ability to attract women. Because it is hard for these men to face their inadequacies and the anxieties that would follow, they strive for money as a panacea for personal ills.

For them, money alone separates the men from the boys. I have seen youngsters drop out of school to make money, just to prove their manhood.

For their part, women have been taught that men who achieve success are the best "catches" in the marriage market. Women have also been taught that the right motives for marriage are love and sexual attraction. Thus, if a woman wants to marry a man with money, she has to believe that she loves him; that he is sexually appealing — even if the real appeal is his money. She has to convince herself – and him – that it is the man behind the money that turns her on . Many women learn to make this emotional leap: to feel genuinely attracted to the man who makes it big: to accept the equation of moneymaking power with sexual power.

There are many phenomenally wealthy men in the public eye who are physically unattractive by traditional criteria; yet they are surrounded by beautiful women and an aura of sexiness and virility. A woman in the same financial position loses in attractiveness; she poses a threat to a man's sense of masculinity. It has been said that men are unsexed by failure, women by success.

Yet why is it that many men who have met the moneymaking standards are still not sure of their masculinity? It should be obvious that money is and always has been an insecure peg on which to hang a masculine image.

Jerry L. is a stockbroker who lost most of his money during a very bad spell in the market in 1987. Distraught as he was over the financial loss, he was devastated over the sexual impotence which followed in its wake. This direct one-to-one relationship may seem pat, but its validity can be attested to by many men (and "their" women) who have gone through serious financial setbacks. Even a temporary inability to provide properly for his family and to justify himself with his checkbook makes such a man feel "worthless."

Even though Jerry L. recouped most of his losses in the course of the next year and a half, he did not regain his previous sexual potency. The experience had made it impossible for him ever again to rely solely on money as proof of his masculinity. It is worth noting that therapy did not really take hold until he made back much of his lost money and he was *still* impotent. He had previously persuaded himself that if he only regained his fortune, he would also regain his sexual potency. It did not work, because he remained uncomfortably aware that money can always be lost again in stock or business activities. Only that awareness permitted him to begin the work to uncover and understand the basic dynamics for his insecure sense of self.

The most extreme and dramatic reaction to personal financial loss is suicide. I have seen several men to whom great loss of money represented such a great loss of self, of ego, and ultimately of masculine image, that life no longer seemed worth living.

The situation today is increasingly complicated when the "head of house" must compete against his wife's paycheck as well as his own expectations. Economic realities have made the two-paycheck family respectable. That is, Jill's income is tolerable to Jack so long as he remains the main provider for the family, and Jill earns enough only to make the "little extras" possible. The current phase of the feminist movement which began in the late 60's has taken root in many women and in society's growing acceptance of women's aspirations for full equality in the workplace and in the home. Despite salary inequities that still exist, women more and more are threatening men's place as number-one breadwinner. Ten years ago a woman made $.63 to the man's dollar; it is now up to $.70. One in four working women today earn more than their husbands. This dramatic change has increased many men's anxieties about their masculine image. They now are not only competing against other men, but against women in general, and their *wives* in particular. This has become a discernible factor in bringing men into therapy for what they describe as dissatisfaction with themselves, their accomplishments, their sense of adequacy and other low self-esteem symptoms. The money problem has also brought couples into therapy because of marital disharmony: fighting, tension, unhappiness, anger, and resentment. A man may come in not realizing that his complaint is directly related to a woman's co-opting his passport to masculinity (thus the stereotype of the successful woman being too masculine, too competitive, too unfeminine). He feels effectively castrated. Many women no longer are willing to be "kept in their place, which is classically "in the home." Here their second-class status assures men that they are first class. Many divorces and breakups that are blamed on "conflict of careers" often mean nothing more than a wife who would not give up her career (and earning ability) in deference to her husband's.

An increasingly common problem in many marriages (and in therapy) concerns men who are "enlightened" intellectually to accept the idea that a woman has as much right to make money as a man does. In practice, emotionally, when it comes to their own wives these "enlightened" men feel threatened and emasculated. Because he is unable to see this in himself, such a man expresses his anxiety by forcing a conflict with the woman in some other area of their relationship: dealing with in-laws or running the house where there really is, in fact, no conflict. In this way he deflects attention from his problem, but he also precludes a healthy resolution of it in their relationship.

Marty B. was caught in this bind. A successful doctor, he divided his time between research, which he found enjoyable but not very rewarding financially, and the practice of internal medicine, which was more lucrative but not so enjoyable. Marty felt it a strain to deal with many diverse people; he was more comfortable with animal research, which also fulfilled his creative talents and led to his writing a number of solid scientific papers. Everything seemed to be going smoothly. But then Marty's wife, Janet, an actress who had had only middling success, became an actor's agent. Her clientele grew and she began doing very well.

Soon, Janet began to earn more money than Marty. At first he joked about it with her and even with close friends, but as Freud said, there are no jokes (there is often a hidden or disguised meaning or hostility present) and as it turned out later, the joking became uneasy, laden with anxiety. Marty decided to increase his patient practice at the expense of his research. He forced himself to make more money, when he actually needed less, thanks to Janet's high income.

They began quarreling about many small things – arguments without resolution because they had nothing to do with the real issue: that her new money-making powers were a threat to his masculinity.

Marty and Janet came to see me because they were considering separating after eight years of happy marriage. After a number of sessions, it became clear that Marty felt that Janet's success meant she didn't need him any more; that he had been diminished as "the man of the house." This was not easy for Marty to admit; he had always claimed he was happy to see Janet doing what she wanted professionally. But this was the first time he had to face her actually succeeding at it. Marty agreed, with some ambivalence, to go into psychoanalytic therapy. As therapy evolved, his problem with "masculinity" emerged even more clearly. He had never felt comfortable competing as a man. He resented Janet's success, but could not admit so unloving a feeling. He was not aware that his manhood was threatened and so he found "other" things to complain and argue about. After three years of therapy and six months of a trial separation, Marty worked through his problems. Their marriage and Janet's success both survived.

There are many marriages with similar tension that do not survive. Often neither husband nor wife is aware of how profoundly money and masculinity are equated or how much a husband's financial security may depend on having a dependent wife.

Another common male defense against the power of the income-producing woman is to belittle her and put her down. No matter how much she makes he may maintain that she doesn't "understand" money, calling upon the stereotyped image of the cute little wife who can't balance the checkbook. Women have become increasingly resentful of being treated in this condescending manner, further fueling marital disharmony.

The fact is that money was always a poor "cover" for an inadequate sense of self, or a definition of masculinity. Like a drug, it masks the symptom but never leads to understanding of the underlying causes of a damaged self-image.

Recently a spate of illegal dealings among Wall Street tycoons raised the question of why multimillionaires would risk reputations and jail to make even more millions they could never spend. If the drive to accumulate money is to neutralize the anxiety stemming from an unstable self-image, then there can never be enough. Money can serve as an addiction where, as with drugs, one needs more and more just to stay in place. And since money does not in fact relate to a man's intrinsic sense of what he is worth, it serves as a Band-Aid when what is needed is major surgery – uncovering the dynamics leading to the obsessive preoccupation with money-making.

For therapy to be successful, it must lead to a changed concept of the essence of "masculinity," a relinquishing of old cultural artifacts such as brute strength, domination over others and, above all, in today's world, "big" money. The fact is that a truly "masculine" man is relaxed and comfortable enough to allow himself to enjoy the traits traditionally associated with women: sensitivity, compassion , emotional expressiveness. He should not have to create a macho facade that keeps him from being in touch with his real self and human values. Cooperation and collaboration are healthier than competitiveness based on the need to conquer and control in order to feel like "a man."

True masculinity may be achieved not through the power of money, but through the power to feel, express, give love and accept (emotionally, not just intellectually) the concept of women being equal with men in every area. This new definition will enhance rather than diminish a man's sense of self and worth. A person more fully accepting of both masculine and feminine traits, within himself, has the capacity to reach fuller human potential, and thus an enhanced sense of self and true masculinity.

CHAPTER 7

MONEY AS A MIRROR OF MARRIAGE

Ann Ruth Turkel, M.D.

Freud's statement (1913) that "money questions will be treated by cultured people in the same manner as sexual matters, with the same inconsistency, prudishness, and hypocrisy" is not yet outdated. As Krueger (1986) says, "Money may be the last emotional taboo in our society."

Fenichel (1938) enlarged on Freud's linkage of money with feces by declaring that money can symbolize anything one can give or take: milk, breast, baby, sperm, penis, protection, gift, power, anger, or degradation. He viewed money as a source of narcissistic supply originating in an instinctual need for food and for omnipotence.

In our culture, money is also a symbol of worth, competence, freedom, prestige, masculinity, control, and security, all of which can become areas of conflict. Money issues may symbolize internal conflicts over dependency, responsibility, exploitation and pride.

Money is endowed by each of us with multiple meanings. It may symbolize self-esteem and regard for others, power and omnipotence, innocence and worldliness, fear and security, caring and disdain, purity and dirt, acceptance and rejection – any individual meaning. Its emotional connotations stem from family values, cultural background, early experiences, and symbolic needs. Unconscious conflicts can give rise to extravagance, hoarding, miserliness, or success phobia. It is indeed paradoxical that guilt can be produced by both money and the lack thereof.

Money is one of the richest fields in which to sow seeds of marital strife. Recent years have seen a shift in the nature and complexity of money issues in marriage as more women have become major earners. According to 1986 statistics, 54.5 percent of all couples have two breadwinners in contrast to 15 years earlier with 33.7 percent. Of course, we have to differentiate between a career and a job: the former involves employment in which financial and occupational advancement are anticipated and possible; the latter offers little promise for increased money and responsibility.

The couples who are described in this chapter are dual-career couples –in contrast to the two-person career. In the latter, the traditional marriage,

Money and Mind, Edited by S. Klebanow and
E.L. Lowenkopf, Plenum Press, New York, 1991

husbands exercise authority over wives by virtue of their economic status. Yet the men are dependent on their wives to provide the emotional and physical support needed to cope with the demands of work. In essence, through marriage the woman became economically dependent on a man who became emotionally dependent on her.

Hertz (1986) suggests that dual-career couples are "more equal than others" in two ways. First, relative economic equality has enabled shifts in their roles as husbands and wives since they are partners with similar goals and pressures. The boundary between "breadwinner" and "homemaker" becomes blurred when neither spouse can claim greater status or importance based on who works outside the home or even on who makes more money. Secondly, "more equal than others" describes the ways in which equality for some couples depends on the availability of others – service personnel – for whom equality is not possible.

The growth of career opportunities for women combined with the increase in white-collar employment has led to a great increase in the number of dual-career couples. Even though they may not have actively championed women's liberation, both sexes have become advocates of gender equality because of equally demanding careers, similar incomes, and the issues of striking a balance between work and family. Thus they behave very differently than their traditional parents and their one-career-family peers.

Today's young adults assume they can cope with both careers and family life. Problems arise when they attempt to juggle these responsibilities. The ideal middle-class couple is now the dual-career couple. The media fills its "lifestyles" sections with glamorous stories about "America's New Elite" as *Time* magazine (1978) named them: "power couples" who have great careers, work hard, and play hard when they come together on weekends. They bring the same energy and enthusiasm to their work as to their relationships. Even those with commuter marriages, who work miles apart, lead wonderful lives.

Earlier generations of young girls dreamed of princes to carry them off so they could live happily ever after. Today they dream not only of princes but also of careers. Boys dreamed of being strong, rich, and independent, with beautiful, supportive wives. Today the dreams may include working wives.

In the media, the successful woman executive is not only accomplished in her field, she is also the perfect wife and mother. She and her husband are mutually supportive and he is an active participant in domestic chores. What was the traditional role of the wife is now a shared one.

In the dual-career couple, neither partner has authority. The couple has been described by Hertz as being composed of two husbands and no wife. There is his career, her career, and what Hertz calls the "third career," the marriage. Since both parties work outside the home, the wife's new role changes the husband's. What had been the invisible work of maintaining the home is now in plain view. The expanded role of each sex is different: the woman has moved outside into the world of earning a living and the man has moved inside into the issues of homemaking.

Ambivalence in moving away from traditional role patterns may stem from stereotypical views or from guilt about not fulfilling conventional roles. Some women are afraid they are emasculating their husbands. Still others are fearful they are losing their femininity, which for them is rooted in the traditional female tasks. Some men are unhappy because they feel they lack the time and attention traditional wives gave their husbands, for women with expanded roles do not have the energy or the time or perhaps even the need to give men so much attention.

The dual-career marriage frees men from sole financial responsibility. They can be less obsessed with work, less aggressive and even less motivated. The women find that careers afford them independent identity and are central to their self-esteem. The money a couple has makes a big difference. It can free them from conscious budgeting and allow for greater satisfaction of material wishes. In most of these couples, either partner's income could really support a family.

If one has a successfully working parent, one develops an anticipation that successful work and material acquisitions are possible. Conversely, identification with a parent unsuccessful in the work area may lead to inability in this area. And some persons may reject or rebel against early role models, thus producing internal conflict. Indeed, a common source of compulsive work is the need to counteract an identification with inadequacy as seen in the family model. Thus, the successful person may view himself or herself as an imposter because of the unconscious link to an earlier identification with incapability.

Jack entered therapy because of depression. He is a 36-year-old lawyer married for 10 years to Carol, a journalist, also 36. Both of them have Ph.D.s as well as their respective professional degrees. Jack's depression led to his becoming increasingly immobilized at work. This created increasing financial problems. It soon became apparent that Jack, in addition to his work inhibition, was also in the habit of vastly undercharging for the work he did produce, so that he was working forty hours and charging for twenty. Carol was threatening to leave him because she felt increasing despair over their economic insufficiency to start having children, made all the more apparent since most of their lawyer friends were making more than twice as much money as Jack.

Jack is the oldest of three siblings. Each year, when he and Carol returned to his family's home in a small New England town, he came back to therapy commenting with wonder on how little he now had in common with his family. Both brothers are factory workers and have no interest in even visiting Jack in New York. Jack's father is a retired factory foreman and his mother was a housewife. Jack was a brilliant student and attended both prep school and Ivy League universities on scholarships.

Carol, being several years ahead of Jack in therapy, stated often that she believed Jack's problems were based on his being passive-aggressive toward her because of unresolved hostility toward his mother. But it soon became clear to the therapist that Jack was terrified of success as it evoked feelings of guilt and unworthiness. He felt particularly guilty at the thought of earning more money than his father. He often dreamed that he was an imposter about to be denounced by a stronger, larger man. Analysis of his parents' attitudes toward money revealed that secrecy was the model. Jack was not raised with a realistic sense about money. His father always disparaged those he termed "rich" – people who Jack now realizes live much the same middle-class life Jack leads; the father always spoke of the family as living on the edge of poverty.

Every child senses the parents' attitudes toward money through their ability to speak about it, their regard for its importance, their ease in dealing with it, how much there appears to be of it, and how they view those with more or less than they themselves have. From these cues, the child develops perceptions about money. A child whose curiosity about parental money is frustrated will mature with an attitude that money is a secret, hence equated with evil and guilt.

The fear of success can underlie problems in acquiring, managing, and enjoying money. These problems are associated with fear of autonomy, fear of wealth, fear of risk, and hoarding of money.

A fear of autonomy reflects problems in separation-individuation and leads to behaviors such as an inability to make decisions or to assume responsibility, maintaining dependency on others, or creating financial crises requiring rescue. If being nurtured and loved means sacrificing independence, then showing skill at handling money involves risking the loss of love. Adrian Berg stated this well: "Women for whom financial care equals love will see their own financial competence as a disastrous loss of femininity."

Some of those individuals who have low self-esteem spend money to attempt to counteract loneliness and emptiness or to relieve anxieties in the same manner that others drink or eat compulsively in an effort to be self-nurturing. A compulsive spender may be trying to show visible "worth" to counteract a feeling of inferiority or to create self-inflicted poverty in order to regress to a dependent status and thus gain needed nurturance.

Mary is a 29-year-old social worker in an administrative position far beyond her years of experience. She is newly married to Steve, a 32-year-old advertising executive in a prominent firm. She entered treatment because of obesity and constant arguing with her husband, primarily over her weight and secondarily over conflicts with both sets of in-laws. What appeared to be successful treatment of her obesity – with a weight loss of 40 pounds – was followed by a new set of arguments created by her newly-developed skills at spending money on clothes and jewelry. It then gradually became apparent that Steve was complaining about her spending because it was encroaching on his spending more and more money on cocaine, marijuana, and alcohol. After two years of individual therapy, Mary insisted they enter couples therapy, following several physical fights. Steve often found work-related excuses to skip sessions and adamantly refused to enter individual treatment, using a fine promotion at work as "proof" of his success.

Both Mary and Steve had experienced early emotional deprivation, having had remote and cold fathers. As might have been predicted from this couple's physical fights with each other, they had both suffered from physical abuse as children. In couples therapy, Steve continued to deny that his hunger for drugs, money, fame, and power were related to emotional lacks.

When Mary regained the weight she had lost, she reluctantly concluded that she could not continue to be married to a man who showed no signs of wanting to change. Within six months of their separation, Mary again lost her excess weight and, two years later, has successfully maintained her weight.

Money continues to be a forbidden issue because it implies power relationships which remain hidden if financial matters are not openly discussed. Yet when the wife earns as much or more than the husband, it is hard to avoid these issues. With two incomes, both parties have autonomy.

The financial systems used by these couples are symbols of power, of who is in charge and who determines how the money is to be used. It is important to understand the source of the arrangement of money for those who express marital conflicts through the use of money. In working-class families, arguments about money revolve around its limits or even its lack.

In dual-career families, the disagreements center around the "rights" to the money: who decides how it is to be spent. They do not question who has the power over money but rather believe that neither should control the other's money.

There are at least four styles of money management in dual-career couples: two pooled and two separate accounting systems – pooled in which husband is major contributor, and pooled in which wife is major contributor. In the two separate systems, there is a common "pot" for base expenses and each contributes a fixed amount. This may be a share proportionate to income or an equal share. But either method may lead to disagreement.

Alice and Joe, both in their late thirties, are mental health professionals. They scrupulously enter every receipt into a basket and several hours are spent every Sunday adding up the sums and dividing them equally, thus carrying the concept of the sharing of expenses to an extreme. Their inability to decide on common expenses was a manifestation of a basic lack of trust. When Alice decided to have a child, Joe reluctantly agreed. (The therapist wondered to herself how they would decide who would pay for the half of the child that eats.) Shortly before the baby's birth, Alice learned that Joe was involved in an affair with her exercise class teacher. Alice was devastated, all the more because this teacher was hardly Alice's equal. She said, "How can I compete with a lightweight like her?" The marriage was dissolved shortly after the birth of a son.

Betty, age 29, and Paul, age 30, are lawyers who recently inadvertently competed for the same position, which went to Paul. Betty remained in a public interest organization while Paul's income doubled. At this point, they renegotiated their separate accounting system, in which each had been contributing a fixed sum, and decided that they would revise it to contributions based on a percentage of their respective salaries. Betty arrived at the analyst's office for her first visit in a veil of tears. "He wants to go on vacation to Bermuda and I can't possibly afford to stay at the hotel he selected. It's bad enough he beat me out for the job. Now he's rubbing it in that he makes so much money." In Betty's view, Paul compounded the problem by offering to pay for her vacation as well as own. To her, this implied even more insensitivity to her position.

In the separate accounting systems, the couple may rotate the task of bill-paying or one spouse may handle all the work. Some couples may bypass a common account and divide up the actual amounts so that, for example, one partner pays the rent and child care expenses while the other pays the remaining common expenses. Yet others may use one salary for ordinary expenses and devote the other salary to "extras": vacation, car, investment, etc. The separate accounting system often reduces quarrels over discretionary income. And where the amounts contributed are proportionate to income, the couples are lessening the impact of inequities in pay between different types of careers as well as between different career stages.

In the pooled system, all income goes into joint accounts no matter who earns what proportion of it. Here the husband more often has primary responsibility for the payment of bills.

In a survey done by Hertz, there seems to be a relationship between the relative earnings of the spouses and the accounting system they employ. Pooled systems are more commonly used when the wife earns less than the husband, and separate accounting systems are more frequently used when the wife earns as much or more. This may be understood by seeing the connection between economic roles and the distribution of power within the family. The power of men has traditionally stemmed from status and resources outside the family. In the separate accounting systems, wives act like husbands, translating external status into familial authority. The pooled system does not alter the traditional power structure and limits the authority of one or both spouses. These couples have a more traditional view of marriage. They conceptualize it as a merger based on mutual trust and dependence. They often have a gender-based division of labor with separate spheres of influence in the home. Pooling income implies an effort to avoid distinguishing between the two incomes and avoids confrontations over disparities in income. In the majority of these couples, the women limit their involvement in financial matters even when they have M.B.A.'s.

Some couples start with one system and change to another because of arguments about money. Pooling income means that both partners have discretionary authority over money but, no matter which method is used, one spouse may feel that money over and above that needed for household essentials is being spent at his or her expense or at the expense of the children. Of course, what partners do with discretionary income affects their mutual life style. If one is a miser and the other a spendthrift, what happens when they decide to buy a new car? And do they hold major investments in both names?

Different value systems can create havoc. In the aforementioned couple, Alice and Joe, in addition to their separate accounting method so painstakingly managed, they had yet another problem related to income. Alice always worked 35 hours a week, not including advanced training time. It seemed to her that Joe had more leisure time than she did, although they were at the same level of study. Encouraged by her analyst to explore this, she discovered (after five years of marriage) that Joe always determined his income by calculating his expenses – both joint and his alone – and then worked exactly the number of hours necessary to produce that income.

What of the family in which the wife is the senior earner? What happens depends on many variables, including how much of their self-esteem depends on money, how they each value their own work and their partner's, if the economic inferiority is offset by other assets, etc. An unthreatened male can take pride in his own identity while acknowledging his wife's ability. An economic disparity can be balanced by the man's commitment to his work and to the partnership.

Yet often the man in these relationships has low career involvement. This was the issue which eventually surfaced in the marriage of Peggy and Jim, both lawyers age 30. Peggy entered treatment because of recurrent depressions after the death of her mother when Peggy was 14. Peggy is an heiress. Her family feels strongly that inherited wealth should be used constructively and has established several notable charitable foundations. In keeping with family values, Peggy worked in public interest law at a meager salary. She was very happy in her relationship with Jim, often expressing her certainty that her money held no particular attraction for him. They had met in law school and married shortly after graduation.

At the onset of Peggy's analysis, Jim was working for a prestigious law firm. When Peggy had been in treatment for about five months, her analyst went on vacation only to discover that Peggy had quit her job in a minor dispute with her superior. She was proceeding to look diligently for another position when Jim came home one day and announced that he too had resigned. To Peggy's dismay, Jim made only feeble attempts to find another position. Then he informed Peggy that he detested working in a pressured situation and he also began to look in the public interest sector. Peggy was troubled by her supposedly ambitious husband's contentment in being supported by her trust fund. Matters did not improve with his next decision that what he really wanted to do was to be an athletic coach at a prep school.

At this point, Peggy's analyst suggested that they enter couples therapy, during which Peggy was able to express her anger at the loss of the implied contract: her fantasy had been that Jim would eventually achieve enough money and prestige in law to outweigh her being an heiress. Peggy had really wanted to marry a man who would be as successful as her father and grandfather; she became angry and rejecting when Jim declined to beat the competition she had constructed. Analysis enabled her to understand that, through her repeated emphasis on doing what one wanted in terms of career satisfaction, she had assisted in setting up Jim's rejection of his own work.

When the woman earns more than her partner, as in about twenty percent of couples, she wants her husband to have some recognizable form of success. It can be traumatic if he flounders while she succeeds. The man may feel emotionally castrated if there is no sense of comparable worth through non-monetary assets.

Diane was 35, a market research executive and five months pregnant when she sought help. She was then married for three years to John, age 38, a college teacher who had been unable to achieve tenure. John had had a first marriage at age 20 and had an adolescent son who had quit high school and was involved with the drug subculture as well as with the police. Diane was highly successful in her work, so much so that she worked only four days a week while making seven times as much money as John. She was furious with him, not because he earned so much less, but because he failed to be successful in any way other than his brilliance at conversation. His first book was moderately successful and he postponed his publisher's deadline for his second book for several years. After he lost his teaching position, Diane helped John obtain a job in a field allied to hers, but he soon found it not to his liking. Diane paid for John's Spanish lessons, his studio where he was supposed to be writing but where he spent most of his time playing the guitar, and for all the necessities. John's salary from part-time teaching and tutoring went to child support for his son.

In couples therapy, John found it difficult to understand the extent of Diane's anger, since he believed he was working as hard as he could. At one point, he became overtly resentful at her insistence on making all the major decisions. She would say, "We'll go on vacation where I want since I'm paying." He replied that this was unfair since he did some of the household chores. In addition to the overt arguments about his failure to live up to his potential, John retaliated against Diane in the same way that women have traditionally retaliated against men's power: by withholding sex. Exploration of this problem revealed that John had both a lack of sexual desire and a deliberate avoidance of sex calculated to demonstrate his resentment of Diane's power in the relationship. Through intensive work on all parts, John was able to secure a tenured university position when he became less depressed and Diane became less hostile.

Just as understanding that all conflicts have an underlying symbolic meaning, so can a couple's financial arrangements represent hidden expectations or needs. Although monetary disagreements are often explained by a couple on the basis of differences in background or personal idiosyncrasies, their money transactions reflect accurately the state of, and can be called, a mirror of marriage. As has been shown, the financial interactions exist often in the service of power needs, dependency needs, for revenge, as a covert way of expressing anger, as an expression of self-destructive tendencies and even of sublimated sexual needs. Exploration of the ways in which a dual-career couple handle money and its discontents can clarify many of their fundamental conflicts.

REFERENCES

Fenichel, O. (1938), The drive to amass wealth, Psychoanal. Quart., 7, 69-95.

Freud, S. (1913), On beginning the treatment, in Standard Edition, Vol. I, Hogarth Press, London, pp. 126-133.

Hertz, R. (1986), More Equal Than Others: Women and Men in Dual Career Marriages, U. of California Press, Berkeley, CA.

Krueger, D.W., Ed. (1986), The Last Taboo: Money as Symbol and Reality in Psychotherapy and Psychoanalysis, Brunner/Mazel, New York.

Time magazine, (August 21, 1978), America's New Elite.

CHAPTER 8

MONEY AND DIVORCE

Naomi Leiter, M.D.

Money often is a language between spouses both in marriage and divorce. In this paper, I plan to discuss money issues that lead up to or help to precipitate a divorce, the financial status of the husband, wife and children, and finally the effect that financial settlements have on the development, emotions and psyche of the persons involved. I will try to present the problems from the viewpoints of both the men and the women involved. Yet it is difficult not to focus on the women since they seem more often to be the injured parties, and since divorce as we know it today has much to do with changing perceptions of women's roles in society.

Since divorce represents marriage gone sour, it might be useful to open by quoting some perceptive comments about marriage advanced by some of its wisest observers. Benjamin Franklin said "keep your eyes wide open before marriage and half shut after marriage." However this advice doesn't always work, and Voltaire is quoted as saying that "divorce is just a few weeks younger in the world than marriage."

Balzac writing in the 19th century in "The Physiology of Marriage" saw marriage as a financial contract, presumably divorce would also be a financial arrangement. He stated "Marriage is a speculation. I have bought the attention and the looking after that I need, and I am certain to obtain all that my old age asks for, for I have made a will of bequeathing my whole fortune to my nephew, and my wife will be rich only so long as I am alive."

Historians are hard put to define the exact moment when divorce became a regular, even if a statistically uncommon, phenomenon in the western world. I will restrict my own history of the subject of divorce to a few significant events in its evolution. Marriage in the Catholic Church was at first a civil contract although it later became a sacrament. As a sacrament, it could not be easily dissolved nor annulled. In practice an annulment was available only to the very wealthy or highly placed, and then only when political considerations made this suitable.

Since money and power were involved and since husbands possessed

Money and Mind, Edited by S. Klebanow and
E.L. Lowenkopf, Plenum Press, New York, 1991

the wealth and political power, men could ask for and be granted an annulment or a divorce more easily than women.

However, divorce became a significant issue almost from the beginning of the Protestant Reformation. Luther said, "It is better to allow wicked and unmanageable people to divorce than to condone vexing and murdering each other, or living together in incessant hate, discord, and hostility." Henry VIII of England broke with the Pope to rid himself of his first wife in order to marry Anne Boleyn so that he might have a male successor to the crown. It would be simplistic to claim that the option for divorce alone led to so major a disruption as the establishment of new religions, but obviously it played its part.

Some of the moral concerns that were raised at the time have persisted through the generations. Does divorce mean free love and total license for wild sexuality? Does it bring about the demise of family life? What happens to the discarded spouse? What happens to the children? Does divorce mean personal failure? Are the separating partners seen as crazy and unstable by society? Why are people still so ashamed of divorce? How much does self realization and self assertion contribute to the increase in the divorce rate?

As we know it today, divorce is the child of the Industrial Revolution and even more so of World War II. The change in work patterns brought about by these two events has led to greater independence for women and a greater range of choices. We all know that during and following World War II, women began to go out and work in factories and in the professions. They began to earn money, to accumulate wealth and to become economically more important and independent. They began to feel more competent and more autonomous, as well as more in control of their own lives. This new-found economic freedom began to change the balance between male and female in the marital relationship. As women were no longer financially dependent on men, they began to see marriage as a union between equals rather than as a state of dependency. In the new state of affairs, men and women are valued equally, at least theoretically, and share equal responsibility in the home, in childrearing, professionally and financially. Neither one is valued more than the other, and both are equally autonomous and independent. A woman who is working and has her own source of income has come to expect more of a marriage by way of equality and thus is more able and willing to leave an unhappy marriage and support herself. She will no longer allow herself to be dominated by a man and his money. And, in such cases, it is usually the woman who will initiate the divorce.

However, the husband may find it difficult, if not intolerable, dealing with a more assertive woman, and may either request the divorce or create a set of circumstances which make divorce inevitable.

Money in any relationship can symbolize commitment, self-esteem, power, love and acceptance. Freud saw money as a medium for self-preservation and obtaining power. Therefore, he who has the money has the power. Fenichel believed that the accumulation of wealth was a derivative of infantile narcissism transformed into a more realistic need to achieve power and self-esteem. In Self Psychology one might try to accumulate as much money as possible in order to enhance one's self-esteem. The more one can accumulate, the more approbation one receives and thus the more there is an increase in one's self-esteem. From a Sullivanian perspective, difficulties with money mirror difficulties with interpersonal relations.

Money is frequently a cause of marital discord in terms of power, control and autonomy. Balzac writing in "The Physiology of Marriage" stated "Keep from your wives the actual amount of your income − because the management of the money should not be put into the wife's hands. It is a popular error which is the cause of many misunderstandings between married people." Thus he who controls the purse controls the relationship. Money frequently reflects difficulties in interpersonal relations between the spouses and it is often a symbolic expression of underlying conflicts, both intrapsychic and interpersonal. On the intrapsychic level, money has been equated with feces and sex as dirty and taboo.

On the interpersonal level, money may represent power, autonomy, security, acceptance and control. In a divorce, money becomes entangled with love, affection, security and self worth. When two people decide to divorce, money often becomes the central focus of the emotional conflict, in effect substituting a concrete issue in place of the more elusive personal ones. This is unfortunate. Instead of the couple focussing on the causes of the break-up or on the short and long term effects of the break-up on the individuals, the children and the family (separation, loss, failure and mourning,) an undue focus is placed onto money and financial issues. In a divorce, money can thus be withheld as punishment or lavished on the spouse as a reward. The cause of the divorce is thus misunderstood and quickly forgotten.

Unfortunately, with the break-up of a marriage, the economic status of most women is greatly diminished. They experience a substantial decline in their standard of living and in their economic life style whereas the economic life style and standard of living following divorce for most men is higher. In divorce, a man might try to hide his assets from his wife so that he will not have to share the spoils of his marriage with her.

One is as secretive and withholding of money as one is secretive and withholding of sex. It is often easier to talk about sex, and one's sexual promiscuities and conquests than it is to talk about money. It is considered rude to ask someone how much he earns, how much he has in the bank or stocks. Sex for millennia has been a commodity to be bartered. Man since practically the beginning of time has bought favors for women in return for sex. Sex for women has long been a commodity to be sold or withheld accordingly. However, when a woman has her own money and her own means of support, she is less easily bought or exploited for her sex and less likely to remain in an unhappy marriage. Only when women have their own cash can they take control over their lives and become more autonomous.

In many marriages an emotional triangulation occurs which is the tendency of two people who are experiencing distress in the relationship to draw a third party into the fray whether this third party is a person or a thing. Instead of confronting the real problem such as loneliness, lack of emotional support, dominance and control, sex, they pretend that the third party is to blame. They project the problems onto this third party, which may be money and money than becomes the battleground.

In divorce, there is a great deal of anger and bitterness directed against the other person. Money is the weapon often used to hurt or to kill. It becomes the focus of bitter rage and hostility. Women are often more bitter and more hostile, perhaps because they have more to lose in the way of real money, self-esteem and ego. They are left in a more vulnerable position. One of the ways a woman might try to recoup her self-esteem is to go after a man for his money.

In a marriage in which a woman feels that she has been demeaned and controlled by a man and his money, she can recoup some of her self-esteem by going after her spouse for his money. If money is a major asset the woman will want "to take" from her divorcing spouse that which he valued most, money, thus making a sort of business deal. Money in exchange for freedom. The more money a woman gets from the divorce the more she is esteemed by herself and others.

There is such a thing as an ideal scenario for a divorce, when two people no longer care for each other and can no longer make a go of it. A husband might say to his wife, "I want a divorce. I still love you, I just can't live with you, and as proof of how much I love you, I will give you half of all that I own. I will always provide for you and take care of you. I will forever be committed to you. I'm simply leaving you to live with someone else." The wife, who has already recognized the truth of his feelings, agrees with his suggestions, and they part to remain bosom friends for the rest of their lives. Obviously, such a scenario rarely occurs.

Most often, when the husband make such an apparently generous offer, he is attempting to assuage his guilt while never truly understanding why the incompatibility arose and why divorce was necessary.

The wife in this scenario, has always felt depressed and alone, hungering for love and intimacy. While the offer of money might serve to keep the wolf from the door, it will not buy her what she longs for and needs. She feels unloved and abandoned. Though money might be helpful, it cannot restore her self-esteem. Self-esteem cannot be bought, and money is never a cure for loneliness or lack of intimacy.

Now for some of the financial realities of divorce. Two people living together can live more cheaply than two living apart. Divorce itself, especially where there are children, can be very expensive, far beyond the capabilities of the individuals involved. In the past, it was assumed that the children would remain with the mother and that the father would pay alimony and child support. Now fewer and fewer courts award alimony. Most states have either community property laws or what is called "equitable distribution" so that the property can be divided up in a more equitable fashion. However, even if there is no fight about money, the couple is bound to find something to fight about, given the hard feelings they have for each other. Now they can be seen battling it out in the courts for custody to the tune of thousands of dollars or even false allegations of sexual abuse.

In divorce there is a need for closure. The "after shock" is greatly minimized the sooner there is closure. However, at times lawyers prolong the divorce process thus preventing closure. At times lawyers interject their own views on the client. They believe they know what is best, right, or wrong for their client. Often it is the lawyer's ego. For example he cannot let the other lawyer (client's spouse) beat him. The attorney has the need to "win", to be victorious even at the financial expense of his client. By focussing on financial issues the attorney prevents the persons involved from feeling the pain and the anger of the divorce. Instead of feeling "cheated" that marriage did not work out like they anticipated or feeling that their spouse has "cheated on him or her", they will not allow themselves to be cheated or taken advantage of financially. Now, they will not allow their spouse to walk all over them. They will not be treated like "Caspar Milquetoast."

Money is perhaps the last gasp of the battle, where both parties need to feel victorious. As ugly as it is, it is better than battling for the children for visitation or custody, or holding the children up for ransom. Lawyers of course bill by the hour. Even the most scrupulous attorney might drag things out because it is money in his pocket. In law, the primary winners are the attorneys. Win or lose they profit.

Marshall Loeb in his 1986 book called *Money Guide* states that more and more divorces are being negotiated in accountants' offices. Splitting up a marriage is like splitting up a business partnership. Instead of fighting over who did what to whom, he advises that smart couples concentrate on tallying up the dollar signs acquired in life together, so that it can be split along some appropriate lines. The new theory is that money and property should be divided fairly and finally so that each partner can move on to the next stage of his or her life.

In the year 1986, only 14% of women divorcing received alimony. Only those over 50 or in poor health are likely to collect though wives do and can receive child support and temporary alimony. It is assumed that women should now work and support themselves. They are thus given temporary alimony just long enough to re-enter the work force or to train for a job. Just recently women have begun to see that they "cut a better deal" under the old divorce laws. Although women want equality as yet there is no equality as far as the earning potential of women compared to men.

Support of the children is now generally considered the responsibility of both parents. The best divorce settlement can come about when each person concentrates on "enlightened self interest." In such cases they accept that neither will come out ahead but each will be able to make a clean break and start anew.

Once the divorce is worked out and the financial arrangements are completed, there are still money problems. Uncle Sam must be paid. Some of the consequences of divorce tax-wise are:

1. Alimony: the wife must pay income tax on this money.
2. Child Support: taxes are paid by the one who earns the money, not by the one who receives it.
3. One can claim a share of a spouse's pension either in a lump sum or in monthly installments. A medical degree or law degree is considered "community property".
4. Capital gains taxes on property acquired during a marriage does not have to be paid until the property or asset is sold.

Since, of the two million marriages a year in this country, one million will end in divorce, more attention is being paid to legal arrangements even before the marriage takes place. Prenuptial agreements are now in vogue. Both men and women are taking inventory of separate assets and liabilities before marriage. There are his, hers and ours bank accounts. In many ways, the new divorce laws with equitable distribution are a step in the right direction. The woman's economic independence need not threaten the man's self-esteem but is simply a shift towards sharing and equality.

Divorce is never a pleasant experience. There is no such thing as a painless divorce. Let me take you through the analysis of a patient who came to see me because her husband was leaving her for another woman. I can well remember her feelings of Rage! Anger! Betrayal! Disappointment! Disillusionment! Shame and Guilt! Marriage was not forever. How could she ever face her friends, family and colleagues? What would they think and say? She thought of herself as a failure. How would her friends line up, with her or with her soon-to-be ex-spouse? Depression, suicidal thoughts, homicidal feelings, finances! How would she be able to support herself and her two children? The private school tuition had not been paid. Mortgage payments were due. Taxes, food, clothing, housekeeper expenses. The children, what was going to happen to them? Lawyers $5,000 just for the retainer. Could she cope? Was there a choice or an alternative? Though she was already an attorney, she was more a full time mother. She now had to go out and work.

Terror, and more terror! The castles they'd begun to build together were crumbling. Could she alone support herself and her two children? Blame! It was all her fault. If only she had behaved differently. Enlightenment. A thought and realization, if all other attorneys could support three wives and seven children, she should at least be able to support herself and her two children at that time, age seven and eleven. Survive, she told herself. She could and would survive the break-up. With determination, she decided that neither she not the children would suffer financially. She took a full time job. She began to work longer hours. Growth and success. She began to see and experience the divorce as a growth rather than a failure. Instead of remaining in an unhappy marriage, with a person who no longer loved her and as a matter of fact who she felt hated her, she had a chance to start all over again. But what a slow process. Re-establishing herself professionally, socially, financially, as a single parent when the world seemed like Noah's Ark. Animals all live in and come in twos. Her friends who went through the divorce with her can remember her saying that she'd lost her best friend. And indeed at the time it felt like she had. Then she began to see her best friend change into her worst enemy. She could no longer turn to him for help or consolation. She could remember the first big purchase she made on her own, a Volkswagen camper to go West in. She felt alone in the world with Paul and Lisa. She was on her own. It was sink or swim. She felt that the tides and currents were against her. Only now as she looks back, eight years later can say she made it. But what about the scar? Will she ever trust again? Will she ever be able to share herself, her life and money with anyone again? Will she ever be able to take the marriage vows again "For richer, for poorer...till death do us part?" Yes, but it will never have the same meaning. Thus divorce was a growing experience for her. It has made her a better person, a better parent and a better attorney. However, she still thinks marriage should be forever, though it is not. If one is fortunate enough to marry, yet unfortunate enough to divorce, one should hopefully try to integrate the trauma and come out as whole a person as possible.

Though she can never forgive her ex-spouse for his betrayal, she now thanks him for forcing her to grow up and become an adult. Money need no longer be the focus of intense hostility. The woman no longer has to give herself to the man, and the man no longer possesses the woman. Each person is responsible for his or her life. Divorce might give each person the opportunity to achieve equality, autonomy, self-esteem and freedom. It is the end to the hostile integration, or the triangulation, or the protective identification, or the blaming of the other person for whatever has gone wrong. Being financially responsible adds to one's self-esteem and sense of self worth. It is not a threat to one's femininity but rather a chance to integrate financial competency into that femininity. It gives each of the two parties the opportunity to recoup self-esteem and to take control over his or her own life. As in every marriage, in every divorce there are important emotional legal, psychological and financial consequences and ramifications.

Hopefully each partner will learn from his or her mistakes. Each will see that although the marriage failed, each divorcing partner is not a failure. Each must go on with life. The divorce becomes a positive growth experience, a chance to learn, to separate, to move on, to take care of oneself, to make decisions and to take responsibility for one's own life.

CHAPTER 9

GAMBLING

Eugene L. Lowenkopf, M.D.

When the first comprehensive survey of gambling was done, in 1974, it was estimated that 68% of all Americans indulged in one form or another at least once in their lives while 61% were currently involved on a regular basis (1). These numbers have probably gone up since in view of two factors: the gambling rate then was progressively higher in younger people who have matured into a more prominent role in our society, and there are now more easily accessible government sponsored lotteries. Most of our compatriots participate in forms of gambling that are apparently innocent and harmless such as bingo games, office pools, off-track betting, card games or state lotteries. A smaller number participates in other forms that are considered less benign like horse and dog racing, jai alai and casinos. However, while different types of gambling may seem more or less respectable, this can be misleading since so-called respectable games can entice the vulnerable to the extent that they lose control while the supposedly heavy gambling scene can attract the casual gambler who is able to stop himself or herself before going too far.

Nevertheless, a lot of people do gamble and it might be a good idea to describe the various kinds of gamblers so that we can eliminate the non-problematic ones from further consideration. Custer, in a 1988 paper (2), classified active gamblers into six categories: the professional gambler, the criminal gambler, the casual social gambler, the serious social gambler, the escape social gambler and the pathological gambler.

The professional gambler is essentially a businessman whose business is gambling. He is a serious student of the matter who bets only when it is a sure thing and who manages money carefully. For such a person, gambling is not fun but work; patience and a cool head are essential. The criminal gambler overlaps with the professional but deals in illegal methods such as running numbers and bookmaking.

Social gamblers include the vast majority of people who gamble. The

Money and Mind, Edited by S. Klebanow and
E.L. Lowenkopf, Plenum Press, New York, 1991

casual gambler indulges in an occasional card game or lotto, or bets on a favorite sport. Such an individual can take it or leave it, and can fill the time spent gambling with any number of other pursuits. The next category, the serious social gambler, participates with regularity, works hard at trying to figure out a system but keeps losses within manageable limits and fulfills all personal responsibilities. Here might be included the elderly who go regularly to Las Vegas and to Atlantic City, but rarely or never spend more than they can afford. For them, gambling serves as a socially acceptable time filler. The escape social gambler does so to relieve tension, frustrations, anger or worry. Such a person may be emotional and erratic about gambling, but the situation arises only sporadically and losses are within tolerable limits.

Most of these categories are easily understood psychologically and require little professional attention, but of much more concern are those individuals whose lives are destroyed along with those of their families by the irresistible urge to gamble beyond reasonable limits. While these are far fewer than 68% of the populace, there are still substantial numbers of both problem gamblers and pathological gamblers. However, it is necessary to define what constitutes excessive indulgence in the activity.

Not until DSM-III, in 1980, included pathological gambling as a diagnostic entity, listing it as in impulse disorder, was there a formal psychiatric definition (3). The essential features were stated to be a chronic and progressive failure to resist impulses to gamble, and gambling behavior that compromises, disrupts or damages personal, family or vocational pursuits. The formal diagnostic criteria were:

A.   The individual is chronically and progressively unable to resist impulses to gamble.

B.   Gambling compromises, disrupts or damages family, personal and vocational pursuits as indicated by at least three of the following:

1.   Arrest for forgery, fraud, embezzlement or income tax evasion.

2.   Default on debts or other financial responsibilities.

3.   Disrupted family or spouse relationship due to gambling.

4.   Borrowing of money from illegal sources (loan sharks).

5.   Inability to account for loss of money or to produce evidence of winning money, if this is claimed.

6.   Loss of work due to absenteeism in order to pursue gambling activity.

7.   Necessity for another person to provide money to relieve a desperate financial situation.

C.   The gambling is not due to Antisocial Personality Disorder.

It will be noted that these criteria do not make mention of premorbid personality, special character traits, other personality problems, reasons why the gambling urge becomes so overwhelming, or any other subjective features. Instead, the focus is on problems in living that gambling brings about, a focus that is consistent with DSM-III's preference for external over internal issues. If gambling was considered a compulsion or even an addiction (as has been suggested over the years), such subjective and intraphysic issues would have to be used as criteria, something that DSM-III does not allow. In 1988, with the publication of DSM-IIIR (4), the criteria were changed to the following:

Maladaptive gambling behavior, as indicated by at least four of the following:

1.   Frequent preoccupation with gambling or with obtaining money to gamble.

2.   Frequent gambling of large amount of money or over a longer period of time than intended.

3.   A need to increase the size or frequency of bets to achieve the desired excitement.

4.   Restlessness or irritability if unable to gamble.

5.   Repeated loss of money by gambling and returning another day to win back losses ("chasing").

6.   Repeated efforts to reduce or stop gambling.

7.   Frequent gambling when expected to meet social or occupational obligations.

8.   Sacrifice of some important social, occupational or recreational activity in order to gamble.

9.   Continuation of gambling despite inability to pay monetary debts, or despite other significant social, occupational, or legal problems that the person knows to be exacerbated by gambling.

At first glance, there appears to be little difference between DSM-III and DSM-IIIR definitions in that both describe behavior and emphasize difficulties in living that gambling brings about; again, there is nothing intrapsychic., However, DSM-IIIR does mention a need to increase the "dosage" to obtain excitement and also speaks of restlessness or irritability occurring when the need to gamble is frustrated. Such terminology is usually reserved for addictions and informs us that there is a growing tendency to regard gambling as an addiction with possible physiological concomitants.

While DSM-III specifically rules out antisocial personality disorder, DSM-IIIR recognizes that this diagnosis may simultaneously be present. Another diagnosis that frequently is associated with the pathological gambler is alcoholism. While manics may gamble in their excitement phase and may get into trouble doing so, they usually do this only episodically rather than chronically. Depressive gamblers who find relief from their distress in the thrill of gambling are more of a problem since the depression may be chronic and the need to escape it continuous, leading to severe chronic gambling.

DSM-IIIR provides us as well with a characterology of the pathological gambler: overconfident, very energetic, easily bored and a "big spender", but also someone who shows signs of personal stress, anxiety or depression at times. The disorder begins in adolescence in males, later in females, and may lead to suicide attempts, drug taking and myriad problems with the law. Predisposing factors are reported to be loss of parents by death, separation, divorce or desertion before age 15; inappropriate parental discipline (absence, inconsistency or harshness); exposure to gambling activity as an adolescent; and a high family value placed on material and financial symbols with a lack of family emphasis on saving, planning or budgeting.

With a more serious definition of pathological gambling in place. Volberg and Steadman (5) attempted to quantify the actual number of people who might be regarded as pathological gamblers. The researchers accomplished 1000 telephone interviews with a population whose demography was typical of New York State where the survey was done. They found that 28 (or 2.8%) of their sample were probable problem gamblers while 14 (or 1.4%) were even worse off, meriting the diagnosis of pathological gambler. Extrapolating from this suggests that somewhere between 230,000 and 486,400 of New York's 12.8 million adults gamble to excess while 89,600 to 269,000 are probable pathological gamblers. Amazing as these numbers may seem, they only confirm previous data available from other parts of the country.

Gambling has been reported in virtually every ancient society from which some sort of record exists: Egyptian, Greek, Roman, ancient Hindu, Chinese, Japanese, Mesopotamian and Persian. It was known among the Scythians and the Huns, and has also been observed with regularity by anthropologists studying less advanced societies in the Pacific, the far North and the far South. Although there are reports that gambling came to America with the first settlers, it was already well established here in various

Indian tribes. Its allure has been portrayed frequently in painting and in literature, it being almost a staple in the 19th century Russian novel.

As the infant field of psychology began to develop, gambling received its share of attention. Clemens France, writing in 1902, examined the subject in some detail and concluded that an environment of uncertain content was necessary to our species, emotional intensity was essential to gambling, chance and risk were a requisite balance to law and order, and humans periodically gave up intellectual pursuits for instinctual (6).

Most psychoanalytic attention to gambling, which did not commence until 1914, is couched in theory and language more of historical interest than useful in understanding the disorder. Von Hattingberg deserves the credit of being the first psychoanalyst to examine the subject (7). He stated that the fear inherent in risks taken by gamblers was an eroticized derivative of urethral and anal strivings, thus uniting infantile anxiety and gambling. Simmel, in 1920, opined that the gambler had regressed to the anal level and was dealing with pregenital anal-sadistic impulses (8).

Freud himself did not address the subject of gambling until 1928 when he wrote a critical study of Dostoyevsky (9). He devoted most of the paper to a consideration of Dostoyevsky's relationship with his father and his strong parricidal urge. This urge produced guilt which required self-punishment; this led him to gamble and acquire a burden of debts. As proof of this hypothesis, Freud mentioned that Dostoyevsky wrote his best when he had lost most heavily; only then did he feel relaxed enough to create. Freud also analogized gambling to masturbation, using as proof certain similarities between the two; the irresistible nature of the temptation, solemn resolutions (always broken) to stop, stupefying pleasure and bad conscience about it all.

In 1947, Greenson wrote a paper reporting on his observation of the gambling scene and his work with five gamblers who entered treatment for other reasons (10). He noted that the sense of excitement in gambling is very similar to sexual arousal and discharge patterns. There was a plentitude of ritual with recourse to superstition and magical thinking, as if thoughts or actions could influence chance outcomes. He concluded that these indicated a background of regression to archaic and primitive modes of thinking. Greenson saw gambling as an impulse disorder resembling addictions and perversions both in its nature and in its treatment.

Lindner rejected the idea that gambling was an impulse disorder (11). He saw it as always being ego-alien and he felt that the gambler was not a psychopath, rather an obsessional neurotic egged on by magical fantasies. When he wins, he is a successful parricide but when he loses, he does not have to contend with guilt, but instead has his omnipotence shattered and is left to face the consequences of his neurosis (12).

Perhaps the most prolific psychoanalytic writer on gambling was Edmund Bergler who wrote a book on the subject in 1957 directed towards the lay public (13) as well as a major scientifically oriented paper (14). He emphasized that the gambler is a masochist with a strong unconscious wish to lose who seeks out unjust treatment as a confirmation of his belief that his parents were depriving him.

Bergler described six different types of gamblers: the classical gambler who rebels against the reality principle and probability, the passive feminine male who has strong feminine identification and who seeks the sexual satisfaction of being overwhelmed, the male gambler who defends against a feminine id by a facade of maleness, the gambler motivated by unconscious guilt, the "unexcited" gambler, and the female gambler.

Fink, in 1961, spoke of gambling as a mental illness, caused by feelings of inferiority and inadequacy (15). The gambler craves mothering and reassurance, and gambles as a form of regression to childhood in an effort to achieve these aims. The gambler is usually unsuccessful in everything he touches and succeeds only in boasts and fantasies. Fink also noted that gamblers have poor sex lives, and saw this both as part of their initial problem and as a consequence of gambling affecting their relations with their wives. He felt that treatment offered only a slim chance of improvement and noted that the inadequate-feeling gambler need a lots of love and gentle treatment from a therapist as well as from this family, something not easy to provide to someone so difficult.

Bolen and Boyd proposed in 1968 that pathological gambling is a complex symptom involving a defensive maneuver against a host of painful affects (16). Identification with a gambler parent is an important etiological factor, and specific episodes are usually precipitated by overwhelming life crises. These authors moved away from libidinal formulations which they found theoretically inaccurate and reductionistic. In describing their therapeutic efforts with a group composed of gamblers and their spouses, they reported criticism of a "jerky" psychiatrist who had previously told the gambler that he gambled because of a need to masturbate (17).

An alternate approach to understanding gambling is suggested by behavioral psychologists who regard it as a pathological habit which eventuates from a high level of excitement and the positive experience of winning. The habit is reinforced when there is a high frequency of wins, easy availability of the activity, and a short interval between wagering and payoff, when real skill is believed to be involved, and when gambling behavior is regarded as socially appropriate and acceptable. Nevertheless, the habit can be broken through application of appropriate negative influences. While gambling has not been the focus of extensive behavioristic research, several therapeutic approaches have been utilized.

Recent years have seen a major change in the psychiatric approach to depression with a reexamination of all problems in which depression is a component; this has occurred in gambling as well. McCormick and his group administered the Schedule for Affective Disorders and Schizophrenia (SADS) to 50 patients hospitalized in the gambling unit of a VA hospital, and evaluated their responses according to Research Diagnostic Criteria (18). They found that 76% had major depressive disorder and 38% hypomanic disorder. The more depressed gamblers stood a much greater chance of having their lives significantly disrupted by gambling.

These results were confirmed by Linden and his co-workers, using standardized clinical interviews on 25 problem gamblers (participants in a Gamblers Anonymous program), and exploring their family trees (19). 76% of their subjects reported one incident of major depression and 50% had recurrent episodes of either major depression or bipolar disorder. 32% had one first degree relative with a major affective disorder, while 36% had at least one first degree relative with alcohol abuse or dependency. Concordant with the hypothesis that gambling represents an expression of major affective disorder is the use of Lithium as a treatment (20). The one paper reporting on this modality presents only three case histories, all of which did well on Lithium but all of whom appear to be diagnosable as manics rather than as pathological gamblers.

Psychobiological explorations of various syndromes have also characterized the recent psychiatric scene, and gambling has received some of this attention. Twenty-four individuals who met DSM-III criteria for gambling were studied for evidence of chemical disturbances known to be present in the urine, plasma and cerebrospinal fluid of patients with impulse disorders (21). The gamblers had significantly higher urinary norepinephrine and CSF levels of 3-methoxy-4-hydroxyphenylgycol than controls. This suggests that the gambler may have a functional disturbance of his noradrenergic system.

In spite of the many insights that psychoanalytic, behavioral and psychobiological examinations of gambling and gamblers offer us, there is no definitive treatment. Historically, the first therapy offered to gamblers was psychoanalytic. Most of the psychoanalytic writers whose papers I have cited treated a small number of patients. Whether the patients improved or not was not usually stated although they did serve as a clinical base for psychodynamic theorizing. Those writers who did comment on outcome generally were pessimistic. In any case, there were no large samples (Bergler is the exception with a reported cure rate of 30 out of 60 patients) and there were no control groups or careful evaluations of outcome. Similarly, behavioral therapies were applied to small numbers of patients without controls (unless the non-treated gambler population at large is so considered) or suitable long term outcome studies. It should be remarked that, in such a condition, however, control groups are almost impossible to establish, and there is a lack of agreement concerning what constitutes a good outcome: is it reduced frequency of gambling, its total elimination, or the actuation of other personality changes?

Behavioral therapy for gambling utilized, for the most part, aversion therapy. This is applied in the form of painful electric shocks which accompany specific component behaviors of gambling such as reading a racing page, or photographs of betting parlors, racing tickets and so forth (22,23). Imaginal desensitization using relaxation techniques accompanying scenes in which gambling urges usually arise has also been tried (24).

A note of caution should be sounded at the outset to any psychotherapist contemplating treatment of a pathological gambler. While gambling is not an addiction in the sense of there being a true physiological dependence, it is comparable in the sense that gamblers are as difficult to engage in any therapy as are addicts. They do not have patience for the deferred understanding of why they do what they do and prefer the immediate gratification of actually doing it. If they do undertake some form of treatment, it's usually reluctantly and at the insistence of their families as the runaway gambling reaches crisis proportions. They don't want to be there, they miss appointments, they tell tall tales and they don't pay their bills. Finally, they terminate treatment, either with or without due notice, the minute the family pressures let up. However, the gambling doesn't get better and some few do eventually make a serious stab at treatment.

Today, probably the most frequently employed means of going about this is through Gamblers Anonymous, an organization begun in 1957 and run very much along the lines of the more familiar Alcoholics Anonymous (25). The gamblers are expected to be totally abstinent and they meet in groups at regular intervals (at least once weekly) when they discuss their problems openly with each other and describe how they were messing up their lives. They also have buddies to whom they turn when the gambling fever hits.

There is a quasi-religious belief in a higher power beyond themselves to which they turn, and they also try to deal with their problems "one day at a time". Critics point out that there is a high drop-out rate, that addiction to the program substitutes for addiction to gambling and that emphasizing the intervention of a higher power demeans the individual and reduces one's autonomy. Supporters point out that GA works for some, and in the absence of good alternatives, it serves a very valuable function.

Even when other modalities are used, GA is often incorporated into these more comprehensive approaches. Russo et al (26) use it as a keystone of their 30-day structured inpatient program which includes group psychotherapy, education, and activities training, in addition to GA meetings. The authors claim that, out of 60 patients, 51% attained complete abstinence as well as better interpersonal and financial status, and had less depression. Post-hospitalization treatment consisted of professional aftercare and GA.

The therapist who does work with gamblers, whether in groups or in individual therapy, will find that certain themes arise with regularity as the treatment proceeds; these must be recognized as cognitions special to gamblers and must be examined and revised if psychotherapy is to have a successful outcome. These are: the paramount significance of money in the gambler's life, his pervasive sense of inadequacy and the extensive defenses he uses against it coming into awareness, and his perception of life as lackluster and dull.

First and foremost is the exaggerated importance of money to the gambler. In a money-oriented world, it is difficult to convince anyone that his or her lust for money is exaggerated, since it can buy so many things that make life more pleasant. The therapist must grant the reality value of money right from the start so that treatment can move on to the more neurotic and problematic expectations: power, success, sexual attractiveness, health and immortality. Unfortunately, these beliefs are shared with gamblers by many others, and it is often hard to dissuade a gambler that his beliefs are erroneous. What is unique to the gambler is that he minimizes the importance of other means towards achieving these goals and believes that only the rapid acquisition of lots of money will accomplish his ends. So, concurrent with the overriding emphasis on money is a devaluation of other important aspects of life: work, love, relationships, and so forth.

Nevertheless, it is apparent that the gambler has a deep and abiding faith in money and a very inflated idea of what it can do and just how much it does make the world go round. The therapist may find himself or herself in the position of espousing a noble and altruistic world view, pointing out repeatedly other virtues and value systems, while minimizing the role of money. It is important not to be moralizing and preachy, but to repeatedly insist on the errors of the patient's devotion to money as the *sole* panacea in life.

The gambler starts treatment under duress and initially seems cowed and overwhelmed, but this appearance arises from recent defeats and does not necessarily indicate any self-awareness. Very quickly, he snaps out of this state and appears quite the opposite; confident, and even swaggering, and he speaks as if he can take on the whole world with one hand tied behind his back. At these times, the glamour of gambling and the possibility of making a financial killing seem very real to the patient, who denies his realities of repeated loss, financial catastrophe and non-stop failure. He is convinced that he has the skills to make a difference, and he knows that he can pick the right horse, has finally figured out the roulette system, can now remember the sequence of cards, and so forth. The therapist should recognize that this grandiose thinking represents a denial of and a reaction against a basically poor self-image. Believing that real skills are involved and denying the total haphazardness of chance suit his need to deny his inadequacies; the odds just do not pertain to him.

From a technical standpoint, these are hard beliefs to shake since overtly denying that the patient has special talents throws him into greater contact with his inadequacies and often stimulates increased gambling behavior. On the other hand, as erroneously held beliefs, they must, at some point, be challenged. A consistent therapist who does not attack the patient's skills, but who assists him in dealing with reality issues often reduces the feelings of inadequacy and the need to gamble to counter these feelings.

Gamblers also describe life as routine, boring and humdrum. To balance this out, they need the excitement, thrill, and challenge that gambling provides. Again, the therapist should not engage in a discussion of how interesting life might be without gambling, but should investigate the patient's lack of success in other areas of involvement that go to make his life so unrewarding, directing the patient to consideration of his personal blocks and inhibitions. The inhibited person cannot get involved in many matters, has a more limited world, and so does become bored even to the point of depression; a turn to gambling produces excitement, even though success here may be totally elusive. Overcoming inhibitions permits greater participation in the world, effectively reduces the boredom and the consequent dependence on gambling for stimulation.

While the major focus in psychological efforts to understand gambling has been on the pathological gambler, it would be a mistake not to mention that it may also have beneficial aspects as well. The very fact that millions of people play weekly lotto games and other games of chance proves this; for all of them, it provides hope that their financial problems will soon mend, and it gives them a chance to dream and fantasize, well worth the expense of a dollar. The fact that they lose every week is only a minor disappointment, and one might even say that the purpose of playing is more to permit the free range of fantasy than to win. In this regard, the therapist may well find it useful to explore with patients the content of their win fantasies; valuable material that might not otherwise appear can be tapped in this way.

For some individuals with impaired social lives, gambling is an activity that provides some interpersonal contact. Although the nature of such contact is limited to the transaction of the game, it does provide some relief to a person who might otherwise be totally isolated. Even for those who do have fuller social lives, it provides an additional area of interest, one that does not require intense interpersonal relatedness, but is satisfying in its own way.

While the therapist has to discourage the rationalization in the pathological gambler that life is boring and routine, the fact is that gambling may be utilized to benefit a variety of charitable and educational causes, effectively raising money where other methods might not be so successful. A case might even be made that gambling provides an education in probability theory and risk taking to the young, as well as teaching them something about mathematics. However, whatever benefits gambling offers, the question always arises whether these positive aspects are outweighed by its potential dangers.

The subject of gambling remains a frustrating one to therapists, since the problem seems so clearly to have psychological roots, and yet the gambler himself remains so resistant to even the best-informed, best-intentioned assistance. But the truth is that we know very little for sure, and there are still many unresolved questions. Do permissive social attitudes produce more pathological gamblers or is a predisposing personality necessary, or some combination of the two? Does the easy availability of state lotteries and other government sponsored gambling encourage early participation which later goes on to produce more severe gambling? What is the relationship of depression to gambling? Is there a chemical predisposition? Do different social classes get involved in different ways? But perhaps the biggest question is how do we, as therapists and as members of society, help a problem which causes so much grief and waste? Perhaps the next few years will provide us with some more answers.

REFERENCES

1. Commission on the Review of the National Policy Toward Gambling: Gambling in America. Washington, DC US Govt. Printing Office, 1978.
2. Custer, RL. The Psychiatric Times, May 1987. PP 19, 20.
3. American Psychiatric Association: Diagnostic and Statistical Manual, Third Edition, Washington, DC APA, 1980.
4. American Psychiatric Association: Diagnostic and Statistical. Manual, Third Edition, Revised, Washington, DC APA, 1987.
5. Volberg, RA and Steadman, HA. Refining Prevalence Estimates of Pathological Gambling. Am Jnl of Psychiatry 145:502-505, 1988.
6. France, C. The Gambling Impulse. Am Jnl of Psychology. 13:364-376, 382-407, 1902.
7. VonHattingberg, H. Analerotik, Angstlust und Eigensinn. Int Zeit Psychoan. 2:244-258, 1914.
8. Simmel, E. On the Psychoanalysis of the Gambler. Int Zeit Psychoan 6:397, 1920.
9. Freud, S. Dostoyevsky and Parricide, in Strachey, J. (ed) The Complete Psychological Works of Sigmund Freud, Hogarth Press Ltd., London. vol 21, pp 177-194, 1961.
10. Greenson, RR. On gambling. Amer Imago 4:61:77, 1947.
11. Lindner, RM. The Psychodynamics of Gambling. Ann Amer Acad Pol Soc Sci 269:93-107, 1960.
12. Fenichel, O. The Psychoanalytic Theory of Neurosis. New York, WW Norton Co., 1945.
13. Bergler, E. The Psychology of Gambling. New York, Hill and Wang. 1957.
14. Bergler, E. The Gambler: A Misunderstood Neurotic. Jnl Crim Psychopath 4:379-393. 1932-1943.
15. Fink, HK. Compulsive Gambling. Acta Psychother. 9:251-261, 1961.
16. Bolen, DW and Boyd, WH. Gambling and the Gambler; A Review and Preliminary Findings. Arch Gen Psych 18:617-630, 1968.

17. Boyd, WH and Bolen, DW. The Compulsive Gambler and Spouse in Group Psychotherapy. Int Jnl of Group Psychotherapy. 20:77-90, 1970.

18. McCormick, RA, Russo, AM, Ramirez, LF, and Taber, JI. Affective Disorders among Pathological Gamblers Seeking Treatment. Am Jnl Psychiatry. 141:215-218, 1984.

19. Linden, RD, Pope, HG, Jonas, JM. Pathological Gambling and Major Affective Disorders: Preliminary Findings. Jnl Clin Psychiatry 47:201-203, 1986.

20. Moskowitz, JA. Lithium and Lady Luck. NY State Jnl of Medicine. 80:785-788, 1980.

21. Roy, AL, Adinoff, B. Roehrich, L., et al. Pathological Gambling: A Psychobiological Study. Arch. Gen Psych 45:369-373, 1988.

22. Goorney, AB. Treatment of a Compulsive Horse Race Gambler by Aversion Therapy. Brit Jnl of Psych 114:329-373, 1988.

23. Seager, CP. Treatment of Compulsive Gamblers by Electrical Aversion. Brit Jnl of Psych 117:545-553, 1970.

24. McGonaghy, N., Armstrong, JS, Beaszczynski, A. and Allcock, C. Controlled Comparison of Aversion Therapy and Imaginal Desensitization in Compulsive Gambling. Brit Jnl of Psych 142:366-372, 1983.

25. Gamblers Anonymous, Los Angeles, Gamblers Anonymous Press, 1977.

26. Russo, AM, Taber, JI, McCormick, RA and Ramirez, LF. An Outcome Study of an Inpatient Treatment Program for Pathological Gamblers. Hosp Comm Psych 35:823-827, 1984.

CHAPTER 10

IN THE MATTER OF SETTING THE VALUE
OF PSYCHOLOGICAL DAMAGES

Marianne L. Sussman, J.D.

Large, some say excessively large, damages awards for personal injuries
are reported daily in the press. Psychological damages, including conscious
pain and suffering, mental anguish and loss of companionship of a loved one,
constitute a major component of such awards. Although the value of such
losses is incalculable, our legal system has developed a means of establishing
their value. The system combines time-honored legal principles and the
collective judgment of the jury to accomplish this result.

When the law strives to find truth and to dispense justice, money is
often the measure of the justice it dispenses. Financial compensation is the
primary means our legal system has developed to compensate victims for
injuries of all kinds.

The range of injuries the law tries to remedy through financial awards
is broad. First there are the many legal transactions which involve money.
A contract is usually entered for the purpose of making money or for
acquiring something of monetary value. If a party breaches the contract, the
other party is entitled to recover the money or value which has been lost
because of that breach. Also, if a person suffers physical injury or injury to
his property at the hands of another, he may be awarded monetary damages
to compensate for financial and other losses.

In criminal cases, fines are often an alternative or additional penalty.
The fine serves, in a sense, as compensation to society at large for the
violation of its order, whether by violence or by other unacceptable conduct.
In the recent highly-publicized case of Bernhard Goetz, who shot his four
alleged muggers on a subway train, a $5,000 fine was imposed in addition to
a jail term. Victim compensation funds have been developed for the purpose
of compensating the victims of crimes in some measure for their injuries,
rather than filling the public coffers.

Although not all civil cases are for compensation, those not involving
money are a minority. In general, in non-criminal cases, our legal system
deals with the demands of plaintiffs for financial compensation. An injured

Money and Mind, Edited by S. Klebanow and
E.L. Lowenkopf, Plenum Press, New York, 1991

party has the right to assert a claim for the loss or damages suffered and, if justified, to have the wrongdoer pay for the loss.

Generally, the extent of the injury suffered provides the measure of the compensation to be paid. The injury for breach of contract is the monetary measure of the innocent party's disappointed expectations. Damages due to personal injury and property damage include direct monetary losses – repair bills, medical bills, loss of earnings. These losses are measurable and can be calculated from actual expenses or projections. The objective in establishing the amount to be paid is to restore the injured party to economic wholeness, the condition he or she would have had if the injury had not occurred or if the contract had been performed.

The more difficult task the law undertakes is to dispense compensation for injuries which are not and cannot be measured in economic terms. Damage to reputation, pain and suffering, loss of a limb, loss of a loved one– –all are serious injuries but elude calculation. They are serious losses in human terms and are recognized in the tax laws as a diminution of human capital: monetary damages collected for such loss are not considered income.

Notwithstanding the difficulty in quantifying the measure, the legal system does not allow the wrongdoer to escape the burden of compensating the victim. If the loss is, in a sense, more than money can measure, it is not fair or just that the person who caused the injury should not compensate the victim at all. While full restoration for loss of the enjoyment of life or for the loss of a parent's nurturing and guidance may not be possible, the law has formulated remedies in the form of monetary awards, attempting to calculate the monetary equivalent of the loss. Whether the injury is to business or property, to person or spirit, the remedy in our legal system is financial.

If the injury cannot be calculated in costs of lost monetary benefit, recoupment of the value of damaged property or medical expenses, the law stretches to set a value for the invaluable, to quantify the unquantifiable human loss. Until injuries can be undone, until more appropriate compensation can be invented, the law compensates by the remedy it is familiar with dispensing – monetary damages.

The jury is the body which attempts to calculate the equivalent of the plaintiff's economic wholeness, and it is directed to measure the extent of the injuries and losses. The courts have recognized, however, that juries may be unduly moved by sympathy for injured plaintiffs; rather than restrict the amounts juries may award, the courts developed doctrines of law which reduced the cases in which damages would be awarded. By this, the system attempted to control the sympathy of juries faced with pitiful plaintiffs with devastating losses.

Various legal doctrines restrict recoveries. The general rules of liability require that a jury first find that the defendant is legally responsible, and therefore liable, for the plaintiff's injuries before it calculates damages. If there is intentional wrongdoing, if the harmful act is intended to cause harm and it does in fact cause harm, the defendant is legally responsible.

Liability goes beyond intent, however. In certain situations, a defendant may be strictly liable, that is, liable even without fault. For example, when a person engages in potentially dangerous or hazardous activities, he or she may be liable for injury caused even if proper care is employed. An owner or keeper of a wild animal is responsible for the injury caused by the animal's attack even if all due precautions are taken. In some states, the same standard applies to a dog owner. This is a departure from the traditional "one bite" rule which gives the owner one chance to know of the dog's dangerous propensities and to take precautionary steps before being held liable. Other hazardous activities for which strict liability is imposed are blasting, pile driving, fumigating, crop dusting, waterway damming and the sale of defective products.

A defendant may also be held liable for personal injuries caused by negligence. Negligence in a legal sense is shown if an accident is caused by the wrongdoer's failure to meet a reasonable standard of care. If the defendant has a duty of care to the injured party and has failed to exercise a reasonable level of care, the defendant is liable to compensate the plaintiff for injuries. The jury, a committee chosen from the community, is expected in its collective judgment to recognize from common experience what was a reasonable degree of care in a given situation.

Other legal doctrines may limit the scope of the defendant's liability. The doctrine of proximate cause is applied to determine whether a wrongdoer's act is the significant causative factor in the plaintiff's injuries. The chain of causation from the act to the injury must not be too long or too tenuous and the outcome must not be too improbable or unpredictable for the wrongdoer to be held accountable.

The 1928 case of *Palsgraf* v. *Long Island Rail Road Co.*,(1) known to all law students, involved the following facts: the plaintiff was standing on a railroad platform waiting for a train; a man carrying a package rushed to catch another train which was already moving at the other end of the platform. Though he caught the train, his footing was unsteady, and a railroad employee pushed him on from behind, causing him to drop his package which contained fireworks. The fireworks exploded, and the shock of the explosion caused scales at the other end of the platform to fall, striking the plaintiff. She sued the railroad for her injuries. New York's highest court, the Court of Appeals, determined that the plaintiff was not entitled to recover because she was not a party for whom the railroad employee could have foreseen injury. A minority of the Court found that the injury was nearly enough caused by the negligent act of the railroad employee to hold the railroad liable, because the chain of causation was direct.

Historically, the courts developed other rules to restrict plaintiffs' rights to compensation, even when the legal elements of liability were shown. While some of these restrictive rules were later discarded, others remain the backbone of modern tort law and govern compensation for personal injuries.

A major obstacle to recovery for injuries was the bar to compensation for wrongful death. The right to sue for injuries was considered personal to the injured person. If one died from injuries, one's right to compensation died also. This caused the anomalous situation in which the wrongdoer would be liable for damages if his actions caused lesser injury, but would have no liability if they caused death. As one commentator wrote, it became "more profitable for the defendant to kill the plaintiff than to scratch him."(2)

Legislatures responded to this anomaly. First in England, then state by state in the United States, they began to allow for the claim for wrongful death by the surviving family or by the estate of the deceased person.

The laws which allowed wrongful death actions at first placed a restriction on the amount that could be recovered, a limit of $10,000 being common. The fixed or token sum was intended to deal with the difficulty of measuring the value of the loss of a life. The courts have, however, continued to develop measuring standards and rules to establish sums which more nearly reflect the magnitude of the injury suffered.

Another rule which restricted recovery of damages was contributory negligence. The injured party was disqualified from collecting compensation if there had been negligence on that party's part. The plaintiff, notwithstanding serious injury, had the burden of showing that he was absolutely without fault himself. If the facts showed that he had been the least bit inattentive himself, that he had a clear view of an oncoming train and could have avoided it, for example, he was precluded from recovering at all from the railroad which had been negligent.

The doctrine of assumption of the risk also restricted plaintiffs' recovery of damages. The rule was applied in instances where the plaintiff "voluntarily" put himself in a position of danger. The doctrine was applied regularly to workers in their workplaces, barring liability in the numerous cases which arose from industrial accidents.

A similar rule which was applied to the workplace was the fellow-servant rule. The rule precluded compensation from an employer for an injury caused by the negligence of an injured party's fellow employee. Consequently, an employer would be liable only for injury caused by him directly, an unlikely occurrence since in most instances the employer was not personally at fault. In effect, these two rules barred recovery for the largest number of workplace injuries.

Imputed negligence was another restrictive doctrine. Certain relationships between the injured party and the wrongdoer caused the negligence of one to be imputed to the other. For example, a driver's negligence was imputed to his passenger, and a parent's to his child. When this applied, the injured person was precluded from collecting compensation for his damages.

While these rules prevailed, the opportunity for compensation was severely limited. Sometimes even the judges who developed them found the rules excessively harsh and modified them to deal with the real cases before them.

Imputed negligence waned; contributory negligence gave way to comparative negligence which allowed for proportional attribution of fault; safety regulations were imposed on industries; and wrongful death actions became possible.

With these changes, the calculation of compensation for injuries and losses posed a challenge. In response, the courts applied the elements of measurement from the basic types of damages which could be demonstrated at trial. Courts award three types of damages: nominal, compensatory and punitive. Nominal damages are token damages, a small sum of money to vindicate the plaintiff's rights and to record a judgment against the defendant. The amount of the award is frequently one dollar. It betokens that the defendant has done something wrong, but that the plaintiff has not been injured other than in principle. A recent case brought by the United States Football League against the National Football League, charging violation of antitrust laws, resulted in such a nominal damage award.

Compensatory damages represent the closest financial approximation of the harm suffered by the plaintiff. The award is intended to restore the plaintiff as far as possible to his economic position before the injury. That, if necessary, includes award of all economic losses, thereby attempting to have the plaintiff's total worth remain equivalent.

There are two categories of compensatory damages: special damages, which have a ready market value of which clear proof must be shown, and general damages, which have no fixed or established market value. For certain injuries, special damages must be shown. For example, slander consists of defamation by spoken words and transitory gestures which lack permanent form. The demonstration of special, that is actual, economic damages is required since the injury is not otherwise considered serious in itself. On the other hand, libel consists of defamation by written or printed words or by oral communications which are likely to affect the plaintiff in his trade or profession. In libel cases, special damages need not be shown, as serious injury is presumed. Acute mental distress or serious physical illness caused by the defamation are sufficient alone in libel cases, but in slander cases there must be pecuniary injury for compensation to be awarded at all.

The courts may award a third kind of damages, punitive damages, to injured plaintiffs. Punitive damages are an additional sum, over and above compensation, which is awarded to punish the defendant and to deter others from similar conduct. Punitive damages are awarded in cases of malicious, wanton or reckless acts, including fraud. The amount is not necessarily related to the extent of harm which resulted. Frequently, the amount is established by governing law at a multiple, often three times, of the amount of compensatory damages. Sometimes the law is silent and the amount of damages may be set by the jury, within its discretion, to warn others of the severe consequences of malicious or reckless acts.

Punitive damages represent a departure from the principle of compensating for the injury suffered by the plaintiff. The plaintiff may instead be overcompensated in relation to his injury, being the beneficiary of society's objective of deterrence. Such punitive damages are construed by some as compensating for the plaintiff's ancillary damages, such as emotional distress and attorneys' fees. Upon analysis, though, the award may be a windfall, more appropriately payable as a fine than to benefit an undeserving plaintiff. In many states, punitive damages may be awarded even if no compensatory damages are found.

Punitive damages which are unrelated to the amount of compensatory damages have been claimed by some to be excessive fines which are prohibited by Article VIII of the United States Constitution. However, the United States Supreme Court recently dismissed that claim in a case which involved unfair competition, with malice, by a nationwide business against a small competitor.(3) The lower court awarded compensatory damages of $51,000 and punitive damages of $6 million. The Supreme Court held that no proportional relationship between compensatory and punitive damages is required.

In calculating compensatory damages, to the extent they are measurable, the jury must consider the evidence of value put forth by the plaintiff and rebutting evidence by the defendant. Measurable damages commonly include loss of past earnings, which is calculated by the period of work time lost and the amount the plaintiff would have earned. Actual medical expenses are also recoverable if proven.

The loss of future earnings or impairment of future earning capacity, another item of damages, is also subject to mathematical calculation. Actuarial tables published by insurance actuaries for both life expectancy and working life expectancy are accepted by the courts as a basis for calculation. In applying these tables, the jury must take into account the plaintiff's earnings, health and prospects for advancement prior to the injury. The jury is permitted to rely on the tables as general guidelines, once the plaintiff has proven the duration of the injuries. Loss of future earnings may also include unrealized occupational accomplishment or training delayed or prevented by the injury.

For long-term injuries, the plaintiff will also seek to collect future medical expenses. These are proven by evidence of the nature, duration and estimated reasonable costs of future needs.

The value of future earnings or future expenses is often reduced to present value. In other words, the sum awarded if paid now would earn interest between the present and the future date at which it would have been received in the ordinary course. Applying particular rates of interest, present worth tables show the present value of a dollar paid over the period of loss. Another accepted method is the use of annuity tables showing the cost of purchasing an annuity for the total recovery over the projected period of time. Some courts have allowed the jury to consider probable inflation in fixing lump sum awards.

Having fixed measurable damages, the jury is then often faced with establishing damages for psychological injuries for which there is no objective standard of measurement. It is the jury's role to set the amount of these damages, applying again its collective reasonable judgment. New York's highest court has described the process as follows:

> A long course of practice, numerous verdicts rendered year after year, orders made by trial justices approving or disapproving them, decisions on the subject by appellate courts, furnish to the judicial mind some indication of the consensus of opinion of jurors and courts as to the proper relation between

the character of the injury and the amount of compensation awarded.(4)

These damages include conscious pain and suffering, future pain and suffering, mental anguish caused by emotional loss and by permanent disability and disfigurement. The elements that the jury is instructed to consider in fixing an award for conscious physical and mental pain and suffering include the degree of consciousness, the severity of the pain, the awareness of impending death and the duration of the suffering.

There may also be claims by others for losses suffered as a result of injury to a loved one. A spouse may claim for loss of support, loss of services and loss of society including love, affection, care, attention, companionship, comfort and protection. Dependent children may claim for the loss of the nurture, training, education and guidance the parent would have given if the parent had not died.

Using the age and life expectancy of the spouse and the ages of the children, the jury may calculate a value for loss of support over time as the first measure of damages to the family. Psychological damages for loss of companionship and nurture are set by the jury in the same way as those for conscious pain and suffering.

Damages for loss of life may be less than for an injury from which the party survives and suffers psychological injuries such as pain, suffering and mental anguish since psychological damages are not recoverable if the injured party dies instantaneously upon injury. Arguably, the loss by death is greater, but the system of compensation dictates that the award may be less. Psychological damages are not recoverable if the injured party dies instantaneously upon injury.

Some new cases have claimed that the comatose, non-sentient injured party who cannot recover for conscious pain and suffering should be compensated for the loss of enjoyment of life. The same would apply to the on-the-spot fatality who has no right to compensation for the value of years of living normally. New York's highest court recently rejected such claims, saying that cognitive awareness is a prerequisite for the award of damages for loss of enjoyment of life. While the court was split, Chief Judge Wachtler wrote that separate compensation for loss of enjoyment would increase awards and that a larger award does not by itself indicate that the goal of compensation has been better served.(5)

For such items as these, there are no precise rules of measurement – – the jury fixes an amount which appears to it to be appropriate. No mathematical guide or per-unit-of-time basis is accepted. In some states the jury is required to specify the amount of its verdict assigned to each element of past and future damages, including medical expenses, loss of earnings, impairment of earning ability and pain and suffering.

The amount the jury sets is subject only to the control of the judge. If the jury has rendered a verdict which the judge finds "grossly excessive," "shocking to the conscience" or which materially deviates from reasonable compensation, he or she may set it aside and grant a new trial. If the trial judge does not do so, an appellate court may strike down the verdict. But, in the first instance, it is the jury's province to quantify such losses in its collective judgment.

Damage awards for injuries are a firmly established part of our legal system. The manifold losses which individuals suffer can be analyzed into greater and greater detail by plaintiffs' attorneys and sympathetic juries. On the other hand, defendants' attorneys and insurers protest the expansion of damage awards. The critical question is whether our society can continue to increase awards to injured parties. As indicated by Chief Judge Wachtler, that is not necessarily a desirable result.

Insurance has been an integral part of the compensation system, ensuring payment of verdicts which would otherwise be beyond the ability of defendants to pay. Insurance rates have risen precipitously in recent years to absorb increasing verdicts to the point where certain activities are now curtailed to avoid the enormous costs. For example, many swimming pools no longer have diving boards and some equipment has been removed from playgrounds. And whooping cough vaccine, considered an essential public health product, was scheduled to be removed from the market until the federal government created a compensation fund to replace the manufacturer's costly private insurance.

It has been demonstrated that the legal system will calculate damages no matter how difficult or unmeasurable, once the predicates for financial recovery conform to the principles established by the law. But society at large must measure the social costs of the compensation system and determine how much compensation it chooses to give for immeasurable psychological injuries.

REFERENCES

1.   248 N.Y. 339, 162 N.E. 99.
2.   William Prosser, Handbook of the Law of Torts (3d ed. 1964) p. 924.

3.   Brown-Ferris Industries of Vermont, Inc. v. Kelco Disposal, Inc., 492
      U.S. ___, 106 L. Ed. 2d 219, 109 S.Ct. 2909 (1989).
4.   Fried v. New York, New Haven & Hudson R. R., 183 A.D 115, 125,
      170 N.Y.S. 697, 704, aff'd 230 N.Y. 619 (1921).
5.   McDougald v. Garber, 73 N.Y. 2d 246, 538 N.Y.S. 2d 937 (1989).

CHAPTER 11

MONEY IN THE OLDER YEARS

Eugene L. Lowenkopf, M.D.

Attitudes and behaviors relating to money in the older years are, at least early on, a continuation of previously held attitudes and behaviors. Additional trends develop with advancing age, some of which are adjustments to new realities of life and new problems while others are either exaggerations of previous adjustments or reactions against them. Towards the end of life, there is yet another shift which directly reflects declining powers of mind and body.

Money, at all ages, is the universal medium for assessing value and for the interchange of goods and services. It enables the purchase of essentials such as food, clothing and shelter as well as non-essentials which make living more pleasant such as better food, better clothing and better shelter, cars, vacations and all sorts of appliances and entertainments. Having money in sufficient quantity permits personal independence and autonomy. It enables each individual to express himself or herself, it allows one to live as one chooses, to make one's own decisions and to pursue one's own goals free from the need to obtain the consent of others. Those who do not have it are dependent on others and often are forced to sacrifice independence and freedom of choice and movement. The wish for material goods and for independence and autonomy is normal at all ages and extends into and permeates the older years as well.

Money also comes to possess personal and perhaps neurotic significances; it may represent power, control over others, success, status, sexual desirability or some combination of these. These meanings also do not vanish overnight but persist into the older years, existing side by side with meanings of later origin which may eventually replace them.

Although the exact age at which the older years begin is arguable, I have chosen 50 as the point of departure, and I will further classify 50-65 as young older age, 65-80 as middle older age and over 80 as old older age. This classification is in general usage since certain life situations are more prevalent in each of these periods, bringing specific expressions in the realm of money.

Probably the earliest change, one that occurs at about age 50, is a

Money and Mind, Edited by S. Klebanow and
E.L. Lowenkopf, Plenum Press, New York, 1991

growing awareness of such realities as illness, retirement and death. Although these may have previously been acknowledged intellectually, they did not seem to have relevance to oneself or to require any special planning. However, by the time one reaches 50, one has experienced enough of these misfortunes in parents, other relatives, colleagues and friends to place beyond denial their inevitability for oneself as well. Recognizing this forces one to pay attention to pensions, annuities, and sickness and retirement benefits. It is striking to observe the growth in percentage of time spent thinking and talking about such issues after 50 compared to prior to then. In the optimistic who look forward to a lengthy and fruitful retirement, the emphasis is on having enough funds to enjoy an extended active golden age. Those who are pessimistic, on the other hand, are more concerned that health needs be adequately underwritten.

In the older years, as at all stages of life, demographic characteristics such as sex, marital status, income level, social class and ethnic background play their part in the ways that money is regarded and handled. Consequently, not every older person shares the preoccupations I have just described. For the wealthy, pension plans and benefits may not be necessary but while they may be unavailable to the poor, both groups may have psychological problems relating to money. Those who live in societies with strong nuclear families together under one roof may also have no great need for planning but, in the United States, these issues have virtually universal significance because such support is usually lacking.

The changing pattern of life during the early older years includes a shift in one's relationship to work with implications for one's attitudes towards money. Previously, one applied oneself to a job and had expectations for recognition, promotion and a higher salary. These are much less likely to be achieved as the years accumulate, and the reality is that most people, as they become older, are shunted into more routine and less challenging tasks. There is a parallel reduction in the possibility of a promotion in title or an increase in salary; changing jobs in response to this blocking of opportunity is not a very viable alternative since older people, even at age 50, are not highly desired as new employees. In other words, the experience and wisdom acquired during their working lives is not very much appreciated in the job market. So, in addition to the frustration of not being allowed to work to one's capacity, one experiences a sense of being devalued.

For those who have relied on money, either its possession or its spending, as a way of overcoming feelings of inadequacy or other negative thoughts and affects, this may lead to either a clinical depression or to the adoption of new defensive operations. One such defense might be a severe cutting back on expenditures, far beyond reality needs, in an effort to save and build up a more substantial treasure chest. Another is to overspend, a counterphobic maneuver, as if to prove that there is no need for caution, rather that everything is rosy. These two themes, excessive caution in the handling of money and its opposite, reckless spending, are themes that occur often in response to various stresses in the older years.

Overspending may also appear in those individuals who have throughout their lives scrupulously stayed within their budgets and denied themselves many pleasures. With the appearance of job limitations or with the first hint of illness, there is a need to kick over the traces and make up for lost time before the course is run and death occurs. Such individuals are often at odds with their families who cannot understand the radical change in life style in their formerly conservative relatives and who attribute it to some emotional disorder. There is indeed an emotional problem but it was present before in the anhedonic life style and it is present now in the inappropriateness of the expenditures, whether this be in the excessive amounts, the unsuitability of what is purchased or in the continuing inability to recognize the motives that underlie the overspending.

Another development which occurs in the young old is that there is relief from many of the large fixed expenses which characterized earlier periods. The house or apartment is paid up, the children have completed their schooling, life insurance policies are no longer a must, and most of the second homes, appliances, cars and so forth have already been purchased. While income may no longer be rising and while purchasing power, thanks to inflation, may be dropping, there is also less occasion to spend. This creates a situation where, perhaps for the first time in one's life, there is a relative surplus of money, and many people in this category have difficulty knowing what to do with it, not being accustomed to such plentitude. This rather strange state of affairs may produce its own dilemma: should it be saved against a rainy day, should it be employed for the next generation or should it be used for self-indulgence? But what is suitable self-indulgence for people who have everything and who do not feel the need for something new? After a lifetime of striving where every penny was earmarked before it was earned, it can be unsettling, even shattering, to have money with no purpose. And those who have lived only in order to make money have now been deprived of the purpose of all their endeavors, necessitating a radical re-examination of who they are and for what purpose they exist.

Parenthetically, a similar situation may be seen in many of those who retire with golden parachutes, that is they are forced out of work at an early age with enough money to cover all their needs and then some. They often respond to this seemingly enviable situation with depression, partly caused by their inability to use their abundant free time and partly caused by being deprived of the financial incentive to work. There can be no question that money, its acquisition, its possession and its spending, help to define one's position in the world not only for others but for oneself as well.

Nor does giving it to the next generation usually solve the problem. Indeed, whether the parents be wealthy or middle class, there is usually a considerable disparity between their views about money and those of their children. Inter-generational strife concerning money matters raises its head repeatedly as we examine the older years and, while the issues differ with the decades, conflict is almost always present. With the young old who have a surplus, there is a tendency to help their children but there is also resentment at the way the younger generation spends the money and at the unspoken assumption that it has a right to it. There is also resentment that the children assume both that parents no longer have needs of their own and that they ought to pass their waning years quietly and modestly while the younger people live it up.

At age 65, the beginning of middle older age, retirement and giving up work become central issues. Too often, it is work that gave meaning to life, and its absence now thrusts the retiree and the non-working spouse into the position of finding new purpose and interest. Occasionally, these are found in accumulating wealth, and this may lead to absorption in counting one's savings or to greater involvement in the world of money, sometimes to the extent of spending all one's time at the stockbroker's. It occasionally leads one to get involved in mad schemes "guaranteed" to increase wealth but more often leading to financial loss. This is related to the growing fear that one will be forced into poverty, destitution and homelessness. While income may be more than enough, the absence of a weekly salary leads to the feeling that one is living on savings which will slowly but surely be used up, leaving one penniless. In view of such a prospect, desperate measures may seem quite logical. Stealing food and other necessities, as a result, may occur for the first time in a previously totally honest and upright citizen when there is no real shortage of money.

In our society, there are a number of bargains offered to help the elderly live on smaller budgets. Restaurants offer "early bird specials" which appeal to people who are not working, stores offer senior-citizen discounts for shopping at off hours, movies and other entertainments sell tickets at lower prices to the elderly, and there are also special rates for traveling, both local and long distance. While it is reasonable for anyone to take advantage of lowered rates for services that would be used anyway, we witness the phenomenon of people who have no need to be careful inconveniencing themselves just to save small amounts. Whether this occurs because they feel they must save every possible cent to guarantee their security or whether actively pursuing such savings occupies time in a socially acceptable way, it makes no sense for financially comfortable people to trouble themselves in this way, to rush dinner, to go to movies at inconvenient times or to go to unnecessary places just to feel they are getting a bargain.

With retirement comes the important decision how to spend the rest of one's life. Since money supplies are finite and life expectancy is uncertain, people have no way of knowing how to apportion out what they have. Should one splurge while one is healthy and then settle for modest living, or should one husband one's resources, making them last as long as possible? The rate of inflation and the duration of one's good health are only two of the imponderables that influence this decision, and other factors such as optimism and the influence of families and friends also contribute. No matter how the problem is resolved, the individual is dealing actively with the issue of his or her own death as an immediate concern, and there is often depression as well as nagging doubt that one has made the right decision, no matter how the issue is decided.

Interpersonal conflicts in couples that had previously been passed over lightly may also become more prominent. These conflicts may have been expressed more as differences in taste or differences in choice of vacation spots. Now, with more time being spent together and with money in shorter supply, such conflicts get played out in the arena of money. For example, one partner may be more interested in cutting back while the other may feel more expansive. One may want to invest in jewelry which is always negotiable should the need arise and the other in more ephemeral treats. Similarly, one parent's preference for one child over another often is expressed by gifts of money, supposedly unknown to the other parent or to other children. Earlier on, such behavior may have been inconspicuous but with a restricted financial base, it becomes more apparent and is a cause of strife.

Such rifts over money are further exacerbated when the partners are of significantly different ages and at different points in their emotional dealing with the retirement situation. The older partner feels that he or she is presently facing up to realities while the younger one is not able to understand what the fuss is about. These differences in stages of life coming on top of personality differences may produce explosive situations. In one case I encountered, the husband verbally agreed with everything the wife did rather than start a battle, but then systematically stole from her to limit her supposedly disastrous spending.

It would be incorrect on my part to convey the impression that the older years are an unending series of crises involving money. However, each new phase of life with its accompanying challenges does seem to be expressed in money terms. One may develop an illness and there is the problem of paying hospital, doctors and nurses. When someone dies, the estate must be settled. And, if remarriage does occur, there are financial questions to be decided. Prenuptial agreements in the elderly are becoming more and more common to ensure that each spouse's property goes to his or her own children and not to some newly arrived, incompletely accepted member of the family. In the elderly poor, the question of whether marriage takes place or not hinges on which arrangement results in the greater allowance from Social Security. Indeed, this consideration also plays a part in whether wealthier people re-marry or not.

At probably any age, the writing of a will is a matter of major concern to insure the smooth transfer of funds and property to heirs. The will is also a way to reward positive acts and to gain revenge on culprits for negative acts committed during one's lifetime. It also may represent for the testator a means of denying death by allowing him or her to continue to be an active, determining factor in the behavior of others through the use of provisions and clauses which may pertain for many years. These all become much more immediate issues to the elderly and lend themselves to the vicissitudes of emotional life. The phenomenon of writing and re-writing wills as different heirs rise and fall in one's affections is well known but these decisions are not purely arbitrary. With increasing age, especially in the late 60's and 70's, one is subject to a series of losses and separations which exacerbate feelings of powerlessness, diminish self esteem and challenge autonomy. At the same time, the support system of spouse and friends gradually disappears, increasing one's isolation and loneliness. Relatives or friends who fill one's needs at this point are likely to be favored in the writing of wills.

Such a situation lends itself to abuse on both sides of the generational divide. Feeling lonely, isolated and unloved on the older person's part increases sensitivity to rejection with great attention being directed onto seemingly small acts committed by the nearest and dearest to determine their significance; do they indicate any falling off of love, do they indicate indifference? Such hypersensitivity may lead to paranoid interpretations of differences of opinion, changes of behavior, or being or not being available. If the elderly person becomes unduly distressed, disinheritance is a possibility. It's one step further to the quite conscious use by the elderly of the threat to disinherit to compel attention and obedience from the young.

Manipulation is not a trick practiced exclusively by the elderly. Children and younger relatives who are concerned about being named in the will often modify their behavior, not out of affection and respect, but out of greed. They learn how to play the strings that appeal to their elderly relative and coldly go about influencing the writing of the will in their favor. They may get into furious and bitter competition with other members of their own generation to see who can beat the other out and win the prize. Many of the elderly realize they are being manipulated and develop deep distrust and suspicion of their families.

Since the elderly are frequently lonely and unsure of themselves, anyone who offers companionship, increases their sense of security or seems interested in their lives becomes very important to them. To encourage and reward this interest, gifts may be offered now in the form of cash or may be postponed to the future, being mentioned in the will. There is a whole spectrum of attitudes encountered in employees, new acquaintances and helpers of the elderly ranging from helpfulness and concern with no care for additional rewards, through willingness to accept gifts as a sign of appreciation, to calculated exploitation of the elderly for financial gain.

Altering wills and giving gifts are two indications of a significant shift in the manner in which elderly people often are forced to relate to others. In many instances, they are no longer viewed as complete people who can maintain a full range of emotional relationships; instead, they are put into the position of having to purchase time and attention from others. It is no wonder that some pretend to be much richer than they in fact are since others will be attracted to them by the promise of wealth. And, conversely, some pretend to be poorer than they are as a means of testing their new-found friends. Will these people remain friends if they are not likely to benefit financially? Having to play such games, feeling that one is wanted only for one's money, contributes to one's feelings of personal isolation and depression.

With some individuals in middle or in old age, a state of disinterest in money may arise. It may look like they simply do not want to be bothered with adding and subtracting, balancing the checkbook and the myriad other activities that are required to keep one's affairs in order. These individuals are only too happy if someone, relative or friend, takes over responsibility for their financial affairs and leaves them alone. However, such surrendering of control over one's life and the loss of independence it entails often create more problems than they solve since rarely has the individual calculated exactly how much autonomy and power will be lost. There will be anger at the invasion of one's privacy, at the imposing of restrictions and at the loss of freedom to come and go, even though all of these are the results of one's own actions. Too often, as King Lear discovered, such abdication produces unexpected agony instead of bliss.

Of course, the abandonment of responsibility for one's own life seldom occurs in individuals with full retention of all faculties. Even though they may appear to be completely rational, their wish for easing of responsibility may be the first signal of a developing Alzheimer's and may indicate that the effort of keeping track of one's affairs is proving to be too much of a strain on diminished capabilities.

Evaluating the diminution of capacity and the strain imposed by trying to keep up are tasks that are often assigned to the mental health worker. It is important not to focus on comparisons between the condition today and the condition of several years back, as families often do since this only highlights the deficits. Instead, one should see how much money management of what level of complexity the individual can handle. Efforts should then be made to simplify matters accordingly; this allows for the optimal retention of autonomy by the elderly person and the maximal retention of dignity. Too often, families are so eager to be sure that money is handled safely that they deprive a still competent person of this right even when they have the best of intentions. Before powers of attorney are implemented and conservatorships arranged, there should be a genuine effort to utilize residual strengths rather than deprive the elderly of all rights. Of course, when these strengths eventually do peter out is the appropriate time for taking legal steps.

With the onset of Alzheimer's Disease begins a very slowly progressive decline in efficiency in handling monetary affairs, and a variety of peculiarities in dealing with money may appear. These do not follow any particular pattern but indicate that there is a lessened capacity as well as attempts to compensate for it. People with this affliction have trouble doing their shopping and keeping track of what change they get and whether it is correct. There is often an awareness on the part of the elderly that they make more errors than they used to; this may result in an increasing scrupulosity in the way they keep their accounts. Hours may be spent in going over their books and there is great anxiety that they might have omitted to write important checks or take care of significant documents. At times, they may get carried away by their need to be correct and they may write out checks for every single charity or mail solicitation that comes along.

When they are relieved of the burden of bookkeeping, the advanced age elderly may develop considerable suspiciousness towards those who take it on. This is not the continuation of a life long paranoia but the reaction of someone who does not understand what is going on and cannot explain any problems that arise except by assuming that someone else is deliberately tricking him or her. Similarly, the very old tend to squirrel away money in various locations in their homes and then do not remember where they put it. This may result in accusing friends and family of stealing when money cannot be found just as they question their motives when they are asked to sign checks.

Some elderly lose the ability to assess the value of goods and services and are likely to estimate prices more in keeping with levels prevalent in their youth. This might be explained in several ways: a reversion to values from childhood; loss of contact with current prices since they rarely shop; or inability to adjust to a changing cost of living. While becoming more susceptible to exploitation, they also become more conservative in the sense that they hold on to money fearfully. They are generally poor spenders and tippers, and less than generous gift-givers. Many are the disappointed helpers who were promised munificent gifts and then find themselves with only five dollars. The intent was not to disappoint but the concept of what constitutes largesse is outdated.

Counting and re-counting money may also occur, not so much to check how much one has to impose some system and organization on a world that is becoming increasingly more confusing. Money in this way retains a substantial symbolic value until virtually the end of life, even when its use as a medium of exchange has been outlived and when other neurotic gratifications that it might have provided are long gone.

Since the number of elderly is constantly growing it is more than likely that every mental health worker will be consulted at some time by some one in the older years or by a family member or friend. And, since money is so important throughout life, it is an issue that is bound to come up. Questions may be raised whether it is being handled correctly or incorrectly, whether its usage indicates illness and what, if anything, should be done about it. As with most presenting problems, it is essential that the context in which the money problem is enmeshed be investigated, and that the underlying explanations for the behavior be understood. As should be clear from this overview, some issues that look like problems may not be, other issues indicate problems that are treatable, and others, while not treatable, point the way towards humane handling of sensitive and troubling life situations.

Part II

MONEY IN THE PSYCHOTHERAPEUTIC SETTING

CHAPTER 12

SIGMUND FREUD AND MONEY

Silas L. Warner, M.D.

Sigmund Freud was convinced that during his early years his family lived in a state of poverty. In a letter to Fliess in 1899 (Complete Letters, 1985, p. 374) he wrote:

> My mood also depends very strongly on my *earnings. Money is laughing gas for me. I know from my youth* that once the wild horses of the pampas have been lassoed, they retain a certain anxiousness for life. Thus I came to know the *helplessness* of *poverty* and *continually fear it.* You will see that my style will improve and my ideas will be more correct if this city provides me with an ample livelihood. (Author's italics.)

An oil painting of the Freud children was painted in 1868. About it Freud said (Freud, M., 1983) "The painter has graciously overlooked the holes in the soles of my shoes." This was thought by his son Martin to refer to the *poverty* of his youth.

In Freud's Autobiographical Study (Freud, 1925) he writes that "Although we lived in   very limited circumstances (in Vienna), my father insisted that, in my choice of profession, I should follow my own inclinations." He decided to become a medical student even though he did not "feel any particular predilection for the career of a physician."

He became engaged to Martha Bernays in 1882 and required an adequate income to marry her. In his autobiography (Freud, 1925) he describes his situation as follows:

> The turning-point came in 1882, when my teacher, for whom I felt the highest possible esteem, *corrected my father's generous*

A similar version of this chapter appeared as "Sigmund Freud and Money", in the Journal of the American Academy of Psychoanalysis, 1898, 17(4) pp. 609-622.

Money and Mind, Edited by S. Klebanow and
E.L. Lowenkopf, Plenum Press, New York, 1991

improvidence by strongly advising me, in view of *my bad financial position*, to abandon my theoretical career. (Author's italics.)

It was Ernst Brucke who advised Freud to enter into clinical medicine. There he could earn money and marry his fiancee Martha Bernays without too long a delay. Freud's phrase, his "father's generous improvidence" is an apparent oxymoron. To be improvident is to not foresee the financial future or to be without thrift. His father's generosity, combined with his thriftlessness, had not prepared Freud for his future financial responsibilities as a married man. His father was generous with the small amount of money he possessed. This allowed Freud to barely get by as a single man. Freud felt entitled to more from his father and took over Brucke as a superior father ideal to make up for his own father's deficiencies.

Another variation in meaning of his father's "generous improvidence" could have been that Jacob Freud supplied money to his son that he did not have or that was beyond his means. This might imply that Freud believed he had been misled by his father into thinking that there were more funds set aside for his future than actually existed. This might have been a purposeful misrepresentation on Jacob Freud's part to spare Sigmund any financial worry. Conversely, it might have been Sigmund's wishful thinking that there would always be plenty of money for his future even though Jacob may have repeatedly told him that this was not the case.

Peter Gay (1986) believes that:

To recall his family's poverty seems to have been painful to Freud; in a disguised autobiographical passage he inserted in a paper of 1899, he describes himself as "the child of originally well-to-do parents who, I believe, lived in the provincial hole comfortably enough." This hyperbole is a mild instance of what Freud would later call the "family romance," the widespread disposition to find one's parents more prosperous or more famous than they are in reality, or perhaps even to invent a distinguished parentage. Freud was simplifying his family's motives for leaving Freiberg and prettying their existence there. After a "catastrophe in the industrial branch in which my father was engaged," he wrote, "he lost his fortune." In the end, Jacob Freud never wholly secured what he had never really enjoyed. For some time, in fact, though gradually their situation improved, the Freuds' move to Vienna brought them little relief: "Then came long hard years," Freud wrote later; "I think nothing about them was worth remembering."

It is very difficult to accurately evaluate Jacob Freud's financial situation at any given time during his life. When he married Amalie Nathanson on July 29, 1855 he had already been married twice before and was a 40-year-old wool merchant living in Freiberg (now Pribor, Czechoslovakia (Krull, 1986). His bride was from Vienna, 19 years old, and the daughter of Jacob Nathanson. It is probable that the two Jacobs knew each other from business transactions in Vienna. It seems likely that they "arranged" the marriage between Amalie Nathanson and Jacob Freud. The age difference of 21 years was uncommon in Jewish couples, but not unheard of, especially if the groom was known to have a respectable income. If Jacob Nathanson was too poor to have given Amalie an adequate dowry, he would have been most pleased to marry her to Jacob Freud who was thought to have a most adequate income. After the marriage the couple moved into a rented one-room apartment in Freiberg. Some Freudian biographers have contended that Jacob Freud exaggerated his wealth and that Amalie was disappointed in her one-room apartment in Freiberg. Other biographers insist that Amalie's new residence in Freiberg was an improvement over the 1-1/2 room apartment that housed the entire Nathanson family in Vienna.

Freudian biographers differ in their estimates of Jacob Freud's financial situation. A typical low estimate is provided by Elliott Oring (1984) as follows:

> Freud did not come from a wealthy family. His father was a merchant and, by most accounts, not a very successful one. In his later years, it appears that Freud's father did not produce any income for his family at all. As a student and during his tenure at the General Hospital of Vienna, Freud was always severely strapped for funds.

In marked contrast to this view is that of Peter Drucker (1978). He believes that Freud purposely perpetuated a *myth* that throughout his life he: "lived with serious financial worries and in near poverty."Drucker is an American economist, born in Vienna in 1909. Both parents had known Freud for years even though his father was 20 years younger than Freud. Drucker's father "would bow with great respect when he encountered Freud on the paths around the Alpine lake on which the Freuds had their summer villa ..."

As a Viennese medical student, Drucker's mother had attended a lecture series by Freud. She owned one of the 351 copies of Freud's 1900 first edition of "The Interpretation of Dreams." When Drucker was eight years old, he was introduced to Freud at a restaurant. His father told Drucker to "Remember, today you have just met the most important man in Austria, and perhaps in Europe."

In assessing Sigmund Freud's finances, Drucker writes:

> The Freuds were not "Rothschild-rich," to use the Viennese term for the super-rich. They were comfortable middle-class. Freud's father was a fairly successful merchant. In the Vienna of Freud's youth – he was born in 1856 just when the rapid growth of Vienna into a metropolis began –this meant a high-ceilinged apartment in one of the new four- or five-story apartment buildings just outside the old "Inner City"; fairly spacious though dark, overcrowded with furniture, and with one bathroom only. It meant two or three servants, a weekly cleaning woman, and a seamstress every month, a summer vacation in a spa near Vienna or in the mountains, Sunday walks in the Vienna woods for the whole family, high school (gymnasium) for the children, books, music, and weekly visits to opera and theatres. And, this is precisely how the Freuds lived. Freud's brother, Alexander – he published a reference book on railroad freight tariffs for the Ministry of Commerce when my father was the Ministry's head – always resented Sigmund's insistence on the dire poverty in which he grew up as maligning their dead father's memory, "who was such a good provider." (Drucker, 1978)

Drucker notes that in the late 19th century Austria enjoyed a very rapid economic climb upwards from its previous low base. Accompanying this trend in Vienna were a few "winners" who became rich. In addition, there was "a much larger group, but still a minority, [who] reached *precarious affluence – the Freuds in Sigmund's youth were just a cut above that level*, I imagine." (Drucker, 1978) (Author's italicizing.)

These were the Austrians from the "Czech areas (Bohemia and Moravia) from which the Freuds had come and from which the Jewish middle class in Vienna was largely recruited." There existed among this particular group a "secret and suppressed obsession with money – the "poorhouse neurosis." (Drucker, 1987).

> According to Drucker (1978), the "poorhouse neurosis" had become a major affliction, and a common one among the older middle class people of my young years (the young people were far less prone to it, for by then Austria was no longer developing and was indeed shrinking economically; the younger people were not obsessed with becoming poor, they were poor). The "poorhouse neurosis" showed itself in a constant fear of ending up poor, a constant nagging worry about not earning enough, of not being able to keep up with the social expectations of oneself and one's family – and one's neighbors – and, above all, in constant obsessive talking about money while always claiming not to be interested in it.
> Freud clearly suffered from the "poorhouse neurosis"; it is etched even into the letters he wrote his betrothed from Paris while still a young man. Yet for all his ruthless honesty with himself, he never could face up to it. That he misrepresented his professional life as being underpaid, under constant financial pressure, and in financial anxiety – these were misrepresentations that evinced the anxiety neurosis which he could not and did not face and which, in a Freudian slip mechanism, he repressed. This also explains why he did not notice it in his patients and leaves it out of his case histories. It had to be a "non-fact," for the fact itself was much too painful for him (1978)

Drucker is convinced that "Even as a youngster, Freud was well-to-do; and from the beginning of his professional life as a young doctor he made good money." Drucker attempts to expose Freud's personal myth of early life poverty as untrue. He also denies the validity of two other similar Freudian myths. The first was that he was victimized by anti-Semitism. The second was that his work was ignored by the Viennese medical establishment and that he was denied full recognition and a university appointment because of being a Jew.

Drucker (1978) claims that Freud:

... never suffered from discrimination as a Jew until Hitler drove him into exile at the very end of his life. He received official recognition and academic honors not only earlier than almost any person in Austrian medical history; he received at an early age honors and recognition to which, according to the fairly strict Austrian canon, he was not entitled at all. Above all, medical Vienna did not ignore or neglect Freud, it rejected him. It rejected him as a person because it held him to be in gross violation of the ethics of the healer. And it rejected his theory as a glittering half-truth, and as poetry rather than medical science or therapy (1978).

According to Drucker, Freud was rejected by the Viennese medical community (the majority of the physicians in Vienna were Jewish) because he would not accept non-paying or "charity" patients. This was because Freud believed that a psychoanalytic patient cannot be helped *unless he pays a fair price for his treatment.* His Viennese medical colleagues felt that every physician should treat some patients free because it was their moral duty and poor patients could not otherwise receive medical treatment.

Freud never wrote about the subject of money, or the "poor-house or money neurosis," but wrote exclusively about sexual anxiety, sexual frustration and how all neuroses have a sexual basis. Drucker claims that the one neurosis that was constantly stressed by others in late 19th century Vienna and Europe was the "money neurosis." Money dominated people's thinking but had become unmentionable. Viennese parents would never even discuss their income with their children; it was a forbidden topic which had to be avoided. Yet it dominated everybody's thinking, partly due to the rapid economic development.

Drucker credits Freud with being:

... a stoic who never complained, abhorred self-pity, and detested whiners. He bore great physical pain without a sound of complaint. And he was equally stoical about sufferings in his private life. But he complains incessantly about imaginary sufferings – lack of money, anti-Semitic discrimination, and being ignored by the Viennese physicians.

Freud was in everything else ruthlessly candid, above all with himself. He was merciless in his own self-examination and tore out root and branch what to an ordinary mortal would have been harmless self-indulgence. It is conceivable that Freud could have knowingly created and propagated fairytales and myths about himself. But it seems equally inconceivable that Freud could not have known that these assertions and complaints were not "facts," but pure myths. Everyone else in the Vienna of Freud's time knew it and commented on Freud's strange "obsessions." (1978)

Freud's referring to his own financial situation as "bad" in his autobiography may have been because he had borrowed money regularly and was bothered by having to repay his debts. During the last two decades of the 19th century Freud accepted money from a few "patrons" who loaned him or gave him substantial amounts of money. These benefactors include Samuel Hammerschlag, Joseph Paneth, Ernest Von Fleisch-Marxow and Joseph Breuer. Hammerschlag was his Hebrew teacher, Paneth and Von Fleisch were his somewhat older co-workers at the Brucke Institute and Breuer was his physician, mentor and co-author of their early joint book on hysteria. Freud felt entitled to being subsidized by these more affluent, somewhat older men. He resented being indebted to them and being financially dependent on them.

In a January 1884 letter to Martha, after Hammerschlag had offered him 50 florins for his support, Freud wrote:

I intend to compensate for it by being charitable myself when I can afford it. It is not the first time the old man has helped me in this way; during my university years he often, unasked, helped me out of a difficult situation. At first I felt very ashamed, but later when I saw that Breuer and he agreed in this respect, I accepted the idea of being indebted to good men and those of our faith without the feeling of personal obligation. Thus I was suddenly in the possession of fifty florins and did not conceal from Hammerschlag my intentions of spending it on my family. He was very much against this idea, saying that I worked very hard and could not at the moment afford to help other people, but I did make it clear to him that I must spend at least half the money in this way. (Letters, #32, 1960)

This letter illustrates a pattern developed by Freud when he borrowed money. At first he felt a shame which betrayed his sense of indebtedness. He was then persuaded by his Jewish benefactors that he was entitled to accept their charity without any sense of obligation. Freud could partly rationalize any indebtedness this way, but he never lost his feelings of resentment from being indebted which automatically placed him in an inferior position. Even after his financial situation had substantially improved some 13 years after he married Martha, he still wrote to Fliess complaining of the helpless poverty he had known and his "constant fear of it." This is what Drucker referred to as Freud's "poor-house neurosis."

Freud apparently never paid back his financial debts to his original four Jewish benefactors. We have no record of any settlement with Samuel Hammerschlag. We know that Ernst Von Fleischl-Marxow was a regular lender of money to Freud and was never repaid. Joseph Paneth died prematurely in 1890 and was never repaid. He had created a 1500 gulden ($600) fund for Freud in 1894. About this Freud wrote to Martha: "Isn't it wonderful that a wealthy man should mitigate the injustices of our poor origins and the unfairness of his own favored position?" (Letters, #41, 1969)

Joseph Breuer lent money regularly and generously to Freud and eventually Freud owed him 2,300 gulden. Breuer appears to have become annoyed at Freud's assumption that the money was his for the asking. In 1884 Breuer turned down Freud's request for funds to visit Martha, claiming that Freud would squander the money on "frivolous extravagances." Freud angrily told Breuer not to interfere with his "adventurous style of life." Breuer relented and gave Freud fifty gulden, but a rift was developing between the two men. Freud sent Breuer a payment on the debt in 1898 which Breuer would not accept. Breuer claimed their financial transactions were gifts to Freud and Freud insisted they were loans. Freud resented his interminable indebtedness to Breuer. Freud referred to this insolvable conflict as follows: "Our intimate friendship later gave place to a total estrangement; –money played a great part among the reasons for my estrangement –" (Freud, S., 1901, PEL).

Oring (1984) has pointed out the connection between Freud's collection of Jewish jokes and his resentment over his continued indebtedness between 1896 and 1898. One type of Jewish joke, that of the Jewish "schnorrer" or beggar, seemed to interest Freud. Such jokes have a theme of the denial of indebtedness. Freud also developed what he termed "schnorrer phantasies." These were scenarios in which he imagined having miraculously received a large sum of money. For example, in 1886 he met an Austrian physician and his wife who were childless. This led him to fantasize their death followed by his inheriting their wealth. In another scenario he heroically stopped the runaway horse of a wealthy person and was offered a huge financial reward.

In 1897 Freud wrote to Wilhelm Fliess (Origins, 1985) "Let me confess that I have recently made a collection of deeply significant Jewish stories (i.e., jokes)." He wrote this after Freud's father's death and at the start of his self-analysis. This temporal connection suggests that Freud's collection of Jewish jokes contain special meaning to Freud. His typical "schnorrer" not only denies his indebtedness but also uses his benefactors' wealth as if it were his own to disperse.

An additional factor of Freud's sensitivity toward money matters and his dislike of being indebted may have come about because of his Uncle Josef Freud's imprisonment for selling counterfeit money. (Krull, 1986) We do not know how much Freud was affected by his uncle's crime, but he does make reference to it in one dream. There is no indication that Freud saw much of this uncle, although he also lived in Vienna. His arrest occurred in 1865 when Freud was 9 years of age. He was caught trying to sell 100 forged fifty-ruble notes which he had originally received from England. There has been a slight suspicion raised that Freud's two half-brothers, Emanual and Philip, who lived in England, may have had some connection to the counterfeit money.

In Freud's dream (Freud, S., 1900) his friend R. becomes his uncle for whom he feels great affection. His uncle's face is changed and a yellow beard is especially noticeable. Freud positively identifies the uncle as Josef Freud for whom "I had naturally never had any feeling of affection ..."

Freud describes his Uncle Josef's situation in his dream associations as follows:

Once – more than thirty years ago – in his eagerness to make money, he allowed himself to be involved in a transaction of a kind that is severely punished by the law, and he was in fact punished for it. My father, whose hair turned gray from grief in a few days, used always to say that Uncle Josef was not a bad man but only a simpleton; those were his words. (Freud, S. 1900)

The extent of Freud's knowledge of the whole incident remains a mystery. Professor Glicklhorn believes that Jacob Freud's house was searched by the police at the time of Josef Freud's arrest. She describes vividly how young Sigmund's classmates teased him about his uncle's arrest and imprisonment. Freud must have had some emotional reaction to it for it to appear in a dream thirty years later. He may have been intrigued by his uncle's grandiose plan to create his own money by forgery. For a child who was his parents' favorite and felt a sense of entitlement, the fantasy of a virtually never-ending supply of counterfeit money must have had a compelling appeal. This could have revived his early wish and belief that his own father's generous supply of money would always be available to him.

WAS FREUD AN ANAL CHARACTER?

In the early Freudian literature there was strong emphasis on the very specific connection between neurotic money problems and the anal stage of psycho-sexual development. The infant learns that the control of his feces becomes an important issue with his caretaker. By withholding his stool he can achieve special attention. This was formulated into the three character traits resulting from a fixation at the anal or toilet training stage of development: orderliness, parsimony and obstinacy. Could it have been that Freud was even describing himself in this description of the anal character? Certainly Freud did show a "basically obsessive-compulsive personality." This meant to Holt (1973) that "he had a good measure of the fundamental anal traits of orderliness and compulsive attention to detail, yet when it came to his mode of working with such details as the slightest turn of phrase in the telling of a dream (which only a compulsive would have noted in the first place), he showed a gift for intuition."

In a letter to Fliess (Complete Letters, 1985) during his self-analysis Freud mentions reading that "the gold the devil gives his victims regularly turns into excrement; –." The symbolic connection between feces and money Freud does mention, but not in a personal context. He also wrote to Fliess that "I can scarcely detail for you all the things that resolve themselves into – – excrement for me (a new Midas!). It fits completely with the theory of internal stinking. Above all, money itself. I believe this proceeds via the word "dirty" for "miserly".

We do know that Freud cherished orderliness and at times could be obstinate. But he could also be very flexible and although not considered wasteful with money, he could be generous. It may be that as his finances improved later in his life he developed a reaction-formation to his earlier fear of poverty.

In Freud's dreams and his other more personal and autobiographical writings there does *not* appear to be a pronounced emphasis on anal material and/or money. This can be interpreted as a sensitivity and avoidance of such material which would confirm that both were topics about which Freud felt inhibited. It is my opinion that Peter Drucker's theory about the myths created by Freud are probably accurate observations on his part. We may have to wait for more of Freud's unpublished letters to be published before we can make a more accurate judgment on this subject.

SUMMARY

I have tried to clarify Sigmund Freud's attitude toward money during the different time periods of his life. Most biographers have written that Freud was born into a poor family which later was elevated to the socio-economic middle-class in Vienna. This traditional viewpoint can be supported by various of Freud's letters and writings.

A very different viewpoint has been proposed by the well known American economist, Peter Drucker. His parents knew the Freud family in Vienna where Peter Drucker actually met Freud. Drucker contends that Freud unconsciously misrepresented his parents' financial situation by creating the myth that they lived in poverty. Furthermore, Freud also developed another myth that it was because of the strong anti-Semitism in Vienna that he was so delayed in being appointed a professor of psychiatry. Drucker points out that the majority of the Viennese physicians were Jewish and that Freud's becoming a professor did not represent a delay and was not affected by the anti-Semitism in Vienna. Another area of conflict between Freud and the other Viennese physicians was Freud's refusal to treat any of his psychoanalytic patients without a fee. Freud believed that treating a patient in analysis for free created a transference-countertransference problem that might doom the treatment to failure. Freud's transference explanation for not taking on charity patients did not satisfy many of his Viennese physician colleagues. They believed that Freud was given an opportunity to accept their traditional standards and turned it down. In their eyes, Freud rejected them, they did not reject him. The same reasoning applied to the Viennese physicians' request for some scientific proof of the efficacy of psychoanalysis. Freud could only provide them with positive anecdotal word-of-mouth testimonials to psychoanalytic treatment. This placed psychoanalysis in the category of a belief system and not a scientific treatment.

Drucker explains Freud's "obsession" with having lived in poverty as a manifestation of his "poor-house neurosis." According to Drucker this syndrome was frequently found among Viennese during the last quarter of the 19th century. It was an irrational and deep-seated fear that an individual and his family were on the verge of being placed in the poor house because they lacked any funds. Freud does not specifically mention his having this irrational fear or obsession, but he made several statements which I have quoted indicating such a dread.

At a recent psychoanalytic meeting I asked Freud scholar John Gedo of Chicago if he the thought Freud experienced a "poor-house neurosis." Gedo replied that if Freud had anything like this fear it was "more of a fear of going to the slammer (jail), the way his Uncle Josef had for selling the counterfeit rubles." It may be that Freud and his family knew about Uncle Josef's illegal financial dealings, and also involved in this were Freud's two half-brothers in Manchester, England. Freudian scholars have not as yet clarified this area.

On the subject of Freud's alleged "poor-house neurosis," I think that there is enough visible smoke to safely assume that there must have been some fire in the past. Freud's having invented a scenario of extreme poverty during his early years provided him with some suffering which expiated some of the guilt which he felt from having clearly won an oedipal victory over his father. His early suffering from poverty entitled him to preferential treatment by his mother. It also cleared the tracks for the tremendous success achieved by psychoanalysis. I rather expect that when Freudian scholars uncover new historical data, including hitherto unpublished letters to and from Freud, it will show that Freud did *not* experience extreme poverty in his early years. This will point to Freud's fears of poverty as having been neurotically motivated. Obviously, I cannot "prove" this thesis, but as a reconstruction of Freud's early attitude toward money I think that it is accurate.

ACKNOWLEDGMENT

I wish to thank Peter Drucker for reading this paper and discussing its contents with me. This conversation resulted in my making some minor revisions in the paper.

REFERENCES

The Complete Letters of Sigmund Freud to Wilhelm Fliess (1887-1904), (1985), edited by Jeffrey M. Masson, The Belknap Press of Harvard University Press, Cambridge, Mass.

Drucker, P. F. (1978), Adventures of a Bystander, Harper & Row, New York, pp. 83-99 (Freudian Myths and Freudian Realities).

Freud, M. (1983), Sigmund Freud Man and Father, Jason Aronson, New York and London, p. 15.

Freud, S. (1900), The Complete Works of Sigmund Freud, Standard Edition, Vol. IV, The Interpretation of Dreams, Hogarth Press: London, pp. 136-141.

Freud, S. (1901), The Complete Works of Sigmund Freud, Standard Edition, Vol. VI, The Psychopathology of Everyday Life, The Hogarth Press, London.

Freud, S. (1925), An Autobiographical Study, Standard Edition, Vol. XX, Hogarth Press, London, pp. 8, 10.

Gay, P. (1986), Freud, A Life For Our Time, W. W. Norton & Co., New York/London, p. 8.

Holt, R. R. (1973), "On Reading Freud", Introduction to Abstracts of Standard Edit. of Complete Psychological Works of Sigmund Freud, edited by Carrie Lee Rothgeb, Jason Aronson, N.Y., pp. 27-28.

Krull, Marianne, (1986), Freud and His Father, W. W. Norton & Co., pp. 97-99, 164-166.

Letters of Sigmund Freud (1960), edited by Ernest L. Freud, Basic Books, N.Y., pp. 32, 104.

Origins of Psychoanalysis, Letters to Wilhelm Fleiss, Drafts and Notes: 1897-1902 by Sigmund Freud (1985), edited by Marie Bonaparte, Anna Freud, Ernst Kris, Basic Books, N.Y.C., p. 211.

Oring, E. (1984), The Jokes of Sigmund Freud, Univ. of Pennsylvania Press, Philadelphia, pp. 13-26.

CHAPTER 13

MONEY AND THE LEFT IN PSYCHOANALYSIS

Mario Rendon, M.D.

Although psychoanalysis has been regarded predominantly as a discipline concerning the individual, it has also, since its inception, been concerned with the fundamental coordinates of the societies in which it flourishes. Psychoanalysis has thus irreversibly influenced society and civilization, and this influence has been, in part, scientific and, in part, ideological. Society, in turn, has modified psychoanalysis in a reciprocal fashion, and psychoanalytic theory bears a clear imprint from the particular cultures in which its theory and practice have become rooted.

Since its beginnings, psychoanalysis has addressed topics in the realm of social issues such as group psychology, values, religion, the family, etc. A psychoanalytic sociology and, similarly, a new anthropology seemed to logically branch out from psychoanalytic psychology. A revolutionary approach to the issues of sexuality, repression and social values was a landmark of early psychoanalysis. As a counterpoint to what seemed a still biologically slanted approach to human nature, however, a number of psychoanalysts started to look more deeply into social issues. Except for the small group of analysts who constituted an ideological left, the psychoanalytic critique of social institutions skirted the issue of capitalism and its money fetishism. The neglect of psychoanalytic studies of money and related issues by the mainstream in psychoanalysis is equivalent in magnitude only to the corresponding emphasis on supposedly biological drives in the explanation of human behavior. Yet, money is as present in everyday life as sexuality or any drive. The difference, of course, is that money is not a biological given.

In this way, the issue of money, perhaps the most central one in capitalistic society, has been essentially left untouched in psychoanalytic theory. Itself a microcosm of all social relationships and the vehicle for the individual's "realization" in our society, issues of money remain to be explored by our discipline. Why such omission, one would ask, in a theory early characterized by its unyielding critical stand. One excuse might be that money belongs in the realm of economics, and has therefore no place in a science such as psychology. The fallacy of such an argument becomes obvious

Money and Mind, Edited by S. Klebanow and
E.L. Lowenkopf, Plenum Press, New York, 1991

immediately, if we consider the fact that psychoanalysis has frequently not only ventured, but tried to supersede other disciplines. So why not explore economics as well? Another answer might be that the two sciences are too different. Although this may be true for technical econometrics and the like, it is certainly not so for political economy which fundamentally concerns itself with social relationships. Yet another answer might be that the analysis of money issues would inevitably lead into politics, and we want psychoanalysis to be a neutral science. This leaves us at the same starting point: Shall we leave politics – the science and practice of the allocation of power in human relationships – untouched by the critical instrument of the psychoanalytic approach?

As a result of the neglect in studying money issues, this most powerful alienating object has been left alone in its egregious and all powerful obscurity by psychoanalytically-oriented social writers. Although there are a few writings about psychoanalysis and economics, these are rare, and the subject of money is usually raised only for its symbolic value, i.e. as feces or the matter of anal fixations, or as the means for greed, narcissism or other human emotions to express themselves. The average psychoanalyst knows little about the reality of money, and his or her concern with it usually does not go beyond the concern of any other alienated consumer. The psychoanalyst, as well as the regular citizen, is often a standard victim of the illusion that places money as the center objective of everyday human activity.

Freud himself, aware of the real meaning of money, touched on it only peripherally. In his *Papers on Technique* he states for example:

> The next point that must be decided at the beginning of the treatment is the one of money, of the doctor's fee. An analyst does not dispute that money is to be regarded *in the first instance* as a medium for self-preservation and for obtaining power... (my italics). (Freud 1913)

Freud makes mention of money issues as early as his letters to Fliess. He expands, however, exclusively on the symbolic aspect. Money for Freud, as is well known, serves as the concretization of a chain of symbolisms including feces-gift-penis-baby. The popular equivalence of feces and money is clearly documented by Freud as based on folkloric data, since the condensed polarity gold-feces was quite frequently used in literature, tales and folklore in Freud's time. Rather than staying with the analysis of money, Freud focused on the organ responsible for the handling of feces. Thus the anus became the seat of a pivotal libidinal stage, and the locus of one of the most frequently observed character structures. With the features of cleanliness, parsimony and obstinacy, the anal character was no wonder one of the most thoroughly studied by Freud himself. But could those character traits have been understood in the light of Protestant ethics? Of course these would be highly regarded character traits in a society based on values such as the accumulation of money and the promotion of the individual.

Money could be "analyzed" from every psychoanalytic theoretical stand: as feces as Freud did, or as a symbol of power or penis, or as greed and domination, generosity and altruism. In more recent Kohutian self theory, money fits perfectly the qualifications to be the universal self-object. Yet, the full analysis of money that starts with its social reality and then moves into the alienating realms of illusion and compensation, remains to be undertaken. The power of money over man is a magic that remains – perhaps wittingly – untouched. There is no more powerful reinforcer and no more universal narcotic than money. Yet money remains a mystery, not so much in its multiple fantasy symbolisms, but in its real social meaning. We all think we know what money is; after all, isn't it obvious? We handle money more than any other object and we transact with it every single day of our lives. There is no desire that cannot be mediated – whether real or fake – through the power of money. We seem, however, happy to leave the understanding of this important matter to those who have trained in economics or who, for better or worse, have concerned themselves in the business of profiting from speculation in money. Our denial is not entirely unconscious of course but we may be afraid to open a Pandora's Box.

Our world is divided into explosive opposites and at the basis of that division is the theory, the belief and the practice of the social appropriation of national wealth. As a result, the world has been at the brink of annihilation on more than one occasion. Freud saw war as the result of an obscure instinct rather than as the outcome of socioeconomic contradictions. May it be that the psychoanalytic emphasis on sexuality and aggression, instincts and drives, is a counterphobic effort within our denial? Sex is one luring object capable of distracting us from the central matter: How to reduce human misery, often times the result not of scarcity at this time in history, but of unequal and unfair appropriation of nature and wealth.

A large part of the psychoanalytic enterprise is to question perceptions and beliefs. Our guide in this is our consensual perception of reality. In the realm of money, we do not examine its reality. If we accept that money is ever present, pervasive, powerful and constituted by social relationships, why don't we? Don't we concern ourselves with the realities of anatomy and biology? Perhaps because the mere fact of being psychoanalysts already places us in a certain social class, the benefits of which we do not want to forfeit? After all, the essence of our social class position is determined by income and material possession, ultimately by money accumulated. We also by and large serve a limited segment of society, those who have enough money to be able to afford our fees. This is how our reality and that of our patients is partially shaped by money. From our practice we develop our theory, such theory being of necessity limited by our position in society and our perception of social reality. Yet, we believe that our theory is universal, that it applies not only to all segments of society, but that it applies to all societies. Coupled to our childlike denial is our narcissistic egocentrism.

Psychoanalysis was born in a capitalistic society and, as a consequence it bears its imprint. The links between psychoanalysis and money are tighter and stronger than one would believe at a first glance. Economics – instinctual that is – is an essential coordinate of psychoanalysis. Such economics however has strict boundaries and is clearly forbidden to go beyond the illusory measurement of drives. Not unlike national wealth, libido is quantified as a fixed amount susceptible of displacements and fixations. Comparably to the way money circulates in a society as a universal equivalent of commodities, unbound libido is exchangeable in all realms of the body and psyche. Like the dollar today, libido is the general token that can be exchanged at any organ, in any part of the body. The concept of Ego – on the other hand – is coined in terms of its strength to mediate. By appropriating enough libido, the Ego, like the capitalist with money, gains strength. The unspoken ideal embodiment of Ego strength is, of course, not the person of color, someone from the third world, a woman, a child or an elderly person. Such ideal can only be thought to be a bourgeois white male, while the Id is reminiscent of the masses of people wherefrom quantums of surplus value are to be appropriated in the name of Ego strength. Freud's concern with quantification may be an interesting side effect not only of the scientific climate of his time, as is usually stated, but of his bourgeois class influence. Although quantitative measurement continues to be the *primum-movens* in mainstream psychology and psychiatry, its claim to this primordial place in psychoanalysis has not been convincing to this day.

From a purely pragmatic viewpoint, Freud was a generous and altruistic person. He renounced a financially regarding career as a neurologist in order to follow the risky scientific leads of his discoveries. His theory however, was necessarily influenced by his position in society and by the Victorian class factors that operated during his time. The displacement of psychoanalysis from middle Europe to the New World already changed its character substantially; England as a first world country, and Argentina from the third world for example, have also given psychoanalytic theory their very unique imprint.

As an anthropologic theory, psychoanalysis has also been influenced by the political ideas of its time, and particularly by capitalism and socialism. This paper examines the psychoanalytic contributions of three authors, Adler, Reich and Fromm, who, having been members of the political left, placed an special emphasis on understanding social relationships, money among them, in their approach to the psychoanalytic theory of man. It is to be understood that, implicitly, most psychoanalysts have, even if it is with their silence, endorsed the predominant ideological positions prevailing in their society; this is what the psychoanalytic silence about money may be all about. By contrast, these three authors saw capitalism from within, not only as the peak expression of alienation in money, but also as a consequent system of social values. They assumed a position that was critical of capitalism, as well as of its values centered on the individual accumulation of money.

It was Karl Marx who, after the classical political economists had laid the groundwork, developed the deepest understanding of money as an object of social relationships. In his *Manuscripts* (Marx, 1844), Marx was able to poignantly describe how man was being dehumanized by his work which was ultimately represented in money equivalents. Marx saw the real nature of work as an expression of creative humankind. He realized however that, not only did workers not see themselves in the product of their everyday work, but that, paradoxically in capitalism, the more they worked, the more impoverished they became as human beings. In his later analysis in *Das Kapital* (Marx, 1867) Marx saw human (social) work as the real essence of value (ultimately capital or money or price) in economics, and he discovered that, inherent in such abstract value, were concrete relationships of human beings in a particular society. Objects had abstract value only in that they were exchangeable between human beings. Objects produced not for exchange, had only the concrete value inherent in the purposeful use their holder made of them. Thus, to acquire a price or market value, an object had to be placed in front of another and compared as to its equivalency in value. This value however was not in the nature of the object or commodity itself, as we often believe, but it was the expression of the amount of work its producer had invested in it, as well as of other secondary and sundry societal variables. The fact that commodities create in us the illusion that they have value, Marx called the "fetishism of commodity", wherefrom the societal aberration of people valuing themselves by the amount of money they held is derived.

One commodity, gold, became the standard for comparison among other commodities. Historically, and for practical reasons, gold was substituted by silver, coins and paper notes. The price of commodities – human work included – is expressed in terms of money. Money thus means commodity which refers to price and value and work and human exchange and ultimately survival (essentially one works to gather the means to continue one's everyday existence), or "a medium for self preservation and for obtaining power" as Freud put it. The important contribution of Marx was to show how, behind the "obvious" value of money and commodities, lay a complex dynamic of human relationships, and how we are alienated in believing that objects we need or desire have value. Put in other words, objects have value only inasmuch as we give it to them in the social processes of production. Thus Marx's theory of value is not only an economic theory, but it ultimately refers to the value of man and to human values. It is an axiology, a theory of norms, morality and ethics. The main question in this paper is how such insight into the reality of money has shaped the psychoanalytic thinking of the authors who became aware of it.

Alfred Adler (1870-1937) was a self avowed socialist and his theory is perhaps the only psychoanalytic theory that has gained some degree of official recognition in the Soviet Union. He was also both an early member and a pioneer dissenter in the Freudian group which he left in 1911; after having been president of the Vienna Psychoanalytic Society, he departed to found the Society for Free Psychoanalytic Research. Like Freud, Adler gave great importance to early childhood in the development of both character and neurosis. He also, like Freud, emphasized the body as a material basis of psychology. His organ inferiority theory is quite different however, from the instinctual theory or the "anatomy as destiny" theory; it is the beginning of a discrete interpersonal theoretical line in psychoanalysis and it refers ultimately to the human need to compensate for weakness. Familial childhood experiences such as overprotection or neglect, among others, were however as important for Adler as the root of neurotic development. A negative self-image, developing as a result of feelings of helplessness and the inability to develop a sense of mastery, was at the core of neurosis. The social environment in these circumstances, was experienced as hostile and prevented the child from developing skills appropriate for the demands of social life. A striving for superiority would start to develop, in order to compensate for inordinate feelings of inferiority. This would result in a fictive self-ideal or a personal myth, as well as an underdeveloped social interest (Ansbacher 1967).

From a practical point of view, Adler's "Individual Psychology" led to the creation of free child guidance clinics in Vienna, where many of his dedicated disciples offered their services on a volunteer basis; his theory thus resulted in social action. To disseminate his views to a wider audience, Adler also held weekly lectures at the auditorium of the People's Institute of Vienna.

Adler's theory is unique in several aspects. It renounces reifying jargon and goes back to plain common man's everyday language. This feature, as well as many of Adler's theoretical formulations, would later be continued by Karen Horney among others, besides the members of the Adlerian school. Adler also anticipates the theory of the "average expectable environment" of the post-Freudians, and the concept of basic anxiety of Horney. It also antedates later concepts about "self-esteem" and particularly the Sullivanian concept of "reflected self-appraisals". Self-esteem or self-appraisal have a completely different economic connotation which is social rather than biologic. The concept of inferiority feelings resulting in a "striving for recognition" is a concept which inserts Adler into the tradition of the philosopher Hegel, and is also reminiscent of the class struggle concept of Marx. In a sense, one could say that Adler picked up the abandoned Freudian thread of the "seduction theory", the so much talked about but today rarely accepted Freudian interpersonal attempt (albeit not in its concrete but rather in its symbolic sense). He gave priority to the relationship with others rather than to any intrapsychic structures or biological determinants.

Another major contribution of Adler is his teleological approach which would find particular resonance in the existential analysis of Jean Paul Sartre and others. Like Sartre, but before him, Adler thought that an essential aspect of all human behavior was its aim or purposiveness.

The psychic life of man is determined by his goal" Adler wrote, and also "... all phenomena of the soul life may be conceived as preparations for some future situations (Adler, 1927).

This approach in Adler's individual psychology is not restricted, as in Freud, to the aim of the instinctive drive. It is, as in Sartre, a part of the dramatic totality of man's life. Again, economic resonance is found here in the emphasis that socialist thinking gives to planning.

Adler also took a strong feminist stand and attributed the unequal position of women in his time to historical facts. Adler's position vis a vis children and women was a progressive one and at odds with the prevalent views of his contemporaries. More than Freud, Adler placed emphasis on education, and, in his practice, it was Adler who inaugurated the today prevalent institutional "team approach".

With his concepts of teleology, organ inferiority and the masculine protest, as well as with his emphasis on the human relationship and on social action, Adler introduced a whole new dialectic into psychoanalytic discourse, that would later be partially developed by later theoreticians.

Wilhelm Reich (1897-1957) started practicing psychoanalysis in Vienna while still a medical student. A member of the Vienna Psychoanalytic Society, he soon became critical of Freud's lack of emphasis on societal factors. While working with patients from lower socioeconomic strata, Reich concluded that social problems were at the root of many of their ills. He joined the Austrian Social Democratic Party and became involved in the study of Marxism as an instrument to understand social issues. To this day, Reich represents the most serious effort to bridge psychoanalysis and Marxism, and his writings during the period of about 1927-1936, (Reich, 1929-1934) were dedicated to this task. Reich focused on the dialectical aspects of Freudian theory, including its criticism of capitalistic values such as bourgeois sexual morality, the family, consciousness and character. *The Mass Psychology of Fascism*, published in 1933, studied the character mechanisms that explained people's attraction to Fascism. In *The Sexual Revolution*, Reich (1936) described what he believed was the close relationship between social and sexual revolutions. In his most known contribution, *Character Analysis* (Reich 1934), Reich undertakes the study of character as an outcome of social repression. Reich died in the Lewisburg Federal Penitentiary, after charges against him from the U.S. Food and Drug Administration for the sale of orgone boxes, and the impounding and burning of his books (for an excellent introduction to Reich see Ollman, 1972).

Reich was a psychoanalyst and a political activist. He created the Society for Sexual Advice and Sexual Research in Vienna and then a similar organization in Berlin which grew to a total of forty thousand members. The clinics organized by his followers were set up in poor neighborhoods and cared for working class people. Theoretically, the main link between Marxism and psychoanalysis was the theory of alienation as it had been developed by Marx, and by Freud and his followers. Reich saw people developing a character armor that basically represented the obliteration of childhood sexuality and curiosity, and resulted in an impoverished life focused on meaningless production for a capitalistic society.

In his preface to the first edition of *Character Analysis*, Reich states that, since there was a split between the owners of the means of production on the one side, and the owners of the working power, the laborers, on the other side, the former established the social norms that ultimately ended up being incorporated by *all* members of society in the form of a character structure. This he saw accomplished through the alteration of the instinctual apparatus by means of repression, and by the effective "anchoring" of this outcome accomplished in the context of the patriarchal family, the educational system and other social institutions.

> The character structures of the people belonging to a certain epoch or a certain social order, then, are not only reflections of this order but, much more importantly, they represent the anchoring of this order (Reich, 1934).

This is how Capitalism, and particularly Fascism, produced the authoritarian character structures it needed for its continuous reproduction and maintenance.

Character structure was thus the result of alienated sexuality, and sexual repression also entailed the repression of rebelliousness and critical thinking, all that was expansive in human development. Submissive and irrational people were the product of such repression. While Freud saw sexual repression as the root of civilization, Reich emphasized the interests of the dominant class in maintaining such concrete everyday repression. Although Reich saw repression as necessary during early historical times in which scarcity prevailed, with the level of industrialization reached by modern society he saw it as unnecessary, being maintained only in the interest of the dominant class' greed. Reich saw the task of de-alienated man as the pursuit of previously repressed libidinal urges in a context of self development and creativity. With the liberation of sexuality, human expansiveness would also be unleashed, critical thinking and revolutionary activity included. Not only was instinctual repression unnecessary in modern times, it was in fact delaying the process of historical change.

As mentioned, Reich saw a major flaw in psychoanalysis' lack of social consciousness. He saw Freudian psychoanalytic practice as paternalistic, patriarchal, authoritarian, and acquiescent to bourgeois morality. He was in favor of therapeutic activity on the part of the analyst and an "unconditional affirmation of the patient's claim for happiness" and the "liberation of morality from its tabooistic features" (Brown, 1973 p. 47). Reich was familiar with Malinowsky's anthropological findings among the Trobriand Islanders where oedipal repression was not found. This was a concrete proof and basis of his theory.

Reich, in contrast to Adler and Fromm, wanted to remain in the Freudian mainstream. His theories and practice, however, led to his expulsion from both the psychoanalytic establishment and the Communist party. His derailment into the orgone theory, as well as his unfortunate end, were a major loss to psychoanalytic thinking.

Erick Fromm (1900-1980) has probably had more popular influence than any other member of the psychoanalytic left. He was originally a psychologist and sociologist, as well as a member of the Frankfurt School (Horkheimer, Adorno, Marcuse) and a follower of Reich. The Frankfurt School's major contribution was the empirical documentation of the authoritarian personality structure in capitalistic society, with the father seen as the representative of the State authority within the family. Initially Fromm believed in the instinctual theory, but he concurred with Reich on the influence of society in shaping the outcome of the individual and his character; later on he believed that the fundament of character was a person's relatedness to the world and not libido organizations. Fromm moved progressively towards a social view and, in the United States, he was part of the neo-Freudian or culturalist ("revisionist") school. Fromm was closely involved with Karen Horney and each had a reciprocal influence on the other's writings. Fromm's later work in his "radical humanistic psychoanalysis", concentrated on the analysis of selfishness and altruism as two basic character orientations. Narcissism was not self love as most psychoanalysts would claim, but its opposite; this was also Karen Horney's belief.

Being a member of a younger generation, Fromm became critical of the application of Marxism in the Soviet Union and shifted his orientation more towards a general humanism that was ecumenical in character and included religious thought. He was actively involved in advancing the cause of socialism and some of his later writings try to sketch his ideal of a socialist society of the future.

Fromm placed emphasis on issues such as biological helplessness at birth, a theme similar to Adler's. He also emphasized the human awareness of death and the human need for meaning and belonging. His characterology, based on the belief that drives are the result of faulty socialization, has a clear sociological imprint second to no other psychoanalytic theory. Thus "receptive", "exploitative", "hoarding", "marketing" and "productive" personalities. In the marketing type, personality is a commodity for sale in the market.

In his late book *To Have or to Be* (Fromm, 1976), Fromm contrasts two modes of existence, one based on the predominant way society conditions its members towards acquisitiveness and greed, and towards a materialistic (commodity) orientation and the other based on an ethical way of being founded on the teachings of different masters of society, including Marx and religious leaders. Fromm attempts to show how these opposite orientations influence the quality of everyday life. Like his predecessors, Fromm illustrates the position of a critical psychoanalyst in the society to which he belongs.

Living in Mexico, Fromm developed an interest in the – up to that point – seemingly antagonistic opposites of religion and Marxism. This would prove to be a pioneering effort, later on translated into a new socio-political phenomenon: the revolutionary movement that condensed the political left and the church as, for example, in Nicaragua and other countries of Latin America. This was a precursor to the flourishing of the new Liberation Theology with which the Catholic Church is now struggling. Although not fully recognized as yet, this influence may prove to be the major contribution of Fromm to the political life of the third world.

In summary, three psychoanalytic authors have been briefly discussed, who may well be the ones to have contributed the most to the critique of capitalism as a system based on the fetishism of money. They all contributed in different ways: Alfred Adler began a discrete line of psychoanalytic thought which replaced biological constructs with social ones, continuing a previous attempt by Freud in his aborted Seduction Theory. Adler's pioneering social orientation would be continued by his disciples and by the neo-Freudians or culturalists. Wilhelm Reich, who ambitiously wanted to bridge the Freudian and Marxist theories, founded his own school also and inspired the rich contributions of the Frankfurt School. Erich Fromm, himself a member of the Frankfurt School and later a Neofreudian, left a rich legacy of sociologically influenced psychoanalytic thought which was focused on social processes. These three authors, whether intentionally or not, ended up outside the Freudian mainstream. They were all members of the political left, and all left rich psychoanalytic legacies, stressing the destructive nature of the social relationships between men in their concrete capitalistic societies. These disturbed social relationships, imbued in individuals as societal values, were seen as the most important psychological factor in neurotic formation. All of them contributed importantly as social activists, not only by trying to widen the accessibility of psychoanalysis to the common man, but also by trying to influence social and political life. They all left solid schools of followers and greatly influenced other psychoanalytic contemporaries. These three authors are neither the only psychoanalysts influenced by Marx nor the only ones to have tackled socioeconomic issues. They represent however, in the context of the reality of money and its many symbolic meanings, the most original and creative leads into a subject that has been left essentially untouched by the silent psychoanalytic majority.

Money, the major preoccupation of modern man, is the least understood social phenomenon in psychoanalysis. The recent psychoanalytic interest on this important subject, perhaps shows a readiness that must be vigorously pursued. Money is, after all, the object of our desire and motivation, the immediate reward of our productive activity, the vehicle of exchange for our survival, the symbol of our status in capitalistic society, the most powerful intermediate in our social relationships and, last but not least, the fetish that causes our greatest alienation. Understanding money will only serve the purpose of enhancing our humanity.

REFERENCES

Adler, A. 1927, Understanding Human Nature, Fawcett Publications, Inc., Greenwich, Conn. 1968.

Ansbacher, H. L. and Ansbacher R. R., 1967, The Individual Psychology of Alfred Adler, Harper Torchbooks, New York.

Brown, B. 1973, Marx, Freud, and the Critique of Everyday Life Toward a Permanent Cultural Revolution, Monthly Review Press, New York.

Freud, S. 1913, On beginning the treatment (Further recommendations on the technique of psychoanalysis), The Standard Edition, Hogarth Press, 1958.

Fromm, E, 1976 To Have or to Be?, Bantam Books, New York, 1982.

Marx, C., 1844, Economic and Philosophical Manuscripts, In Fromm, E. Marx's Concept of Man, Frederick Ungar Publishing Co., New York, 1972.

Marx, C., 1867, Capital, A Critique of Political Economy, Vol. 1, International Publishers, New York, 1967.

Ollman, B. 1972, Introduction to the Sex-Pol Essays, Random House, New York.

Reich, W., 1949, Character Analysis, The Noonday Press, New York 1968.

Reich, W., 1929-1934, Sex-Pol Essays, Random House, New York, 1972.

CHAPTER 14

THE SEDUCTION OF MONEY

Arnold Rothstein, M.D.

Mr. X is a sixty-year-old married, childless, wealthy retired lawyer. In the fifth year of his analysis he began a session by announcing that he was rewriting his will and would like to make me beneficiary in the amount of $250,000. When I suggested that he elaborate upon this fantasy, Mr. X became annoyed. He told me that I had helped him a great deal and was one of the most important people in his life. He wished to make my old age a bit easier. In the ensuing sessions, Mr. X became aware that, in spite of the reality of his considerable wealth, his wish to make me a beneficiary in his will expressed certain unacknowledged concerns of his own. He was anxious about being alone and uncared for as he grew older and wished I would never leave him and would instead take care of him.

Four months later Mr. X brought to his session an article on therapeutic nurseries that appeared in the newspaper. He was very touched by the report of these preventive interventions with young children and their families and expressed his wish to help. Mr. X had lost his mother as the result of a postpartum psychosis when he was six years old. He was by nature very generous and philanthropic and was moved by the article to think about how he might help develop these preventive services. Mr. X reflected on the facts that he was childless, had generously fulfilled his obligations to his alma mater, had millions of dollars to decide how to bequeath, and thought that nothing would be finer than to create a foundation to facilitate the development of these wonderful services. He related that there was not one whose judgment he respected more than mine. He wondered if I would consider being the administrator of such a foundation. As far as I could determine, Mr. X had no conscious knowledge of my long-standing interest in working with handicapped children. I was aware of the powerful

---

This chapter originally appeared in the Psychoanalytic Quarterly, 1986, LV: pp. 296-300. Reprinted by permission.

countertransference temptation to accept this seemingly rational and morally acceptable impulse toward generosity. Nevertheless, its relationship to the earlier offer to be my benefactor was obvious. Further analysis eventually revealed more about its concealed intentions.

About a month later Mr. X began a session by reporting: "While walking to the session, I had the thought that we could call the foundation the X-Rothstein foundation." He laughed and noted, "That way we would be united forever." This gratifying fantasy of union was particularly poignant for Mr. X, as it reflected, in part, his wish to repair the shockingly traumatic loss of his mother at the height of his oedipal phase. Later in the session he reported that he was thinking about termination and wondered if I would consider the idea of being put on a permanent retainer to insure my availability on short notice if he felt the need for a session. In exploring this fantasy, we were able to analyze his mistrust and his fear that I would not be there for him, just as his mother had not been there for him after he was six years of age.

Some other data are noteworthy in regard to Mr. X's use of money, both as an expression of his transference love and as an attempt at seduction.

Mr. X sought psychotherapy for the first time at the age of thirty-seven when he was single, successful professionally, and deeply troubled by his homosexual proclivity. Although he found both men and women attractive, he confined consummated sexual experiences to bathroom encounters with men whom he considered beneath him socially. His abhorrence of a homosexual way of life influenced him to seek help. He worked in psychotherapy two or three times a week for fifteen years. The interpretive approach of his therapist emphasized Mr. X's masochism and its expression in the extratransference sphere of his life. Mr. X had no memory of their having worked on his childhood experiences in general, or on his oedipal conflicts in particular. In addition, he could not remember exploring his feelings and/or fantasies concerning his analyst. The therapy was helpful to Mr. X in achieving his goal of marrying a woman and in obtaining moderate pleasure in sex with women. After Mr. X terminated, he visited his therapist yearly. On one such occasion, in response to Mr. X's complaints about his wife, his therapist suggested that Mr. X should accept his wife as she was; she would probably never change significantly. The therapist added that perhaps he ought to find another woman. This remark terrified Mr. X, who left feeling that his therapist had become quite successful and had lost interest in him. This thought influenced Mr. X to find another person to work with when he sought help for a second time.

During the second year of his analysis with me, Mr. X received a letter from his first therapist seeking a contribution to a fund to support a psychiatric foundation. Also of note was a *dream*, perhaps six months prior to the emergence of his fantasy of leaving me money, which foretold Mr. X's subsequent attempt to seduce his analyst with money. Mr. X reported:

> I'm being conducted through a bank. If I'm not the guest of honor, I'm clearly a very important participant. This bank was previously directed by Harold Quieter. I was very fond of him. (Mr. X associates, 'When I think of Harold I think of you.') As I approached the entrance to the bank, there was a large billboard. I thought this is an odd display for the entrance to a bank. I thought that although it was hard to believe, Harold seemed to have a conflict of interest here.

Mr. X was silent for some time. I noted, "In the dream Harold's integrity is doubted." Mr. X remarked tersely, "Money corrupts." I said, "It never corrupted you." Although the content of this intervention was ambiguous, my tone of voice emphasized the transference. Mr. X responded: "I can't believe I have even a subconscious thought that it would corrupt you." He paused and conjectured, "I suppose I have a need to make you larger than life."

At this point in the analysis I conjectured that Mr. X was tempted to test my corruptibility both in response to his past therapist's appeal for money and in response to residual homosexual impulses that seemed part of the latent fabric of the more manifest maternal positive oedipal transference.

DISCUSSION

In the seventy-odd years since Freud wrote his papers on technique there have been many contributions to the literature on technique and on the subject of transference-countertransference. However, there is a striking paucity of discussions about the meanings of money in the transference-countertransference aspects of the analytic situation. As I worked to understand my countertransference responses to Mr. X's attempted seduction, I found that Freud's (1915a) final paper on technique contained guidelines that seemed as valid today as they were seventy years ago. In that paper Freud discussed male analysts' heterosexual conflicts in working with women analysands who had fallen in love with them.

I am suggesting that the fantasied gratifications associated with money may be as much a problem as those associated with sex. The guidelines that Freud (1915a) proposed for "not giv[ing] up the neutrality towards the patient, which we have acquired through keeping the counter-transference in check" in relationship to working with heterosexual material are pertinent to working with the issues discussed in this paper.

Some of the foundations of technique Freud established bear repeating. First and foremost, "The welfare of the patient *alone* should be the touchstone" (italics added). Second, "The patient's falling in love is induced by the analytic situation and is not to be attributed to the charms of (the analyst's) own person". Third, "Anything that interferes with the continuation of the treatment may be an expression of resistance".

In a sense that the task is simple, but it is far from easy. The offer of money in any form and for any reason should be regarded as a transference fantasy. Like any fantasy, it is an overdetermined compromise formation that needs to be analyzed. To do otherwise is to perpetuate a countertransference enactment.

The analyst's attitude toward the future and particularly toward the post-analytic phase is especially important in regard to the issue of money. Because of the analyst's narcissistic investments in his professional endeavors and institutions, he might be tempted to rationalize the feasibility of accepting contributions from an analysand after termination. In this regard, it is important to remember that the unconscious is timeless (Freud, 1915b), and that analyses are all, in a certain sense, interminable (Freud, 1937). Any other attitude may interfere with the analysis of an analysand's attempts at seduction with money.

Although some analysts suggest the appropriateness of soliciting and/or accepting contributions from former analysands,I think the analytic material presented here supports my contention that to do so has powerful transference implications. From the perspective of this brief communication, such behavior may reflect a countertransference enactment that is a potential interference in the analysand's independence and post-analytic self-analysis. In addition, such behavior might interfere with the analysand's possible need to return to the analyst for further analysis.

REFERENCES

Freud, S.(1915a), "Observations on transference-love" (further recommendations on the technique of psycho-analysis III), S.E., 12.

(1915b), The unconscious, S.E., 14.
(1937), Analysis terminable and interminable, E.E., 23.

CHAPTER 15

MONEY AND COUNTERTRANSFERENCE

Marvin G. Drellich, M.D.

I am going to make some observations and ask some questions about what money means, personally, to the psychoanalyst or psychotherapist. The material I draw upon comes from over thirty years of psychoanalytic practice during which I have worked with patients who are physicians, psychiatrists, psychoanalysts (both medical and non-medical) and with a significant number of candidates in psychoanalytic training. I have also had numerous discussions with colleagues and friends within the profession; mostly informal, anecdotal conversations about fees, income, referrals and the psychoanalytic "business" in general. Most analysts have such informal discussions and yet this subject is rarely included in psychoanalytic training curricula or, for that matter, in the psychoanalytic literature.

FREUD AND MONEY

The realities of money, by which I mean the earning of one's living and the support of one's family fell upon the shoulders of the first psychoanalyst, Sigmund Freud, from the beginning of his professional career.
Jones, in his biography of Freud, describes the economic hardship of Freud's early life, continuing into his years in medical school, his hospital years, his months of study with Charcot in Paris and into his first ten years of medical practice in Vienna. Freud borrowed money from Breuer and other friends well into the 1890's because his practice was growing very slowly. In May 1896 he wrote to Fliess that his consulting room was empty for an entire day and that he had had no new patients for weeks.
In the early 1900's, as psychoanalysis became more widely accepted, Freud's practice became very busy and his fees are described as being fairly high for Vienna at that time, eight dollars per session.
World War I brought Freud new economic hardships. His practice was very slow and inflation was rampant. In 1916 Karl Abraham proposed Freud's name to the Nobel Prize Committee and Freud, having no patients at all at the time, was quite pleased. In addition to the great honor of such

Money and Mind, Edited by S. Klebanow and
E.L. Lowenkopf, Plenum Press, New York, 1991

an award he said that he could use the money that went with winning the Nobel Prize. As we know, Freud never did receive this coveted award.

By 1917 he feared that he might have to declare personal bankruptcy. In 1919 he was still in dire financial distress and was depleted of most of his patients. The terrible post-war inflation had seriously reduced the real value of his savings. In 1919 he once again had to borrow money from friends, in this case, mostly from Max Eitingon. Fortunately in the last two decades of his life his financial condition became more prosperous and secure.

MONEY AND PSYCHOANALYTIC PRACTICE

The practice of psychoanalysis has many meanings and values for its practitioners. One very important and rarely discussed meaning has always been the livelihood, the monetary income of the psychoanalyst.

In this sense the analyst is no different from any wage earner, businessman or investor. He makes an oral agreement with a patient (customer) to sell his professional skills and services for a fee; in business terms, for a profit. The profit from patient's fees provides home, sustenance, discretionary income and in some instances a wide range of luxuries for himself and his family. This income must also take into account the current inflation in the cost of housing, clothing, food, medical and dental expenses, education of children, vacations, etc., which the analyst must face along with the rest of the population.

Over and above these material considerations, the analyst, like many others in our society, has status and prestige values associated with money and life style.

Comparisons and competition are common in the area of money. Psychiatrists and psychoanalysts are among the lower income groups in the medical profession. Most other specialists, excluding pediatricians, among our friends and colleagues, among our peers in age and experience, are earning more money and living in a fashion which reflects their higher income. Even among our psychiatric colleagues the psychopharmacologists, hypnosis specialists and others appear to earn more money than the psychotherapists do as a group.

How much are one's personal self-esteem, sense of achievement and feeling of reward for long years of study dependent on the measure of money earned and the material aspects of one's life? The answer may be different in the case of each psychoanalyst but money and material well-being are rarely totally irrelevant factors in a psychoanalyst's self-esteem system. I have heard psychotherapists and psychoanalysts wonder out loud if they had made a mistake choosing their specialty. Money was usually one of the elements behind such doubts.

THE FIDUCIARY RELATIONSHIP

The practice of psychoanalysis is, of course, much more than a commercial enterprise which generates money, material well-being and self-esteem. It is also a fiduciary relationship, that is, a relationship of trust wherein one person, the patient, is needy, dependent, helpless or impaired. He puts himself in the care of a fiduciary, the analyst, who for an arranged fee promises to carry out his specialized services which are supposed to be exclusively in the best interests of the patient. A fiduciary is a person of professional skills but must also be a person of the highest integrity, trustworthiness and scrupulous good faith. Except for the fee which should be fair and reasonably compensating, all the activities of the fiduciary, the analyst, should be directed toward the well-being of the client, the patient. That is what society expects of us and what we should expect of ourselves.

There are, I regret, a small number of analysts who, blatantly and cynically, violate this trust and exploit the patient in ways which include, among others, the inappropriate monetary benefit of the analyst. I know of two analysts who acknowledged without shame or regret that each had contrived to be named as an heir in a wealthy patient's will. In June 1988 a newspaper reported that a prominent mid-western psychoanalyst "has been charged with serious improprieties in dealings with a now deceased former patient." The analyst is accused of using undue influence in causing the patient, before her death, to establish trust funds for the analyst, his family and his professional institution. The analyst was also named as one of three executors of the patient's multi-million dollar estate.

In addition to such occasional blatant exploitations of patient, I am concerned with the more common, more subtle exploitations which occur. The analyst who quietly invests in a stock or a stock option based on insider information which he heard from the couch, the analyst who accepts expensive personal gifts, paintings from an artist patient, expensive products from a manufacturer patient, these may also be violations of the fiduciary trust for the financial benefit of the analyst.

These "innocent" exchanges are not inconsequential. They contaminate the transference and constitute a collaborative transference-countertransference resistance in the patient's analysis.

IRRATIONAL ATTITUDES TOWARD MONEY

Now – beyond the analyst's conscious and realistic concern with earning a living, beyond the possible conflicts between the commercial and the fiduciary aspects of his practice, there may be other unconscious and unrealistic attitudes toward money which can truly be called countertransferential in the classical psychoanalytic sense of that word.

Irrational attitudes about money are rife in the general population, in our patient population and may well exist in some of the psychoanalyst population.

These include:

1. Fantasies and wishes to acquire enormous wealth, far in excess of one's needs or even one's most expensive appetites for the luxuries of life.
2. Compulsive work schedules which may be in the service of accumulating more and more wealth.
3. Compulsive gambling, while due to many factors, is also due to irrational fantasies about money.
4. Hoarding money to the point of self-denial and even impoverishment of one's material life.
5. Compulsive spending and compulsive picking up of a restaurant check are clearly derived from irrational attitudes about money.
6. Compulsive stinginess over small expenses as in the person who walks eight or ten blocks out of the way to save two cents on a can of tuna fish.
7. Successful cheating of small amounts of money in transactions with friends and relatives as well as strangers.
8. A constant fear of being cheated or tricked out of money, over and above the realistic caution and alertness one must exercise in this area.
9. Irrational fear of imminent economic failure in business or profession with grave expectations of poverty.
10. Excessive generosity or charitability which goes beyond what one can afford.

Any of these elements in a psychoanalyst's personality would invariably have an effect on the character of his work.

MONEY ISSUES IN THE PSYCHOANALYTIC PROCESS

My chief concern is with the money issues that directly and specifically involve the psychoanalytic process, the analyst-patient relationship.

The analyst may feel competitive toward a patient who has or earns more money than himself. The patient may be in another branch of medicine, another profession, a lucrative business or even a person of great inherited wealth.

A distinguished analyst of an earlier generation told me in 1951 when I was a student in analytic training that he once had had a super-wealthy patient whom he, Zilboorg, charged three times his otherwise highest fee and still felt that he was not charging enough.

If an analyst feels competitive with such patients, if he resents the patients' greater affluence, does it influence what he says, what he interprets and how he interprets?

When patients are paying the analyst's maximum fees and thus make a major contribution to the analyst's gross income is there a danger that the patient may be kept in treatment longer than is needed in order for the analyst to maintain this income? I heard an analyst describe someone as a "one-hundred fifty dollar an hour patient" who was terminating and causing the analyst some concern about income. Such a label is significant as to the importance of that patient and his money to that analyst.

When analysts have, for whatever reason, lower fee patients, do they resent them? When such patients are making very slow progress does the analyst become impatient for their time to be available for a higher paying patient? Do these considerations influence the content and quality of the analyst's interventions?

Are there countertransference issues involved in an analyst's excessive willingness or excessive reluctance to discuss the money issues that arise in analysis; the patient's attitudes about money, property, and real or neurotic anxieties about money?

Are there countertransference factors involved in (1) setting fees both maximum and minimum (2) adjusting fees due to inflation or due to the patient's earning more money or conversely, losing his job? Is countertransference ever a factor in an analyst's policy regarding missed sessions? The traditional psychoanalytic reasons for charging for missed sessions involve the analyst leasing time to the patient, or the patient should feel some sense of sacrifice but I wonder if these are ever rationalizations to protect the analyst's income?

Tulipan sees all aspects of an analyst's fee policy as an extension of his personal style. I would add that this personal style affects the analyst's non-professional, social and personal relationships as well. Inherent in this style is the analyst's self-image as well as what he wishes to portray as a public image: Two contrasting pictures would be (1) an analyst who wants to be seen as a caring person, a warm and giving human being who has little greed or acquisitiveness or (2) a pragmatic realist who has no illusions of altruism or guilt-induced selflessness; hard-nosed, worldly professional who does not let false sentiment contaminate his professional skills or influence his fees.

ADDITIONAL RELATED QUESTIONS

It is useful to compare an analyst who has all or nearly all available hours filled with one who has considerable unfilled time in his schedule. The latter may actively seek referrals from busier colleagues but he may be reluctant to do so for fear that it might tarnish his professional image. I can remember a time when many prominent, sought-after analysts had waiting lists of new and prospective patients but I have not heard of such a situation in over twenty years.

Competition for patients is a reality at the present time. I have heard medical psychoanalysts complain that the large number of non-medical psychoanalysts is reducing the potential patient population and they have taken a strong political and "scientific" stand against the training and recognition of non-medical analysts. Could unstated economic factors be involved in such behavior?

Additional competition for patients comes from the large number of therapies which have entered the area in the past few decades. Many are, of course, legitimate and useful alternatives to psychoanalytic therapy but some are clearly wildly unscientific, "get-well-quick" schemes which will lead to no therapeutic gain for the patients.

COUNTERTRANSFERENCE AND MONEY

The bed rock countertransference issue involving money is simply the analyst's economic dependence on his patients.

Silverberg once said, "money is the patient's protection against the analyst's countertransference." He was implying, I believe, that the analyst disciplines himself to maintain a strictly professional (therapeutic) stance, does not yield to his countertransferential temptations to act out (socially, sexually or with hostility) because he is economically dependent on the patient's fees. Alas, we know of all too many instances where analysts have acted out, both sexually and otherwise, have continued to call it "therapeutic" and have continued to charge, even as the acting out was going on. Overall I suggest that the analyst's personal integrity and secondarily the threat of malpractice are the major deterrents to countertransference acting-out.

Apart from acting out I am emphasizing that every psychoanalyst has a strong sense of economic dependency on his patient population as a whole. If his practice is small that sense of dependency can become focused on individual patients whose fees make up a significant part of his income. Such dependency may generate resentment, hostility and any or all of the reactions which anyone may have toward any person on whom one feels dependent and hence, ambivalent.

This dependency is an irreducible element which inevitably affects the way the analyst participates in the analytic relationship. The most important corrective requires the analyst to be aware that money is indeed a factor in *all* his professional decisions.

ANALYST'S FANTASIES OF INDEPENDENT WEALTH

To put some of these issues to a test I have asked a number of my colleagues to imagine themselves to be independently wealthy and to comment on how this would affect their psychoanalytic work.

Very few said they would retire outright and lead a life of leisure and recreation. Most said that they would continue to practice but make significant changes. They said that psychoanalytic work was a source of great personal satisfaction for many reasons besides money. Their sense of identity as practicing psychoanalysts was an important feeling they would be most reluctant to give up, but they added that they might conduct their practices in somewhat different ways.

Some of the changes they fantasied are interesting and significant." I would clear out some of the dead wood in my practice," meaning patients who are not making progress, who do not work in the therapeutic alliance, who are in a kind of maintenance therapy with no likelihood of movement, who remain in therapy because of their intractable dependency needs. For some analysts they may be like an "annuity" who could be discharged if the analyst had no need for their money.

"I'd lower my fees to make therapy available to worthy patients who cannot now afford it," said another who had a strong interest in treating artists, writers and other young creative patients. Another analyst spoke of selecting only the most highly treatable, analyzable patients with whom the satisfactions of successful analytic work are much more probable.

Still another spoke of making tougher, more confronting interpretations without the fear that the patients might flee from treatment and the analyst would lose their contribution to his income.

The majority of the analysts volunteered that if they were independently wealthy they would work fewer hours each day and take more frequent and longer times off. Their current schedules are maintained, in part, to assure a certain level of income. For the sake of that income they work long hours, experience fatigue, sometimes inattention, boredom and resentment which are the inevitable consequences of such schedules.

What is exposed by these fantasies is that some analysts work certain hours, see certain patients, refuse to see other patients, make or withhold certain interpretations or confrontations with the analyst's income as a significant determinant for these decisions, rather than consideration of the optimal therapeutic interventions.

REFERENCES

Jones, E., (1953), The Life and Work of Sigmund Freud, Basic Books, New York.

Masson, J.M., (1985), The Complete Letters of Sigmund Freud to Wilhelm Fliess 1887-1904, Belknap Press, Cambridge, Mass. and London.

Silverberg, W., (n.d.), Personal Communication from Lilly Otenheimer

Tulipan, A.B., (1986), Fee Policy as an Extension of the Therapist's Style and Orientation in Krueger, D.W. ed., The Last Taboo, Brunner/Mazel, New York.

CHAPTER 16

COUNTERTRANSFERENCE PROBLEMS WITH MONEY

Natalie Shainess, M.D.

BRIEF REVIEW OF THE DEVELOPMENT OF TRANSFERENCE – COUNTERTRANSFERENCE CONCEPTS

A search for references on the significance of attitudes toward money in the psychoanalytic literature produced little. Before exploring this, it seems worthwhile to review briefly the meaning of those terms, since at times 'countertransference' is used very loosely today. It is also an area frequently overlooked in supervision, both psychotherapeutic and analytic. Goin and Kline (1976) found in reviewing video tapes of supervision that countertransference in the resident was largely overlooked by the supervisor, and dealt with only indirectly in a few cases. This is a touchy area, and one could propose that the *supervisor's* countertransferential responses interfered with good supervision.

Going to the source, Freud (1912) described transference as "a special individuality in the exercise of the capacity to love...which every human being has acquired. It forms a cliche or stereotype in him, which perpetually repeats and reproduces itself as life goes on...Of feelings which determine the capacity to love, only a part has undergone psychical development; this part is directed toward reality...The other part...has been held up in development, withheld from conscious personality and from reality...this is the transference." So, often forgotten is the fact that *love* is involved, meaning for the analyst the capacity to respond in an appropriate (and thus empathic and caring) way. The countertransference is exactly the same as transference, but in the analyst, pointing to bits of unsolved developmental problems.

In 1913, Freud spoke, perhaps a bit indirectly, of countertransference in relation to money, citing a special instance: "Gratuitous treatment enormously increases many neurotic resistances, such as the temptations of the transference-relationship for young women." Inferred in such a full-blown relationship is the part of the countertransference of the analyst–usually male. There is a further extension of this by Freud (1915) in a statement that capsulizes the ultimate disaster of countertransference, be it in relation to

Money and Mind, Edited by S. Klebanow and
E.L. Lowenkopf, Plenum Press, New York, 1991

erotic 'provocation' by the patient, or others, including money. "It is a triumph for the patient and a complete overthrow of the cure." To avoid this pyrrhic victory for the patient, Freud believed that the transference problem must not be ignored, but faced boldly and treated as unreal (which, of course, it is) and used to bring to light hidden developmental factors. The analyst's major task is to "do battle against the forces which would draw him down below the level of analysis." Later, Freud (1937) again remarked on the importance of overcoming countertransference, by quoting Ferenczi on the fact that successful analysis largely depends on the analyst's having profited by the lesson of his own 'errors' and mistakes, and (having) got the better of the weak points in his own personality—that is, having overcome the blindspots or irrational areas of countertransference.

Spensly (1977) devoted himself to this issue in analysis, stressing the importance of the analyst's appropriate communication, and Sandler's (1973) view that countertransference is a specific *emotional* response aroused in the analyst by specific qualities of the patient, and always inappropriate. This implies, since the analyst *is* the authority in analytic therapy, that countertransference is usually manifested in the irrational and destructive use of authority. The analyst must not use the analytic situation in a hypnotic-like way; the analyst must be devoid of traits which tend to unconsciously perpetuate the originally destructive or authoritarian situation.

WHY ANALYSTS DEVELOP COUNTERTRANSFERENCE IN RELATION TO MONEY

This leads into the question of why the analyst, who has undergone at least one training analysis, has not overcome gross distortions in relation to money. One explanation is that the analyst in training is often young, has not fully developed a practice, or even a feeling of satisfaction or *dis*satisfaction in relation to financial success. Further, in the training analysis, sibling rivalries are rarely considered in economic terms, because the rivalries of young children generally do not focus on money, although envious feelings may begin to develop that include this.

Also, in an earlier day, the economic side of practice was rarely discussed, so that irrational attitudes were not very likely to come up for consideration. It could be added that discussing fees in practice among colleagues is rather rare, even today, suggesting that the analyst's feeling of worth is reflected in the fees he commands, and that he is reluctant to reveal this. Krueger (1988) has reminded us that in 1913 Freud wrote that "Money questions will be treated by cultured people in the same manner as sexual matters, with the same consistency, prudishness and hypocrisy. Perhaps the word 'sophisticated' might be substituted for 'cultured' today; and while sex today is revealed in all its minutiae, there is still something secretive in talk about money (perhaps this suggests what is considered most precious today!).

Much appears to remain hidden with regard to money, on both sides of the analytic equation. It seems to have been felt, in years past, that any bright young practitioner or analyst who kept his or her eyes open would know what to do. Obviously, such is not the case. The very first monetary hazard is fee-setting. Practical issues enter in: how experienced the analyst is; how well-connected with other professionals (in relation to the likelihood of referrals); what the prevailing fees are in the analyst's location; how well-regarded the analyst is; publications and special expertise; and to some extent, what the market will bear.

But then other factors may enter in, especially distortions from early experience with money in the family--the family's attitude towards money; how comfortable the family's circumstances--whether wealthy or impoverished, and whether generosity or niggardliness represented the main economic approach; how acquisitive the family was; whether parents' attitudes were geared toward giving freely to the child routinely (when possible) or demanding a period of waiting before satisfying the child's longings; or whether over-indulgent to the therapist-as-child, and what kind of expansiveness--or its antithesis--may have resulted from parental attitudes toward giving. Also involved is the family's treatment of siblings--whether fair or unfair, generally *and* in relation to money. A patient of mine, who tended to hoard his allowance as a child, was constantly being told by his parents that "You have more money so why don't you give your brother some to help him get what he wants." His resentment grew as he did, especially as his brother was a spendthrift.

Then, there is the question of whether the potential analyst was greedy or envious as a child, and to what extent these traits were analyzed or continue to exist. Vindictiveness as an unanalyzed trait (where it is subtle) may still affect the handling of money matters and evoke sadistic response in the analyst. Fear of losing a patient by being too firm, or its opposite-- allowing inadvisable arrangements (as suggested by Rothstein's patient) may also have deep roots, in addition to immediate causes. Passivity may also affect actions in relation to money, and some of these factors may slip through the analytic net, leaving the analyst inadequately prepared to cope with the realities of the business side of practice. Patients, like children, are very resourceful in 'tripping up the analyst'.

One of the unexpected ploys that I have run into more than once, though never brought up initially, is that of the patient trying to tie payment to the receipt of his/her biweekly or monthly paycheck. It sometimes requires much discussion and ingenuity to place this demand (that the analyst accommodate to a special situation) in proper perspective, and occurs when the analyst is unclear about his or her own responses.

In my own experience of being supervised, I can recall only two comments from analysts which helped deal with my inadequacy in the area of payment--and they were in the nature of advice, rather than analytic scrutiny. One supervisor suggested that I tell the patient "If I have to be concerned about being paid, it might interfere with thought about your problems, which is where I would like to place my effort." The other, to a patient who used money and payment as an ongoing means of expressing scorn (and fear of treatment's-and his-worthlessness): "Treatment is either priceless or worthless-the fee does not determine its worth, and we will both have to do our best and see which it will be."

THREE CASE ILLUSTRATIONS

At the very outset of treatment, in discussion of fee, an analyst's undue (countertransferential) sensitivity to the patient's view of what treatment 'should cost' may elicit a problem from the start; or else, there may be denial of the patient's manipulation in relation to fee. Denial or delay in dealing with the patient's special needs as expressed through money will inevitably result in further difficulties or failure. Of course, I am *not* saying that the analyst should be inflexible, or never make concessions, where appropriate.

1. Postscript to a 'completed' analysis--bouncing check

Certainly, something must have been overlooked or denied (on both sides) in the following case: A patient who had paid her monthly bill with relative regularity had reached the endpoint of treatment. The last session ended on a positive note, but the analyst was surprised to find that the check in final payment 'bounced'. This was something that had not occurred in the several years of analysis. The patient was called but had left town as anticipated. A letter was mailed to the new address. The patient called and expressed great surprise that there had been insufficient funds for the check, and insisted this was sheer chance.

The analyst was tempted to let it go at that, but she decided to ask if the patient had a few minutes to talk on the phone, and said "I always had the feeling that you felt rebellious about something, but we were never able to clarify this in the course of treatment. Is it possible you were expressing something belatedly when it felt 'safe', and testing me also?" A few silent moments were followed by a burst of laughter from the patient, and some clarification. She added: "I'm sorry for the inconvenience, and I'll get a check to you at once."

One could not say that the analysis would have been a total disaster without this postscript, but it certainly was better with this belated consideration of a problem.

2. Rothstein's Report

Returning to the one documented case in the literature—in which the analyst did *not* have counter-transferential problems: Rothstein, in a brief paper titled "The Seduction of Money" (1986) reported on a patient who was a wealthy, 60-year-old childless married lawyer, who decided after 5 years of analysis to re-write his will and make his analyst the beneficiary of a quarter of a million dollars.

His analyst demanded time for further consideration of the idea, which seemed some attempt to bind him to the patient so that he would not be alone and uncared for in his old age. The patient then decided some months later that he would like to give money to a therapeutic nursery, and asked his analyst to be the administrator. But the analyst found that that, too, had concealed intentions. The patient then wanted to put the analyst on permanent retainer, so that he would not be deserted as his mother had done at age 6 (by dying).

There are further ramifications to this briefly reported case, but it serves to illustrate the complexity of issues relating to money, and the fact that Rothstein rightly commented on the paucity of discussion about the meaning of money in transference-contertransference considerations. However, while he spoke of working on understanding *his* countertransference responses, he kept the door closed on them, revealing nothing in his paper, although it would have been informative. He did point out that Freud emphasized maintaining neutrality toward the patient, stressing that the *welfare* of the patient *alone* should be the touchstone (1915). This brief case, and the lack of psychoanalytic literature in relation to money suggests that countertransference problems abound here.

3. The Rescue Fantasy

A common countertransference problem not yet considered is the grandiose need to 'rescue' the patient and play the 'good mother or father'. This may appear positive on the surface, but it is actually destructive to successful therapy, because it does not help the patient develop insight into the distortions of early development and subsequent related behavior.

A window into this particular area of countertransference opened via a referral. It is an area relating to one of the reasons analysts may enter their field–a desire to be of help to others–a healthy reason, also accompanied by the growth of self-esteem deriving from successful efforts. But often because of early difficulties, this latter becomes distorted and takes on a grandiose quality. The patient's transference – often parasitic in nature – drives the analyst to extremes in the desire to be the good all – giving mother or father.

In the following case, money became the central area of the analyst's weakness and resultant exploitation:

The wife of a man in analysis with a colleague was referred to me. She was a bright, attractive woman who was filled with rage at her husband. She felt she could stand the situation no longer. It was a second marriage for each, and each had a child of the previous marriage. They met when she became his secretary–he was a professional man–and shortly started an affair. His protestations of love over a number of years did not result in willingness to leave his first wife, but somehow she finally prevailed and he divorced and married her.

The 'big issue' appeared to be money. He did not feel that he should pay her for coming in to his office to work for him several days a week; he did not give her a household allowance; and she was reduced to 'begging him' for money and 'selling' herself, since he was more willing to part with money after sex. She became very indebted and pursued as she charged things in order to manage. (She was not a spendthrift.)

They had bought a large and lovely old house, but over eight years had passed, and he could not get around to allowing some repairs in the dilapidated kitchen. He indulged the wishes of his daughter, but gave little to hers; and complained that *she* played favorites.

No sign of countertransference yet? Well, he drove a Ferrari, bought expensive clothes, said his analyst was wonderful and so helpful–AND had not paid his analyst for about 2 years, owning her at least $20,000. If the daughter was upset and called the analyst, an emergency session was immediately set up. There is more–but this is sufficient to offer a picture of the situation.

This man's control via money had spread like the tentacles of an octopus over everything he contacted, and his rages did not help. I asked the wife how she proposed to pay me, if this was the situation. She said she had managed to save some money from her first marriage and had put it aside – now that she was desperate she would use it. I asked if I might speak with the referring analyst, and she agreed; but when I called the analyst, I was told she would have to get permission from him, and called back to say that he did not agree to her speaking with me. The vicissitudes of how he played on this analyst and her need for omnipotence (while in fact being impotent) are largely hidden, but the report helped me examine myself and avoid contertransferential involvement with the wife, so that I could deal with some money problems which eventually came up.

In contrast to this, deprivation and manipulation in the analyst's childhood sometimes lead to sadistic behavior of the analyst in special instances, and sometimes in relation to payment. An example of subtle sadism and vindictiveness was the report of a patient who had left her analyst and come for consultation.

She had felt he was helpful during the period of turmoil in her marriage when her husband started an affair and then left her, starting divorce proceedings. But with her new economic circumstances, she approached her analyst with some trepidation and said that she had a practical matter to bring up; and went on to say that when her husband was paying for treatment, she had no reason to question his fee. But now that she had limited means, and wanted to continue in treatment, she could not afford what she had been paying. She reported that everything seemed all right to that point. But when she tried to bolster her request by saying that friends had mentioned that his fee was high in comparison with others in the area, and she would really appreciate it if he would reduce it, his face took on an angry expression and he said: "I have always suspected that you are an aggressive bitch." She described herself as "reeling towards the door," and walked out immediately.

Firstly, the analyst's response was unprofessional – ordinary or street language such as "aggressive bitch" is inappropriate to the therapeutic endeavor. Further, its aim was to wound, and it was vindictive and sadistic in the timing of the statement, as this woman was in a period of great distress and needed support, not attack. But more sadistic was the revelation of secret contempt and anger, not previously revealed nor dealt with therapeutically, if valid.

It appears it was not only the potential loss of income, but the fact that the patient had inquired of others about fees, that set off the analyst's response – he apparently felt he had been 'snooped upon'. How simple a rational response would have been! He simply could have said "I'll do what I can," or "I am sorry but I cannot reduce my fee – I'll try to help you find another analyst".

Among other countertransferential trends, competitiveness and rivalry with the patient may occur, especially with wealthy or powerful patients.

SOME PRACTICAL CONSIDERATIONS

It must be acknowledged that in the early 40s–the time of my training –the business side of medical practice was not discussed. It is only recently that physicians, particularly women physicians, have realized that it is necessary to be as knowledgeable about running a practice as about medical expertise. The monetary aspect of practice was generally little discussed in an earlier day, where idealism (or at least the desire to appear idealistic) led the practitioner to be inattentive to fee-collecting. This often led to difficulty, rather than appreciation of the doctor or respect, and it is possible that countertransference from the doctor to the patient accounted at least in part for this. Thus, the setting of fees and manner of collecting payment are difficult but important areas. It is my impression that the analyst is every bit as vulnerable to transference distortions in relation to money as the patient, unless careful and deliberate consideration has been given to this, making countertransference less likely to occur.

I touch briefly on a number of issues:

1. Fee-setting

Among other considerations, analysts need to have a sense of what the prevalent fees are, where they should stand on this scale, what their sources of referral are, and what other factors may affect the fees they hope to command, such as special expertise. In some locations where analysts are scarce, they may be guided by what the market will bear. Indebtedness or special needs of the analyst's family may also enter into fee considerations. But then, distortions from early experience with money in the family have their effect; the family's attitude toward money, how acquisitive the family was; whether in comfortable circumstances; whether money was used to reward, bribe, discipline or control. Then, there is the question of whether the potential analyst as a child was envious or greedy, and to what extent these traits continue to exist. Vindictiveness, when subtle, may escape notice and may affect the handling of money matters. So may the trait of passivity.

2. Inadvisable Arrangements

Fear of losing a patient by being too firm, and thereby inappropriately reducing the fee (and resenting it); or allowing uncomfortable arrangements (for the analyst)—for example, by allowing the patient to tie payment to receipt of a paycheck, are usually contertransferential in origin, as is permitting deferral of payment without exploring the reason for it.

3. Allowing Unpaid Bills to Accumulate

Large unpaid bills are rarely paid later on, even if a formerly impoverished patient becomes successful, because the patient's needs seem to expand—which is usually an expression of continued acting out of transference attitudes. But on a few occasions I have had the surprising—and restorative—experience of being sent a check many years later in complete payment, when the patient has come into an inheritance. Even though the money was a 'windfall', it speaks of a good and positive relationship with the analyst when it is parted with, since failed payment was accepted.

4. Fee-collecting

In relation to fee-collecting, sometimes many factors enter in, especially the analyst's sense of authority, or lack of it, or fear to exert it. The important point is that if financial arrangements are not handled in a practical and emotionally neutral way, problems inevitably arise. Of special importance – the analyst must be able to deal with the patient's attempts to control through delaying or withholding payment.

In an earlier day, when patients themselves were totally responsible for payment, there seemed to be *less* resentment than today, with help from third party payers; and of course, this may elicit countertransference. In addition, special problems arise both in relation to poor and very wealthy patients. I gave never charged wealthy patients a higher than usual fee. I feel it is my time they are paying for and they should not be unfairly charged because of their good fortune. Yet occasionally, I have found that very wealthy patients do not seem to have a well-developed sense of obligation, nor do they understand the *other* person's need for money. If the analyst denies the problem, there will be unresolved areas. But if clear, the patient can be 'educated' about monetary attitudes, and they will change. It is, after all, an ethical problem, and requires attention.

I want to offer a few practical points with regard to fees and collecting, which I came to out of self-examination. Early in my practice, I had little experience and no guidance with regard to these matters. I gave patients monthly bills, but did not set limits with regard to payment, so that weeks – or months –would pass. I was surprised to find that this happened even with patients who could easily pay. I never asked to be paid at the first visit – I guess it did not seem 'nice'.

Now I have evolved the following procedure: When I am called by a new patient, whether referred or self-referred, before the end of the conversation I state my fee if I have not been questioned about it. I also tell my initial consultation fee, which is about 1/3 more–because the first visit is more demanding and often more time-consuming. I also make it clear that I expect to be paid at the end of the first visit. So, patients cannot claim that they were uninformed. However, at the first interview, and sometimes even in the course of the initial phone conversation, if my fee seems genuinely beyond the patient's capacity, I indicate that we can discuss fee and I will lower it if possible and appropriate. Of course, we all see some patients at reduced fee, and in a few instances, only a token fee.

As a final point with regard to fee-collecting, after the initial consultation and once it is clear that the patient is continuing in treatment, I give a monthly bill promptly at the last session of the month, having made it clear that I expect payment that session or the next (after all, I have given quite a few hours in the course of the month *before* compensation, and further delay is not warranted). I make a point of a monthly bill because it indicates trust of the patient. I have only once accepted payment at the end of each session–in this case I felt that the patient was asking for my help to prevent acting out. But generally, I feel that payment each time is disruptive, and at times a grave interference. But I hope it is clear that I am not suggesting inflexibility with regard to any of these points, but rather careful thought, and hopefully, clarity.

In concluding, I have only brushed the surface of an important topic with many ramifications. I have had occasion to wonder why Moses warned his followers not to make graven images nor worship the Golden Calf. Why Golden Calf? What does it stand for? Youth, Wealth and Mediocrity (calves are not the brightest animals) and certainly not subject to one of the 'gravest' accusations of today–that of being 'elitist'. (After all, what could be worse?) It is good that the meaning of money, and distortions of attitudes and actions in relation to it, are now coming up for consideration.

REFERENCES

1. Freud, S. (1912), The Dynamics of the Transference, Collected Papers Vol. II, Basic Books, pp. 312-322, 1959.
2. ibid. (1913), On Beginning the Treatment, Further Recommendations in the Technique of Psycho-analysis, Collected Papers Vol. II, Basic Books pp. 342-65, 1959.
3. ibid. (1915), Observations on Transference Love, Further Recommendations in the Technique of Psycho-analysis, Collected Papers Vol. II, pp. 377-391, Basic Books (1959).
4. ibid. (1937), Analysis Terminable and Interminable, Collected Papers Vol. V, pp. 316-357, Basic Books, 1959 or Standard Edition Vol. 23, Hogarth Press 1937.
5. Goin, M. & Kline, F., (1976), Countertransference: A Neglected Subject in Clinical Supervision, Am. J. Psychiat., 133:41-44.
6. Krueger, D. W., (1988), Money: Meanings and Madness, The Psychiatric Times, pp. 4,5, June.
7. Rothstein, A., (1986), The Seduction of Money: a brief note on an expression of transference love, Psychoan. Quart. LV, pp. 296-300.
8. Spensly, J. & Blacker, K.H., (1977), Countertransference and Other Feelings in the Psychotherapist, Diseases of the Nervous System, pp. 595-598, August.

CHAPTER 17

MONEY ISSUES AND ANALYTIC NEUTRALITY

Althea J. Horner, Ph.D.

It is not likely that we can separate payment for psychoanalytic treatment from transference and countertransference. Freud (1913) notes that the transfer of money is an integral part of the treatment with possibly decisive consequences for the course of treatment. Although Kubie (1950) thinks that both therapist and patient should behave as if "money did not exist", it does, in fact, exist and such behavior is in itself also a stimulus to which the patient may be likely to respond.

Mrs. G. had been the go-between in childhood, her parents going for long periods without speaking to one another. Every week her mother would ask her to go to her father to get the weekly household allowance check, and each week she would have to listen to his diatribe against mother before he would then have the child write the check which he would then sign. The asking for and receiving of money continued to be traumatic for Mrs. G. in her adult life. When her analyst told her that he did not send bills, but that the patient was expected to pay at the last session of each month, Mrs. G. found a way to avoid a replication of the original situation. At the beginning of every last session of the month she set the pre-written check down on the corner of the analyst's desk. She said nothing and neither did he. Both behaved as if money did not exist. The avoidance led to the failure of the treatment to deal with her money anxieties and the underlying chronic trauma of being torn between warring parents.

Setting aside the unconscious meaning the payment of fees has for the patient, Freud refers to the "psychoanalytic mechanics," the kind of transactions that are dictated by the society in which we live. I have chosen to refer to these mechanics as the pragmatics of money in the analytic situation.

Confrontation with the inescapable realities of life – death, taxes and the analyst's bill – will certainly mean different things to different people. When we speak of maintaining the therapeutic frame (Langs 1976), which must include the exchange of fees, we cannot assume that the frame is inherently neutral. It may be a challenge to the patient's overtly or covertly

Money and Mind, Edited by S. Klebanow and
E.L. Lowenkopf, Plenum Press, New York, 1991

held illusion of specialness, in which case the need to pay a fee constitutes a narcissistic wound. Narcissistic wounds are never neutral, in spite of the patient's capacity to endure them without overwhelming shame or paranoia. The pragmatic aspects of billing and collecting will be taken in and processed in accord with the patient's character structure. Pre-existing defenses and coping strategies aimed at maintaining narcissistic equilibrium will be brought to bear. This will be as true of the repression of the neurotic patient as it will be of the splitting of the more primitively organized character disorder. Even in those instances where the payment of the fee is a relief to the patient who characteristically and cynically wonders what interpersonal price will have to be paid in important relationships, something is effectively hidden by the frame itself. As with Mrs. G., the frame prevents the emergence of the conflict within the transference.

In his discussion of the payment of fees, Eissler (1974) makes it clear that no general statements can be made, that the specific meanings to specific patients will cover a wide spectrum of effects. A wealthy patient who is charged a high fee may see this as further evidence that he is only sought after because of his money, or that if you have anything people will be out to exploit you. In contrast, another wealthy patient may not believe he is getting optimal service unless he pays a corresponding fee.

The analyst's approach to financial arrangements with his or her patients is likely to be multiply determined. Issues such as prevailing peer community standards will enter in as well as the analyst's issues of competition, envy, or masochistic self denial with respect to his or her peers. The analyst may gain superego gratification by not being as "greedy" as those peers. The analyst's relation to money and what meaning it holds symbolically and dynamically will also be a factor. One's professional ego ideal, one's social values will certainly play a role. Countertransference issues may be indistinguishable from social values, and they may both be active within a single clinical situation.

For example, an analyst holds values related to helping certain individuals who would be denied treatment unless they were assigned a greatly reduced fee. It is not unlikely that a judgment as to the worthwhileness of the patient enters into a decision to make such an offer. Already the dynamics are becoming complicated. Having made this offer, our hypothetical analyst feels good about himself insofar as he is living up to his values. He is taken aback when the patient reports that he or she feels humiliated by the offer, or, that he or she feels burdened by it, feeling the necessity to make the financial sacrifice up to the analyst by having to make his work pleasant or easy. The patient may also be suspicious of the analyst's motives and wonder what will be asked in return. Instead of trust being generated, it is shaken. Our hypothetical analyst may feel wounded, his altruism having been misunderstood or unappreciated. Countertransference may now be in full swing. Eissler writes of the benefits for every analyst of seeing at least one patient without fee. In addition to the social benefits he writes, "...it would enable him to accumulate experience from analyses in which the fee factor plays no role as a motivating force (either in the patient or in the analyst) and should...[also] contribute to the refinement of the psychoanalytic technique...". In my view, in a society in which the patient surely knows that the payment of a fee is usual and customary, I do not understand how Eissler reasons that money, in its very absence, will not be a significant factor in the therapeutic relationship.

This all goes to say that practical, day-to-day decisions with respect to money matters in the therapeutic relationship are never simple matters of policy. Yet, policy decisions are required on a regular basis in one's practice. Assuming that the analyst is, for the most part, aware of his own dynamics with respect to money, I would like to suggest a clinical principle that will guide clinical decisions entailing the payment or non-payment of fees. This principle, simply stated, is that one's policy decisions should not traumatize the patient, that the analyst adhere as closely as possible to a stance of clinical neutrality in making those decisions. This brings us to the question of what is neutral, since that will vary from patient to patient and from situation to situation.

For the answer to this question I turn to Greenberg (1986) who provides us with a creative and clinically useful definition of neutrality that allows for its application in a manner specific and appropriate to the uniqueness of any given patient. He agrees with Schafer (1983) that there is an intimate connection between the analyst's neutrality and the patient's experience of safety, without which he or she would continue to "feel injured, betrayed, threatened, seduced, or otherwise interfered with or traumatized". In terms of a relational model of psychoanalysis (as contrasted to a drive model), Greenberg notes that "the atmosphere of safety would depend on the analyst's ability to create conditions in which the patient perceives him as a new object". However, he adds, if the situation is too safe, there is no room for transference and for confronting the threatening feelings that are part of an archaic relationship. Neutrality embodies the goal of establishing an optimal tension between the patient's tendency to see the analyst as an old object and his capacity to experience him as a new one. Greenberg writes:

The patient can become aware that he is assimilating the
analyst into his world of archaic internal objects only when
he has already become aware that there is an alternative
possibility...If the analyst cannot be experienced as a new
object, analysis never gets under way; if he cannot be
experienced as an old one, it never ends.

The closer our decisions with respect to money matters in treatment
can come to being true clinical decisions based upon our understanding of
the patient's character structure and dynamics, the less likely we are to act
out our countertransference motives even when countertransference issues
are operating. The principle of neutrality provides us with a secure frame
within which we can operate with relative equanimity and within which the
patient and the clinical process are protected from serious therapeutic errors.

One man had two long term therapies before coming to see me.
The first entailed a dual role situation in which the patient was a student
assistant to his therapist. The bill was never paid, despite many arguments
about it and the relationship ended with an accumulation of many thousands
of dollars owed the therapist. The patient had almost exclusively negative
feelings towards the former therapist. The patient felt entitled to free
treatment because of the special nature of the relationship.

His second therapist was a woman who did not charge him above
what his insurance paid, supposedly out of a stance of supporting his growth
and professional maturation. His feelings towards her were predominantly
positive.

The patient was established with a respectable income when he came
to me. Although other factors were also operative, the therapy bogged down
because, for the first time in many years of treatment, he would have to pay
money out of his own pocket for therapy. His sense of specialness and
entitlement, iatrogenically reinforced, did not yield to interpretation. His
rage at having to pay seemed to him to be too realistic to be viewed as a
transference issue in view of his previous therapy experiences. Together with
the humiliation of having to be in treatment at all, the money issue was used
to justify ending treatment.

Eissler refers to the patient who believes he is so remarkable that he
is not only entitled to free treatment, but deserving of it. Eissler notes that
for such a person paying a fee constitutes so grave a narcissistic injury that
the patient will not be able to start analysis. Eissler advises taking him into

•

treatment without pay, anticipating that after adequate analysis, the patient will be willing to compensate the analyst. However, Eissler also notes:

> ...it is advisable at this point to turn him over to another analyst, inasmuch as the transference situation has become too involved to be disentangled; moreover, as a result of the analyst's initial willingness to comply, the transference has become too libidinized to warrant any expectation of a promising course of treatment.

The iatrogenic complexities of this maneuver boggle my mind.

With 20-20 hindsight, I wonder how the treatment might have gone if I had started with my patient with a brief therapy contract with the focus on payment for treatment. If this approach were successful, the humiliation of dependency on the therapist would have been minimized insofar as brief psychotherapy aims at avoidance of a dependent transference through its specific techniques of once a week face-to-face treatment, coupled with a time limit and with constant attention to dissolution of the transference by interpreting it within the focus whenever it emerges.

In the service of neutrality, he would not have been faced with becoming a dependent hostage to a powerful object who only took from him, leaving him depleted and impoverished. Thus, he might have been able to experience me as a new object. Yet, I would also be experienced as an old object insofar as I did indeed want *something* from him, namely, my fee.

With a theoretically sound, clinical rationale informing my decision with respect to payment of a fee, I would not have been caught up in a rigid, ex-cathedra position of being unwilling to work without a fee, whatever its justification. On the other hand, I would not have been bullied into submission to his demands nor manipulated with guilt into acceding to them. Beyond these, I might have found a way to work within what appeared to be an unworkable situation.

There are many situations that come up around the payment of fees, such as payment for missed sessions, third party payment, raising fees, reducing fees, or allowing a bill to accumulate. Taking the maintenance of analytic neutrality as a guiding principle, one cannot make across the board statements about any of these. When we try to do so, we inevitably get caught up in our own beliefs, values, needs and rationalizations of them, or in theoretically narrow concepts that inevitably do a disservice to one patient or another. Other elements that may not seem as prone to evoke transference reactions may well do so, such as the conduct of the business end of one's practice by a secretary, or the mailing of bills and checks with no hand to hand exchange of money taking place.

In Eissler's comprehensive discussion of the payment of fees, it is clear that from time to time he turns to personal values and standards to support clinical judgment. He is not unaware of this when he writes:

> It may cause unnecessary pain to a patient to be told that it is for economic reasons that he is being refused analysis by a therapist by whom he wishes to be treated. It may be preferable, in such a case, to give 'lack of a free hour' as the excuse. Here, however, I am uncertain about the extent to which my suggestion is influenced by personal idiosyncrasies.

When I have taken this very approach, I have found myself faced with a patient who then insists on waiting until I have a free hour. Even this "excuse" does not shield the individual from a narcissistic wound and envy of those for whom the analyst does have time.

Eissler also turns to his considerable past experience as a guide, yet there may be pitfalls if one were to make a clinical decision based on anyone's past experience alone, even someone as eminent as Dr. Eissler. The idiosyncratic nature of analytic work requires a metaguide, a theoretical rationale for the moment to moment decisions that arise with respect to the pragmatics of money in the analytic situation. Knowing that judgment as to what is or is not neutral for a given patient itself will not be infallible, I still view it as the most reliable principle on which to make these decisions.

REFERENCES

Eissler, K. R., (1974), On some theoretical and technical problems regarding the payment of fees for psychoanalytic treatment. Int. Rev. of Psycho-Analysis, 1: 73-102.

Freud, S., (1913), On beginning the treatment. (Further recommendations on the technique of psycho-analysis. I.) S.E. 12: 123-144.

Greenberg, J. R., (1986), Theoretical models and the analyst's neutrality. Contemp. Psychoanal., 22: 87-106.

Kubie, L. S., (1950), Practical and Theoretical Aspects of Psychoanalysis. New York, Int. Univ. Press.

Langs, R., (1976), The Bipersonal Field, New York, Aronson.
Schafer, R., (1983), The Analytic Attitude, New York, Basic Books.

CHAPTER 18

PSYCHOANALYTIC UNDERSTANDING AND
TREATMENT OF THE VERY RICH

Silas L. Warner, M.D.

I. GENERAL CONSIDERATIONS

Children of the very wealthy are vulnerable to many problems
brought on by affluence. The term "Affluenza" has been coined to describe
the syndrome from which the very rich and their children may suffer. Many
Americans believe that money solves all problems and give the very wealthy
little sympathy or understanding when they develop emotional problems.
Certain well known sayings illustrate the negative feelings that the non-
wealthy hold against the affluent. Matthew says in the New Testament: "It
is easier for a camel to pass through the eye of a needle than for a rich man
to enter the kingdom of heaven." A frequently heard folk saying is, "Behind
every fortune lies a hidden crime."

The most frequent basic cause for the affluent having their special
problems is having a deprived childhood.(1) They lacked a close empathetic
relationship with their parents, especially their mothers. Having a surplus of
money may be accompanied by a wealth of crippling emotional problems and
fears. Their home environment has been called "a golden ghetto without
walls." Frequently they are raised by surrogate parents such as a "nanny".
Their closest confidants may be one of the family servants or their nanny or
governess. They may have other special individuals teaching them in special
areas, such as their academic tutor, their piano teacher, their tennis
instructor, and their dancing teacher. If they develop childhood emotional
problems they will have their own child psychiatrist. They may gain from this
special help but it may also lessen their self-esteem and make them believe
that they are unable to do much on their own.

As a spin-off of all this special attention they begin to feel entitled
to the very best, whether it be in teaching, riding or clothes. They may
develop true respect for their special instructors or they might experience
contempt for them and treat them like servants. They soon learn that anyone
who is hired by their parents can also be fired. The best feed-back for a

Money and Mind, Edited by S. Klebanow and
E.L. Lowenkopf, Plenum Press, New York, 1991

child to receive is always an honest response from their parents. If this is not available they will have to ask for it from others. This may be unavailable and result in a lack of confidence and a poor self-esteem. This in turn can make them non-competitive and chronic underachievers.

Their sense of reality can become distorted because if they get in trouble they know they will always be "bailed out" and never have to face the consequences of their actions as others do. This serves to increase their already hypertrophied sense of entitlement.

Also characteristic of the very rich is that they either always talk about money or never talk about it. Either extreme creates problems for their children. If the child talks a lot about money because the parents do, it creates hostility in their peers who have less money. If they never talk about money they cannot gain any perspective on the subject and become suspicious of those who ask them about it. They are never certain whether or not others really like them or are after their money.

If the child's parents are both rich and famous they can suffer from attributed identities. They are always known as so-and-so's children and not for their own identities. They can be easily bored because immediate pleasure has become part of their lives and they have difficulty in sustaining interest in anything requiring work. This can lead to serious addiction to alcohol, drugs or gambling.

II. PSYCHIATRIC TREATMENT FOR THE AFFLUENT

An apocryphal story is told of a dialogue between F. Scott Fitzgerald and Ernest Hemingway. Fitzgerald reminds Hemingway that in America the rich are very different from others. Hemingway replies, "Yes, they have much more money!"

Nowhere does this difference show up more clearly than when the rich seek psychiatric help. I will point out and illustrate some of the *problems* which inevitably surface in trying to give psychological help to the rich.

Their sense of *entitlement* and *denial* of the problem often presents a major block to good psychological help. The rich are convinced that having achieved affluence they are entitled to "*the best*". It matters not whether it is their car, home or health, they demand the finest that money can buy. In health matters, this is translated into their search for "the best doctor". They will often ask other highly successful affluent persons whom they recommend as the best psychiatrist, psychologist or psychotherapist. They may not even use the same sound thinking used in their business transactions. If they were to introduce a new product they would first have their marketing research department study the situation and come up with sound recommendations. In selecting a doctor, they usually do not seek advice from the experts in the field such as the local chairman of the medical school department of psychiatry. Instead, they will ask a non-expert such as a friend. His "expertise" is knowing somebody who was a patient of a Dr. Jones and who "liked him". He also might rely on his wife to ask her friends to come up with a recommendation. This may lead to the name of whatever doctor is currently "in vogue", irrespective of his professional reputation and ability. Moreover, the rich man does have a built-in protection against making a mistake in selecting a doctor. He can easily "fire" the doctor and "hire" another one. This can lead into wild scrambling and a second, third or fourth medical opinion, along with attempts to coerce the doctor into telling him exactly what he wants to hear. Let me provide an example of this.

Mr. Jones' son Bill has been showing increasingly bizarre behavior at college and is seen in the college counseling service. The consulting psychiatrist phones the family and suggests that they work together in formulating a long-term plan to help the son with his serious mental health problem. This can lead to very difficult responses from the very rich parents. The first one centers around a denial of the seriousness of the problem. Such a parent (usually the father) might reply: "Bill is a fine young man who is going through a difficult phase in his life. I remember being in college and going through the same thing. It was a turning point in my life. I shifted my major to business administration and went on to be a highly successful stock broker. I know Bill has the stuff to make it; he'll come through. All he need is a little guidance and T.L.C. You people can give that to him better at college than we can miles away. So why don't you counsel him, give him good advice, talk to him like a Dutch uncle and tell him we are completely behind him. As a matter of fact, you can tell him that we have rented a house in the Caribbean for the month of March and he can spend his spring vacation with us there. He loves to swim and snorkel and the sun and water will do him good. In the meantime, tell him to keep his nose to the grindstone and study harder. If he wants to change his major or even transfer to another college next fall, we can arrange it. I have a friend whose son switched to M.I.T. and he's done fine. Remember that Bill was in good shape when we sent him to your college two years ago. It's up to you to get him felling good again. In the automobile business they give out a warranty which guarantees that their product will do what it's supposed to do or you get your money back. I think that colleges should have the same policy. I will consult with our legal department on this, but it only makes sense that if anything should happen to Bill mentally, you should be held responsible".

Mr. Jones has shown some of the frequently found rich man's ways of reacting in this vignette. First of all, he does not like being told that his son has a serious mental health problem and so he denies that it exists. Instead, he calls it merely a transient phase or stage. The obvious fact that an expert in the mental health of college students has warned him that his son has a serious mental health problem is not addressed and is arbitrarily denied. This defensive denial is not limited to the rich. However, when used by them they can rapidly muster tremendous support for their position. In this instance, Mr. Jones could easily find an "expert" who will agree that Bill is only going through a temporary phase. Mr. Jones is familiar with court cases in which an "expert" favorable to his viewpoint can easily be "located" and will testify for him.

Mr. Jones is also subtly suggesting the possibility of a malpractice suit against the counseling service by claiming that Bill came to college "in sound mind" and that the college could be held responsible for any subsequent mental problems. There is something sinister about dealing with a parent who makes such a not-too-thinly-veiled threat. The psychiatric consultant then empathizes with Bill and his life-long struggle with this powerful and manipulative father. One can predict that attempts at doing meaningful psychotherapy within the counseling service could be sabotaged by the father. If the therapist is manipulated by the father, the therapeutic alliance will be undermined. Even attempts at family therapy can be ruined by the powerful and exploiting father.

In one such instance, a schizoid, frightened young female college student was seen in regular psychotherapy by a sensitive and talented outside therapist. The therapy was going well and the therapist received an appreciative letter from the father. In this letter he mentioned that "a little research had revealed" that the therapist "had also attended the same college as Mary". Since the therapist could not ethically receive extra money, above and beyond your normal fee, "I have made a contribution of $25,000 to yours and Mary's college in your name". The therapist was non-plussed at this turn of events. The gift had already been sent to the college in her name. It was, of course, necessary to bring this subject up in the therapy with Mary and hope that she would not see the therapist as having caved in, under the impact of her father's power and wealth. As it turned out, a very useful discussion took place with Mary which instead of contaminating the therapeutic alliance, strengthened it. Suffice it to say that if this situation had not been skillfully handled, the therapy might have reached an impasse with a resulting negative therapeutic reaction.

Another personality feature of the rich is their tendency to see mental problems *alloplastically*, or as having been caused by the outside world. Rarely if ever does the problem exist within the personality of the rich patient. Since the problem is alloplastically caused by the environment, it can only be resolved by changing the environment. I have already mentioned how Bill's father suggested an alloplastic solution – that a few weeks in the Caribbean would "do wonders for Bill's mental health". Such a currently popular phrase as "stress-related burnout" provides a marvelous rationale for solving a problem by an environmental manipulation. It's the Rumpelstiltskin effect all over again. First you label the condition, and it then becomes a legitimate "disease". After the diagnosis, an environmental improvement will alleviate the condition. Along with "burn-out" and "excessive stress", I can also mention such often misused diagnoses as "hypoglycemia", "hypotension" or a "situational maladjustment". If and when any of these terms gain authenticity such as by being included in DSM IV, it makes the underlying condition all but untreatable by any other method than by environmental improvement.

Years ago there was a well known Philadelphia psychiatrist who treated only the very rich. He had a very bright and able secretary who also functioned as a travel agent. It was her job to book Dr. Smith's psychiatric patients on the QE2, on a cruise to the South Seas or on a plane to the Riviera. Naturally, when the patient returned, he or she temporarily felt better and as long as their finances held up, their life happily consisted of an endless series of trips. If they were very wealthy, a private duty psychiatric nurse was "assigned to their case" and traveled with them. Any other psychiatrist who inherits such a case will be hard-pressed not to continue in this deluxe cruise form of psychiatric treatment. Even a gentle confrontation of the patient with some of his or her own internalized self-defeating patterns is a risky business. It is necessary to make a slow and gradual transition to a more meaningful kind of therapy or else these patients quickly find another therapist who will give them the self-gratifying kind of therapy they want and are used to.

Part of improving the patient's environment is prescribing "proper" medication which will magically solve problems. The "proper" medication is either what has recently been reported in newspapers or magazines as new and effective or what other affluent patients report as "doing miracles".

Again, the psychiatrist's authority is undercut because if he holds out against prescribing the medication on which the patient insists, he takes the major risk that the patient will not respond favorably to his own prescribed medication. He may then lose the patient and be "bad-mouthed" by the patient as being stubborn and incompetent.

With no chance to defend his choice of medication or explain his reasons, his reputation can be harmed by a vindictive rich patient who is angry at him for not prescribing the medication he wanted. Ironically, this phenomenon is not found only in rich patients. The studies of Redlich and Hollingshead (2) showed that lower-class psychiatric patients without much education always expected to be prescribed medication by a psychiatrist. If they only received psychotherapy, they felt cheated and would go to another psychiatrist and insist that medication be prescribed for them.

The rich do not always expect medication, but they feel entitled to get good results from whatever psychiatric treatment they receive within a "reasonable period of time". Even if the psychotherapist warns them in advance that they should not expect to feel better until at least a year of intensive psychotherapy, they will soon become impatient and question why the results are "so slow". Inevitably, they will have heard of somebody else whose depression or anxiety state was cured within a few weeks. Soon this theme will lead them into seeking another psychiatric opinion and then to giving this other new kind of psychiatric treatment a try. To assuage their conscience, they will always add that if the new treatment does not work, they will return to the original psychotherapist. But one can be reasonably certain that there will be no such return, as "getting cured quickly" is much more important to them than any sense of loyalty to a psychotherapist who has worked hard to help them with their presenting problem.

One other characteristic of the rich is their self-concept of being a very important person (VIP). VIPs expect and know how to get special privileges. They never have to stand in a long line with the public to buy a ticket. A word to their secretary or a quick phone call to their ticket broker and presto, the desired ticket is theirs. In health matters they expect the same kind of special privilege. If normally a diagnostic procedure cannot be done until another screening test is first done, they will insist that both be done the same day or that an exception be made for them and the screening test be omitted to speed up the diagnostic procedure. They expect these special favors and it is often difficult for the physician to not give in to them. The prudent physician should tell the rich patient ahead of time that no special privileges or VIP treatment will be accorded them because it is important that all details of the diagnostic and treatment regime be meticulously followed. There is a danger in making exceptions to the routine and taking a chance of missing vital data required for a thorough evaluation.

A wealthy woman entered the hospital with a gradual onset of paranoid thinking. She had ideas of reference and delusions of persecution. She wore very expensive clothing which she insisted be kept locked in the closet of her open-ward room. Because of her hostility and suspiciousness, the staff was fearful of going into this closet and searching her clothes for drugs or alcohol. The attending psychiatrist also warned the staff not to unnecessarily confront her and to avoid any disagreements. After she had been in the hospital for three weeks without any improvement, the psychiatric resident asked the attending psychiatrist if he could run a screening test on her urine for abusive drugs. The patient refused to allow her urine to be tested as she saw "no reason for it". The resident then took it on himself to get the key from the nurses and search through her clothes in the closet while the patient was at group psychotherapy. After a brief search the resident found a bulge in a special inner pocket in her raincoat. He reached in and found a large container full of pills. These were examined in the hospital lab and found to be amphetamines. A rather nasty confrontation took place with the patient and the attending psychiatrist. The patient threatened to sign out against medical advice and also to sue the hospital and the attending psychiatrist. Fortunately, the attending psychiatrist had done his homework and had consulted his own and the hospital's lawyers and knew how to proceed. He was able to obtain a temporary commitment and withdraw the patient from the amphetamines. After twenty days the patient signed a voluntary commitment and entered into a long-term rehabilitation program. As the patient stabilized emotionally and gained insight, she was finally able to accept the rules and regulations of the hospital. She was even able to express gratitude to the attending psychiatrist and the resident.

III. TRANSFERENCE-COUNTERTRANSFERENCE PROBLEMS WITH THE RICH

In 1975 Wahl (3) noted how three respected colleagues had recently made inappropriate disclosures of patient identification and material to him. He attributed this unprofessional "name-dropping" of a rich and well-known patient to the analyst's need for praise and recognition. Since psychoanalytic therapy is such an intensely solitary undertaking there is a need to share its "triumphs and defeats, difficulties and achievements" without compromising the patient's identity. If a rich and well known patient's identity is revealed it probably comes from the analyst's countertransference problem. He is saying to his colleague that he is prized and valued by a rich and famous patient. This may result from a childhood need for parental recognition. It stems from his own unresolved sibling rivalry and/or oedipal striving.

Another important issue in treating the very rich comes from the fact that most analysts have middle-class origins. They may share in the frequently found middle-class "covert hatred or envy of the rich". This culturally-shared prejudice limits the analyst's ability to do effective analytic work with the very rich. It is not a countertransference problem per se, but a consciously held pejorative attitude with a sociological basis. To cover it up the analyst can either show a reaction formation and become excessively ingratiating or act out his hostility by putting down the rich patient. In either case the analyses will be failures.

Another significant transference problem is the attempted seduction of the analyst through the affluent patient's money, charm or power. Those rich patients who have made their own fortune and have not inherited wealth often have very powerful and charismatic personalities which have brought them success in the marketplace. These personality qualities will surely be used on the analyst to gain his favor and tempt him into being controlled in some fashion by the rich patient. An instructive example of an attempted seduction of an analyst by money is given in a 1986 paper by Arnold Rothstein. (4) His patient was "a sixty-year-old married, childless, wealthy retired lawyer. In the fifth year of his analysis he began a session by announcing that he was rewriting his will and would like to make me beneficiary in the amount of $250,000". Rothstein treated the offer of the money as an overdetermined transference fantasy which he proceeded to analyze. He recognized his own fantasied gratification associated with being given money to be similar to a male analyst's heterosexual fantasies and conflicts in working with an attractive female analysand who has fallen in love with him. In reviewing the literature he found virtually no mention of the meanings of money in the transference countertransference aspects of an analytic situation but many papers on the meanings of sexual feelings. He successfully followed the guidelines outlined by Freud (5) in his 1915 paper, "Observations on Transference Love." He therefore did "not give up the neutrality toward the patient, which we have acquired through keeping the countertransference in check". Rothstein concludes:

The analyst's attitude toward the future and particularly

toward the post-analytic phase is especially important in regard to the issue of money. Because of the analyst's narcissistic investment in his professional endeavors and institutions, he might be tempted to rationalize the feasibility of accepting contributions from an analysand after termination. In this regard, it is important to remember that the unconscious is timeless and that analyses are all, in a certain sense, interminable. Any other attitude may interfere with the analysis of an analysand's attempts at seduction with money.

Although some analysts suggest the appropriateness of soliciting and/or accepting contributions from former analysands, I think that the analytic material presented here supports my contention that to do so has powerful transference implications from the perspective of this brief communication. Such behavior may reflect a countertransference enactment that is a potential interference in the analysand's independence and post-analytic self-analysis. In addition, such behavior might interfere with the analysand's possible need to return to the analyst for further analysis.

IV. DISCUSSION

In my own forty years of experience in providing psychoanalytic treatment for the very rich, I have experienced a mixture of good news and bad news. As patients they cover a wide spectrum from being the very best, most satisfying patients to being the most difficult of all patients.

Starting with the good news, they can be the best, most satisfying patients to an analyst. In these cases they are cooperative, bright, appreciative, honest and very worthwhile human beings. They can afford to pay your top fee and always pay promptly without quibbling. If the patient is a young adult who has inherited his money he oftentimes is well educated and sensitive to humane needs. He may have put his money into a foundation which is geared toward helping others who are handicapped or less fortunate. In providing more self-awareness to such a worthwhile rich person, the analyst is helping someone who is helping others.

Now for the bad news. Among the very rich who seek psychoanalytic help there are individuals with warped values who have been corrupted by the power of money and show a destructive mind-set which undermines the analyst's efforts. Their cynical, skeptical attitude helped them to succeed in the world's marketplace and prevented others from exploiting them. Nevertheless it prevents them from entering into a therapeutic alliance in psychoanalysis because of their lack of trust.

This patient defends himself with a narcissistic coating which delivers a message to the therapist that he is dealing with a VIP and consequently should put forth his very best effort. This may be conveyed by the secretary phoning the therapist to inform him that Mr. Gotrocks has just returned from his board meeting and will be a few minutes late to the appointment today.

Mr. Gotrock's basic attitude toward psychiatric treatment is similar to his attitude toward buying a car or arranging a business merger. Paraphrasing this attitude: "I can afford the best and I intend to find it in my psychoanalytic treatment. You have been recommended to me as a topnotch psychoanalyst. I know that psychoanalysis is a young and controversial field but I will ask you to create a treatment regime which will benefit me. I will check out any doubts I have about your proposed regime with other well known psychoanalysts. I am placing you in competition with your distinguished peers to propose the best treatment plan for me. I will not stop at a second opinion, but will continue to get additional opinions until a consensus is reached over the best program for me. I will then monitor the program and make certain that I am making progress. If there is unsatisfactory progress I will make changes (much as an owner of a professional baseball team fires the manager during a slump)."

It presents a major problem to any psychoanalyst to have a patient assume such a hard-nosed adversarial role. We normally work with patients who seek our help and who are perfectly willing to trust us and believe in our basic integrity. This atmosphere promotes the patient's free expression of feelings and thoughts which in turn promotes good psychoanalysis. It is unnatural for a therapist to feel under pressure to prove his worth to the patient. There are even a few rather unscrupulous therapists whose technique consists of trying to favorably impress the affluent patient. Their expertise is more in the area of promoting good public relations for themselves and not in the realm of understanding the patient psychodynamically. These analysts are the mirror image of the difficult affluent patient and the two tend to find each other. This analyst is often unduly concerned with external appearances and believes that psychological changes can best be accomplished by making external changes in the patient's life. This has been called alloplastic treatment in contrast to the autoplastic changes sought by the more psychodynamic analyst.

Our patients expect us to do certain things to help them. With the poor and less educated patient there is an expectation that the psychoanalyst give them direct advice plus prescribing pills. With the well-educated middle-class patient, there is usually an expectation of some form of psychotherapy. With the very rich patient there is frequently an expectation that some environmental change be effected to improve the patient's mental health. If these expectations are not met, the patient will search for another analyst who will fulfill them.

Most of us have been asked to prescribe medication when we believe that psychoanalytic psychotherapy is preferable. We risk the possibility of refusing to prescribe the medication and having the patient go elsewhere for help. With the recent furor over the detrimental side-effects of psychotropic medication there is always some risk of a malpractice suit if the patient develops side-effects. The very rich patient is more apt to sue you than the less affluent because that is often part of his mind-set.

Although Rothstein does not specifically refer to an earlier Freud quotation he seems to be aware of its substance and uses it. I am referring to Freud's 1913 paper "Further Recommendations on Technique (I) On Beginning the Treatment:

The next point that must be decided at the beginning of the treatment is the one of money, of the doctor's fee. An analyst does not dispute that money is to be regarded in the first instance as a medium for self-preservation and for obtaining power; he maintains that, besides this, powerful sexual factors are involved in the value set upon it. He can point out that money matters are treated by civilized people in the same way as sexual matters — with the same inconsistency, prudishness and hypocrisy. The analyst is therefore determined from the first not to fall in with this attitude, but, in his dealings with his patients, to treat money matters with the same matter-of-course frankness to which he wishes to educate them in things relating to sexual life.

(St. Edition of Freud's Works, Vol. 12)

V. SUMMARY

Money can be likened to fire; it is a vital and integral part of our modern civilization and has the potential for great good and great harm. It is important that we understand how it can achieve its good and harm. Everybody should learn about the benefits and dangers of money. Very little education is provided to our children about the positive use of money and also how destructive it can be. We as psychoanalysts should learn more about the psychological effects of too much and too little money. It is a subject that has been neglected by psychoanalysts. The probable reason for this neglect is Freud's preoccupation with childhood sexuality plus his own inhibitions about discussing money. Freud had a "poor-house neurosis". This made him very fearful of not having enough money even though during most of his life he seemed to have had ample funds.

Children raised within an affluent family may show signs of parental deprivation and usually develop a strong sense of entitlement. It is most rare to have a family like the Rockefellers in which all five children were trained to feel responsibility, a sense of noblesse oblige and who became leaders in their respective fields. It shows that with some preparation and education even children of affluent parents can become responsible humane leaders.

Psychoanalysts treating the very rich should become aware of the typical transference-countertransference problems inherent in working with the very affluent. They should also become aware of the syndrome of "Affluenza" with its various manifestations.

Working psychologically with the very rich can be a very satisfying experience, a challenge or a humiliating failure. The analyst who can prepare himself to face some of the aforementioned problems can lessen the possibility of a negative experience and improve his changes of having a positive experience in helping the rich patient.

In closing I want to quote F. Scott Fitzgerald's well known statement about the rich.(6)

Let me tell you about the very rich. They are different from you and me. They possess and enjoy early, and it does something to them, makes them soft where we are hard, and cynical where we are truthful, in a way that, unless you were born rich it is difficult to understand. They think, deep in their hearts, that they are better than we are, because we had to discover the compensations and refuges of life for ourselves. Even when they enter deep into our world or sink below us, they still think they are better than we are. They are different.

REFERENCES

1   Stone, Michael and Kestenbaum, Clarice, "Maternal Deprivation in Children of the Wealthy: A Paradox in Socioeconomic U.S. Psychologycial Class. History of Childhood Quarterly (The Journal of Psychohistory), Summer 1974, Vol. 2, #1, pp. 70-106.

2   Hollingshead, A. B. and Redlich, F. C., Social Class and Mental Illness, N.Y., John Wiley and Sons, 1958.

3   Wahl, Charles, Psychoanalysts of the Rich, The Famous and the Influential, The PSA Forum, Vol. 5, 1975, pp. 90-120

4   Rothstein, Arnold, The Seduction of Money: A Brief Note on an Expression of Transference Love, PSA Quarterly LV, 1986, pp. 296-300.

5   Freud, S. (1915a), Observations on Transference-love (further recommendations on the Technique of PSA III), SE, 12, pp. 157-171.

6   Fitzgerald, F. Scott, Short Stories, The Very Rich Boy.

CHAPTER 19

MONEY MANAGEMENT IN THE BORDERLINE PATIENT

Lawrence Cuzzi, D.S.W.

INTRODUCTION

In many situations where people are being treated on an outpatient basis for substance abuse, the personality configuration often recognized is that which has been labeled the Borderline Personality. Specifically, for the purposes of our discussion, the primary personality organization is that described by Kernberg (1) and Masterson (2), as the Borderline Personality Organization.

Kernberg's writings regarding the adult borderline personality describe a stable disorder due to developmental arrest with specific observable symptoms, ego defects and psychopathology of object relations. The term "borderline personality organization" is used to emphasize that this patient does not exhibit different (and transitory) points along a continuum from neurosis to psychosis. Rather there is a definite, stable personality organization with typical symptomatology, specific ego defenses, instinctual difficulties, and pathologic object relations. Kernberg paints a clinical picture of a patient with borderline personality organization as having serious difficulties with interpersonal relationships with some alteration of the experience of reality. Also present may be direct expression of "id contents", some pseudo-insight into one's own personality without real awareness of how conflicted one really is, and a lack of understanding of other people.

All of the above is combined with what Kernberg identifies as "non-specific ego weakness", meaning lack of impulse control, lack of anxiety tolerance or sublimating capacity, and presence of primary process thinking.

Masterson's view is that this clinical picture occurs as a result of feelings of abandonment created by the mother's withdrawal of various physical and emotional rewards when the child attempts to separate and individuate. What is seen, and needs to be treated, is that the patient attempts to defend himself or herself against the feelings of abandonment and becomes developmentally arrested; depression results and acting out behavior occurs. Where the acting out occurs as substance abuse the self-destructive

Money and Mind, Edited by S. Klebanow and
E.L. Lowenkopf, Plenum Press, New York, 1991

aspects need to be addressed before any reconstructive or insight focused work can be attempted. To love and to work - Freud's concept of the goals of psychoanalysis – are Masterson's essential building blocks for gratification in adult life. His stance is that all borderline patients have serious defects in these two capacities. They need to defend themselves against intimacy by clinging and/or distancing; the satisfaction at work is made impossible by their need to avoid individuation.

The introduction of money as a variable into this personality organization results in interesting and often confounding dynamics within the therapeutic relationship. One of the primary reasons for this is that money as a generator of conflict is a well-described concept in art, theatre and real life. However, money in therapy, as resistance or as a tool, in the repertoire of a competent therapist has been less carefully considered.

The case to be presented and the resulting theoretical discussion is illustrative of money and its importance in the treatment of an adult substance abuser utilizing techniques espoused by James Masterson in the treatment of a patient with a borderline personality organization as described by Kernberg.

CASE PRESENTATION

Mr. L. is a 39-year-old stockbroker who had recently left a position in a large Wall Street firm to begin his own brokerage business in partnership with two colleagues. Mr. L. is married with one child and expects to earn approximately $50-60,000 this year, after earning as much as $125,000 in his previous position. He is the only child of professional parents, both living, who "doted on me and gave me everything, at least my mother did". His father was unnoted by the son until adolescence was reached when they occasionally attended baseball and football games together. His mother is by far the dominant person in his life. Mr. L's earliest memories are of his mother dressing him in "nice clothes", sending him out to play with others and then making him come inside because there was the possibility of his getting his clothes dirty or getting hurt roughhousing with his friends.

Mr. L. was an indifferent student, obtaining excellent grades, combined with terrible conduct marks, at other times failing tests and being labeled an underachiever. The maternal response to such behaviors was to yell and threaten to prevent him from playing sports (a lifelong treasured activity). This always worked and hence was used whenever he did something to displease his mother. Often it was done, in his perception, for no reason other than to punish him in general for behaviors which he felt were minimally offensive, i.e. staying out fifteen minutes past curfew; answering back in a "disrespectful tone".

Mr. L. wanted to go away to college and was not allowed to do so, even though he was accepted to several academically fine schools. He went to a city school where "my mother could keep an eye on me". He reports being enraged at such restrictions but "what could I do?" His father completely abdicated the disciplining to his mother whose stated position was that he could be on his own soon as he demonstrated the ability to function independently in an appropriate manner. At this point his drug use, heretofore experimentation with marijuana, gradually expanded to alcohol and cocaine. Cocaine would consciously be used as "reward" when he was under stress, either at home or at school. Alcohol was used to enable him to sleep after prolonged cocaine use.

He abruptly married in his senior year a woman he had known only a short time. His parents, especially his mother, were upset about the precipitousness of the marriage and the woman he married (a different faith). His mother did not speak to him for six months and never invited the newlyweds to her home. The marriage dissolved of its own accord after a year – "neither of us knew what it meant to be married so we failed". The parents wanted him to return home, he refused and lived in his own apartment which again resulted in parental (read maternal) ostracism. His father did call once a month.

Mr. L.'s subsequent second marriage was ignored until a child was born. This led to a reconciliation between Mr. L. and his mother. He reports this as the normal course of events throughout his life. Whenever he displeased or disappointed his mother, she withdrew both emotionally and concretely, i.e. no money, no special occasions or not being driven to friends. Mr. L. always "gave in" because his mother's perseverance in her behavior was by his account phenomenal. She could literally go for weeks without interacting with him in any way other then to criticize. He always apologized or provided the behavior she required.

His second wife is described as a strong-willed woman who initially in the relationship readily shared his use of cocaine, marijuana and alcohol. However once they decided to start a family she stopped completely and has been consistent in insisting that he cease. She had refused to participate in any sexual activity until he stopped, which he did until their child was conceived. He then commenced the drug use which placed a heavy burden on the marital relationship. His wife reacted to his behavior by going through his clothes and possessions searching for drugs, refusing any affectionate contact and ultimately contacting his parents to inform them of the problem. She requested their help in forcing him into a treatment situation.

Mr. L.'s early life including his relationships with friends and other family, and its "fit" with many of Masterson's and Kernberg's borderline patients are important to understand, especially as they occur within the context of a therapeutic relationship with money and caring as a central theme.

The presenting problem in treatment was that Mr. L. had finally been convinced that he was "out of control" with the cocaine use. It was costing him too much money and that was unacceptable with his new business. He was increasingly convinced that he had made a mistake with this venture. He had never liked the stock business, considered it mechanical and unsatisfying though lucrative. Because of his family he now felt trapped in an uninteresting work endeavor. He resented his wife and child for forcing him to stay. Also his wife was becoming increasingly insistent regarding her demands that he discontinue cocaine. This had become more of an issue after the birth of their daughter. The agreement to seek help was a begrudging one especially since a previous foray into the world of therapy had been unsuccessful because the "therapist was only interested in his fee: I could never get him to concentrate totally on me".

In the incipient stages of the therapeutic relationship, there are two clues that money will be a major factor in therapy.

First, although his wife has been pressuring him for several years to quit, Mr. L.'s expressed reason for entering treatment is that he had no money because he was spending so much on cocaine that there was nothing left for his family or business. The prior week he had taken $1,700 from the firm's petty cash to pay off drug debts, and had no way of returning it. His initial presentation was wanting to cut down the habit to "manageable" proportions, both financially and maritally. (At the time of this treatment cocaine was selling for $100 per gram. Mr. L. would use from 2-4 grams per week).

Second, the unsuccessful previous attempt at therapy ended because of the therapist's alleged focus on money as a priority.

Reportedly the therapist refused to see the patient after several hundred dollars had been unpaid for several months. The therapist even declined to provide medication (anti-depressants) until the bill was paid in full. Mr. L. experienced this as an incredible position for a physician/psychiatrist to assume given the fact that a therapeutic relationship had ostensibly been formed. How much could the relationship (and he himself) mean to the therapist if money would end it. Mr. L. was terribly disillusioned by this experience which he called being "abandoned by someone who is supposed to help you no matter what".

COURSE OF TREATMENT

The first few sessions with Mr. L. were fairly routine. The initial meeting at which fees were set and attendance guidelines enumerated were unremarkable except that Mr. L. thought the fee would be higher than quoted. It was explained that the fee was based on twice weekly sessions and would be adjusted as planned sessions were reduced to once weekly. The commitment of paying for sessions not cancelled in advanced by mutual consent was agreed to easily and then immediately tested via several car-related "unavoidable" no-shows or last-minute cancellations i.e. for flat tires, or towaways for illegal parking. The fee was to be paid under all such circumstances.

Mr. L. quickly focused on the unfairness of such rules and openly questioned the therapist's motives. Money was immediately the cornerstone upon which resistance to treatment was based and as such required immediate attention. Masterson's therapeutic confrontation approach is the intervention of choice here. The function of his technique is to enable the patient to identify how his maladaptive defenses contribute to his here and now negative life experiences. Masterson's statement that while working with (patient's) personality disorders, it must be remembered that where there is acting-out there cannot be constructive insight; "..in fact the promotion of insight prematurely may escalate acting-out behavior to fend off intensification of feeling".

The following is an example of confrontational interchange that has proven useful in enabling this patient to recognize his resistance. This particular exchange occurred during the fourth session:

Therapist: We've agreed that you are to pay after each session. Each of the last 2 sessions you've left without paying and we've had to begin the next session by discussing payment. It's getting in the way of treatment and we cannot continue to function this way.

Patient: What do you mean, you can't see me unless I pay? I'm miserable, my job is falling apart, my marriage is gone and all you can talk about is money!

[Notice that the patient's immediate response is to accuse the therapist of rejection based on money.]

Therapist: I wonder why you experienced what I said as a threat to end treatment [and abandon him]. I'm attempting to help you understand that what you do affects others and affects the way in which you are treated.

Patient: I tell you I'm miserable, I'm doing drugs, my firm is losing clients, my wife is a policeman and all you can talk about is money.

Therapist: You'd rather blame me or "them" for your problems than begin to take responsibility for understanding why all these things are occurring.

Patient: Well, that's what I come to you for. Aren't you supposed to give me the answers?

Therapist: You are still refusing to work on this yourself. I'm just here to help you, not to do it for you. Your payment of the fee allows me to do that. Non-payment stops it because as we're doing now, we discuss money, not helping you.

Patient: That's your fault. You keep on bringing it up.

[One of the caveats at points like this is for therapist not to feel guilty about treating money as a resistance or defense, but use it as one would deal with denial or projection. The fact that successfully working through the resistance has an immediate positive financial impact on the therapist is immaterial. What is really being discussed are the topics of caring, self-worth and maladaptative behavior.]

Therapist: You consider my discussion of money as inappropriate. Yet it is only an issue because of your behavior and our agreement.

Patient: How come you're so different from everyone else? Everybody else changes the rules. My mother said to grow up and the minute I tried she had a fit. My God she's still calling to check up on me now! My father said he understood what I was going through and then never said a word to my mother. My wife did drugs with me until we got married and now I'm a damn criminal because she stopped and I didn't. I'm good for the money. My own therapist doesn't trust me!

[What we see here is a verbalization of the difficulty in separation and individuation. The use of money is apparent in the avoidance, denial and clinging manifest in the interchange. We can recognize how focusing on money triggers the maladaptative functioning of the patient. He is in treatment for drug abuse yet he is angry about money and is spending valuable time challenging the therapist's functioning.

There is no attempt by the therapist to use insight quickly. The emphasis is always on the here-and-now maladaptive behavior.]

Therapist: Do we need to discuss a fee reduction?

Patient: No, since I'm not doing drugs I have money. It's just that I don't have enough to redo the house, pay you and what I owe (to the drug dealers).

Therapist: So your choice is to redo the house, pay off the dealers and not pay me. What effect does that have on your expressed interest in treatment?

Patient: It would have none if you'd cooperate.

[Here we have the patient attempting to use money as a way to have the success or failure of treatment be a function of the therapist's willingness to make it a major treatment issue.]

The connection must be made to the patient that his use of cocaine (drugs in general) and money both serve the purpose of preventing him from "doing" anything about his problems. Drugs, especially cocaine, had always been consciously used to relieve pressure and cope with the stresses of home and work. It had not been successful for all of the usual and obvious reasons that such behavior never works.

Yet when he is faced with the unavoidable (therapy), in order to salvage the positive aspects of his life, he employs another defense, money, where the goal is to prevent the identification and working through of his internal conflicts.

Unless money is approached quickly and directly it provides Mr. L. a whole host of defense maneuvers from which to choose i.e. projective identification, denial, omnipotence and devaluation.

With patients in whom reality testing is basically intact it is vital that the reality of therapy– "You are paying me to help you"–be consistently emphasized. Once those boundaries and agreements are established and adhered to by the therapist, the form of therapy becomes that which is most appropriate to the therapist's understanding of the patient's emotional life. In the author's experience many of the substance abusers had demonstrated refraction to the more conventional forms of therapy. Kernberg's explanation of this is quite specific. Psychoanalytic approaches generally fail with borderline personalities because their weak ego development does not allow them to tolerate the regression necessary in analytic treatment. In addition, the acting out of their instinctual conflicts within the transferential relationship gratifies their pathological needs and blocks analytic process.

An example with Mr. L. is illustrative of this point. His yelling at the therapist, if allowed to continue without comment (or with analytic interpretation) would have resulted in increased verbal outbursts precisely because it made the patient feel good to be able to behave in such a way without the emotional recriminations which would have occurred within his family or work situation. It would have resulted in tension release which would have had him leave the session feeling satisfied and perhaps optimistic regarding future sessions. The problem, of course, is that there had been no "working through" of the dynamics underlying the outbursts, hence there would be no significant behavioral modification.

The interchange which occurred in our illustration forces the patient to examine his behavior immediately, and allow a modicum of therapeutic discomfort to occur, in the hopes of facilitating behavioral change and understanding.

Likewise, supportive psychotherapy attempts fail because the defenses characteristic of these patients (splitting, repression, denial and projection) interfere with the establishment of an effective "therapeutic alliance". It leads to the patient establishing negative transferential feelings towards the therapist ("good" vs "bad" mother). For reasons similar to that expressed above, these negative transferential feelings lead to acting out outside the therapy session, very similar to the behavior which occurred in his earlier attempts to cope with feelings towards his mother. This behavioral sequence nullifies whatever support may be offered within the therapeutic environment because the patient is not required to work them through in therapy. The interactions described earlier make it difficult for the patient to do anything else but relate to the "here and now" of the interaction with the therapist. Money as the conduit through which the interaction occurs only makes the effects more concrete and visible.

In Mr. L.'s case the use of money as resistance was a consistent aspect of the therapeutic relationship. It never was resolved. Under pressure either externally applied (wife, work, therapist) or internally generated (fear of abandonment or failure) money would reappear as a subject in therapy. It always was introduced by the therapist and was usually greeted with a "here we go again" response from the patient. The purpose of such a reaction was to induce guilt in the therapist for discussing such a mundane, self-indulgent topic while the patient was in such psychic pain. The approach taken by the therapist at each occasion was a replica of the dialogue previously described.

SUMMARY

The therapeutic approach described above borrows from Kernberg, Fenichel and the Masterson Group. It is by no means the only way of treating substance abusers who may exhibit much of what can be labeled borderline personality organization. Kernberg in fact discusses several different therapeutic approaches to treating borderline personalities. ([1]Chapter 3) An important aspect of treatment is that this approach has proven to be useful with borderlines presenting different addictive or behavioral symptoms. Gambling is a currently recognized behavioral problem in which borderline personalities appear to be well represented. This technique would be applicable in such a treatment situation.

However, what has proven to be successful in treatment of such patients is a combination of their unique personality characteristics, the training of the therapist and the setting within which the therapy occurs. On an outpatient basis, money is one of the most important variables in the environment and needs to be addressed quickly, relevantly and consistently. It provides a necessary linchpin upon which much of subsequent therapy may be based.

REFERENCES

1   Kernberg, Otto F., M.D., Borderline Conditions and Pathological Narcissism, Jason Aronson, Inc., New York, NY 1975.

2   Masterson, James F., M.D., Psychotherapy of the Borderline Adult: A Developmental Approach, Brunner-Mazel, New York, NY 1976.

CHAPTER 20

PSYCHOTHERAPY WITHOUT FEE

Richard C. Friedman, M.D.

The fee has been a topic of interest to psychodynamically oriented clinical theorists from the inception of psychoanalysis. It is well known by now that the capacity to form a working alliance may be adversely affected in those who are so wealthy that no fee, no matter how large, is necessarily meaningful. A subgroup of patients whose fee is paid by third parties may have similar difficulties participating in the psychotherapeutic process. Since psychotherapists are frequently in private practice, the ethical and practical aspects of setting appropriate fees has also been commented on by many clinicians.

In 1950 Frieda Fromm-Reichmann discussed the issue of fees in psychoanalytically oriented psychotherapy as follows:

"Psychiatric services – that is, the attempt to help a person overcome his emotional difficulties in living – are priceless if successful or worthless if they fail. It is through these attempts nevertheless, that the therapist makes his living, so that the settlement of his fees has to be determined by the market value of psychiatric services at a given time and in a given area. The degree in variation of these fees must be in proportion to the financial status of the patient and according to the number of patients whom the psychiatrist has accepted at both average and reduced fees at the time."

Concerning patients who need treatment but cannot afford to pay Fromm-Reichmann stated:

"Patients who cannot afford adequate payments for their treatment should be treated for nominal fees or *without pay*. The old psychoanalytic concept that psychotherapy will not be successful with patients who do not make a financial sacrifice to obtain it regardless of their economic status, is

Money and Mind, Edited by S. Klebanow and
E.L. Lowenkopf, Plenum Press, New York, 1991

an unfortunate misconception engendered by misleading teachings of our modern culture. This does not mean to deny the desirability of nominal payments where possible for the sake of the maintenance of the self respect of the patient who does not wish to obtain something for nothing."

Despite the recognition by Fromm-Reichmann and others including Freud (Gay, 1988), that it may be appropriate for some patients to be treated without fee, this topic has been underattended to in the literature.

In 20 years of practice of psychoanalysis and psychoanalytically oriented psychotherapy, I have found that most patients do indeed find that payments of an appropriate fee enhance their self worth and sense of autonomy. Sometimes, however, the exchange of money is not required for psychotherapy, and sometimes it may be an obstacle.

The present chapter focuses on such situations. I discuss below cases of people who were treated with long term psychotherapy in a private practice setting and who, for very long periods of time, paid no fee. In this area, where there are few established guidelines, it was necessary to consider treatment principles on a case by case basis. My stance in this article therefore is subjective and experiential. I present one case in particular detail, and another two in more compressed fashion. I also discuss an unusual situation of a long term relationship with a psychotic man, which I felt was helpful to the patient but not explicitly psychotherapeutic.

In each case discussed below treatment was begun in a private practice setting, and each patient initially paid a reduced fee. This was ultimately dropped, and years of psychotherapy were carried out for no fee. In the discussion section of this chapter, I comment on general guidelines for practice derived from these clinical experiences.

TIMOTHY

I worked with this 31-year old Catholic, single research scientist for 14 years. Psychotherapy terminated a few months prior to the writing of this article, at the time Timothy moved to another city to join the faculty of a distinguished research center.

When I first met Timothy we were both rather young. I recognized that he was, of course, but had no such awareness about myself.

He was referred by a college health service psychiatrist, for treatment of depression. At that time Timothy was a 17-year old college freshman who lived with this parents in a lower income area of New York City.

After a few initial sessions it became apparent that he was a gifted person struggling to stay afloat in a sea of familial, social, financial and psychological problems.

He had never before received individual treatment although he had been involved in family therapy throughout his childhood. This was primarily focused on helping his parents carry out tasks necessary for family life. His father, a civil servant, was paranoid schizophrenic; his mother, a homemaker, suffered from incapacitating severe depressions lasting for months at a time. Timothy was an outstanding student. He did not view himself as being particularly bright, however; others simply seemed slow to him. In lower school grades he rarely did homework, preferring to finish assignments on the day they were due. When called on, he always found himself knowing the correct answers no matter what the subject matter was.

To his surprise, Timothy was advised to apply to a prestigious Ivy League college on the basis of high grades, and the highest scores on the S.A.T. exams in his school. He did well his first semester but, despite scholarship aid, had trouble making ends meet. Although tuition was paid for and he made some money as a waiter, he still could not pay for necessities. He walked to save money on subway and bus fare. He ate only two meals a day, of which one was coffee. His winter coat was torn, and he could not afford to have it repaired.

Timothy had decided to transfer from a private to a state college when I met him. This decision precipitated the depression for which he consulted his school's psychiatrist and was referred to me.

Before seeing me, however, he did something that I later came to realize was characteristic of him, a matter of personal style. Feeling alienated, detached, and pessimistic as he walked through the halls of the college library, he noticed an advertisement for a national poetry contest posted on one of the bulletin boards. Timothy had long loved reading and writing poetry (an interest no one else knew about). The deadline for entry into the contest was midnight of that very day. Timothy impulsively decided to become a contestant. He went to the library where he composed a poem and, on his way home from school, mailed it to the contest officials.

"After I dropped it in the mailbox I forgot it completely." Timothy was quite surprised to learn that he had won first prize, the considerable amount of $1,000. This was not enough to keep him from transferring colleges, but it did give his self-confidence a boost.

Timothy's past history was that of a neglected child with psychotic parents, left to fend for himself as best as he could on the streets of New York City. He had no sustained friendships despite anguished loneliness. His father vigorously discouraged visits to their home by other children or play dates at their homes. His mother was withdrawn, preoccupied with her own problems. Timothy's childhood and early adolescent years were spent in his words, "roaming the streets as much as possible to be out of my house."

Despite expressed disapproval of Timothy's "sissiness" his father also admired him – calling him "the only good thing in life." The father was particularly in awe of Timothy's intellectual capacities. Both parents were opposed to Timothy's leaving home until some indefinite future date.

The initial diagnostic assessment of Timothy seemed ominous. He suffered from a major depressive episode, and a borderline obsessive-compulsive character disorder. There was no personal or family history of mania, alcohol or other substance abuse, suicide, attempted suicide or self mutilation. Schizophrenia occurred in members of his father's extended family; unipolar severe depression in his mother's. There was far more to this person's character, however, than can be expressed in diagnostic terms. Before discussing treatment, which progressed in large measure because of his unusual coping abilities, a brief review of the daunting problems at the time I first met Timothy is indicated.

This was a young person whose psychotic family environment resulted in apparent absence of appropriate social interactions with peers. Negative input from his father about his masculinity produced fears of age-appropriate romantic and sexual involvements. He was unsocialized in many ways, lacking in knowledge of normal middle class manners. He felt alienated from all groups he had ever been exposed to and was often perceived as alien.

Despite all this, Timothy possessed intellectual brilliance, an ineffable quality of inner determination. This in itself was remarkable in light of his feelings of ugliness, stupidity, worthlessness and identify diffusion.

The Fee

The referring psychiatrist working with his parents' therapist managed to get them to agree to support Timothy's treatment. The fee was modest but acceptable. The parents continued to pay during the first year until shortly after Timothy moved to his own apartment.

Timothy realized the need to do this after the first few sessions. He also recognized that both parents would be extremely opposed to any move he made towards autonomy.

Timothy's father threatened to cut him off financially if he moved out. His mother passively supported her husband's position. Nonetheless, Timothy found an unfurnished room for rent and took it. He also got a second after-school job to pay for day to day expenses.

Timothy's parents then discontinued financial support of his treatment. By this time I had come to know Timothy quite well and recognized his unusual assets.

He never missed a therapy session, nor was he ever late. During these years I had two offices; one outside of the city at a hospital where I worked, and one in Manhattan. Whereas I usually saw Timothy in New York City, in view of the fact that we met three times per week, it was sometimes necessary for us to have sessions at the other office. The hospital was about five miles away from the railroad stop and visitors from New York City would usually take a taxi cab or van to the hospital complex. One bitterly cold winter day I learned during Timothy's session that he had walked from the railroad station in order to save money. Needless to say, he had appeared on time as usual.

Despite poverty, Timothy never complained about his circumstances. He expressed no envy of more advantaged peers.

Timothy continually set interpersonal, psychological and academic goals for himself, and despite great anxiety worked to meet them. He made friends with classmates and used these young people (without their knowledge) as role models. He copied their manners and dress style. As much as he could he tried their leisure activities and some, such as going to museums, became his own. He soon discovered that girls found him attractive. Although he had experienced sexual and romantic fantasies about women (never men) he had avoided dating because he was painfully shy. He worked hard to overcome this during treatment and was ultimately able to become sexually active and to fall in love.

In the academic realm, Timothy succeeded in achieving outstanding grades. His teachers encouraged him to pursue an academic career in light of usual talent in theoretical physics.

When his parents cut off funds, Timothy saw three possible options with regard to paying for treatment.

1. plead for continued help from his parents
2. cut down on frequency of sessions or discontinue treatment temporarily
3. take out a loan.

We evaluated these possibilities together and none seemed promising.

1. It was most likely that his parents would either refuse to give him money he needed or would insist that as a condition for receiving it he move back to their home.
2. He not only felt deeply involved in and committed to psycho-therapeutic treatment, he felt that he needed it in order to function (this despite simultaneous pharmacotherapy). I agreed with his assessment.
3. He was already in debt to both universities he had attended. He had no additional source of funds; and no immediate prospects for paying back a loan.

At this point, I decided to support Timothy's treatment myself. I initially suggested this to him as a loan which he gratefully (albeit guiltily) accepted. As the debt accrued, it became clear to both of us that he could never afford to repay me. He was not satisfied with this, however, and insisted on a schedule for repayment ("even if it takes 20 years"). By the time Timothy terminated therapy with me, having obtained a Ph.D. degree at a major center and achieved acclaim as a leader in his field, we had done enough work on his vicious superego for him to accept my offer to cancel the debt. Although we had accomplished much, it was clear that he still needed treatment for a variety of reasons. He is presently in twice per week therapy in his new home city. The fee is modest but he pays the bills as they come in. As a scientist he lives frugally but comfortably. He and I are now making a transition from therapist-patient to friends.

At this point I wish to comment on aspects of this treatment experience from my personal point of view. The area I am addressing falls under the heading of subjective reactions of the therapist to financial dimensions of psychotherapy.

First, I both admired and identified with this patient from the start. Fortunately for me, my own parents were not as disturbed as his were. My family did not have much money, however. Like Timothy I had depended on scholarships to get an education. I recall being visited by a distant relative when I was about the age Timothy was when we started our work. This middle aged successful entrepreneur found himself in the city where I attended school and looked me up. We did not know each other well, having last met when I was one year old. After an enjoyable dinner we were shaking hands and saying goodbye, when he abruptly took off his Harris Tweed jacket and had me try it on. He made some excuse and insisted that I keep it. I was astonished, but I sorely needed the jacket and kept it. I never forgot that act of kindness, which became an organizing experience for me.

Subsequently, when I found other people who were spontaneously charitable, I tried to get to know them well. I have learned much from this (including the knowledge that openly expressed altruism is not terribly frequent in day to day life).

Meanwhile, during these years a dear friend needed psychiatric help. This person bankrupted himself in order to afford sessions with his therapist. This seemed to me fundamentally unjust.

These are only two examples of the kind of events from my own life that led me to regard the opportunity to work with a patient such as Timothy as a gift in itself.

This was not only because his talent made it likely that he would contribute to society in general. It was also because of his moral integrity, courage to face his own fears, uncompromising determination to grow beyond his limitations, and uncomplaining nature.

Had Timothy been in a position to repay me without undue hardship I would have accepted his money gratefully and (hopefully) gracefully. That not being the case, I found that the rewards of being able to be giving to him were payment enough. I hasten to add here that I was only able to do this because my other patients paid their bills.

Psychotherapy was carried out for 12 years without fee. In looking back on this today, I feel confident that Timothy's progress would not have been greater if he had refused this gift.

In discussing with him my motivation for cancelling the debt, I mentioned that people had helped me when I needed it and I was grateful to be able to pass this giving spirit along. I was confident that he would meet people during the rest of his life who would profit from his altruism.

Had my financial circumstances not been such as to allow me to treat Timothy he could have obtained psychotherapeutic help at a clinic. It was clearly good for his self-esteem, however, to be treated in a private office setting. He saw many other patients come and go during the years of our work. This in itself was educational and acculturating since most of these were from the middle and upper classes. He learned to feel that he too belonged in this type of environment. I am reasonably sure that this welcoming stance enabled him to make the leaps required for his career. Looking back on the treatment, it was apparent to me that Timothy would have to leave the culture of poverty (and of psychosis) in which he was reared, in order to enter an academic culture compatible with his abilities. In order to facilitate this, it was important that he receive treatment in a private setting and not be transferred to a clinic (where he secretly feared he belonged).

TWO BRIEF CASE REPORTS

I have treated two other patients with long-term psychotherapy without fee. Space does not permit extensive discussion of these cases here. They were each unique in important ways, but in other ways had much in common with the patient described above and with each other.

One such person was Louise, a 60-year old, childless, divorced, unemployed lawyer with a fixed modest income. Her diagnosis was Borderline Mixed Character Disorder with paranoid and obsessive features, and Dysthymia with occasional major depressive episodes. As a result of progress in psychotherapy, she divorced a husband with whom she had long been unhappy. After a year had passed she decided to emigrate to the country of her birth. She had left this country many years before as a refugee from the Nazis. We discussed this move in psychotherapy, and she terminated treatment. The next year, having occasion to be in her reclaimed homeland for a scientific meeting, I looked her up. She was a gracious hostess, and our relationship naturally became more personal and informal than before. A number of months passed and then, to my surprise, my ex-patient called for an appointment in New York. She had decided to reimmigrate to the USA and take up life in New York again. She needed psychotherapy once more and initially I urged her to consider working with someone else (I felt that a fresh perspective might be helpful for her). She saw many therapists in consultation both from the private sector and from clinics. She rejected them all and refused to work with anyone but me. I came to understand the underlying transferential meaning of her insistence. Her beloved father had been murdered by the Nazis shortly after she had initially left her country of birth – I had come to replace him. It became apparent to me that my ex-patient would either have me as her therapist again or do without treatment. I decided to resume our therapeutic relationship, but discovered that I was reluctant to charge a fee, and she had become reluctant to pay one. In neither case was the reason due to the money itself; rather it was what the money symbolized. To the patient it stood for a certain kind of coldness which abraded the wounds left by narcissistic injuries of her childhood. I responded to her feeling and was uneasy about challenging it. The apparent enactment of a transference relationship seemed to me to provide this patient with something vitally needed. I elected not to bill her and to proceed without a fee, albeit cautiously. The relationship remained (what I judged to be) optimally supportive. There was no escalation into the more pathological aspect of transference love. To the contrary, this patient proved able and willing to see me infrequently; usually once every few months. This minimal contact, however, was and is necessary for her stability. She often brings homemade cakes, bread, and artwork which I am pleased to accept without discussion. This is in keeping with a general guideline to avoid interpretation of the positive transference.

In retrospect I formulated that her traumatic history and character pathology resulted in severe impairment of her capacity to trust. In fact the only durable intimate relationship in her life was the one with me. This relationship had been therapeutically helpful to her in the past. Even more important to her was the fact that we had continued to enjoy each other's company during an interval when she was not formally labelled "patient." Having become sturdy enough to survive time and space stresses, our relationship had evolved into something unique in this person's life. She was therefore able to allow it to support weakened psychic structures.

A second patient and I have worked together on and off for more than twenty years. Unlike the previous two people, this latter patient is psychotic. She belongs to that subgroup of schizoaffective patients who are able to benefit to some degree from psychotherapy. This person is unemployable and lives on disability income. Her inner world is highly eccentric, and money does not mean the same things to her as it does to most people. Both her inability to hold a job and to pay a fee for psychotherapy are an intrinsic part of the schizophrenic process from which she suffers.

I began working with this person during my residency years. I have no doubt that our relationship will continue as it is now until one of us dies. Psychotherapy has clearly been helpful in keeping her alive and out of the hospital. This is particularly evident since she is rigidly pharmacophobic and refuses antipsychotic medication.

The issue of fee in her case has to do with setting realistic treatment goals. She seems to have made as much progress in psychotherapy as she is capable of and, as a result, is able to live outside of a hospital. She is chronically delusional, however: unable to work, or to tolerate either sexual or nonsexual intimacy, or isolation. (Two suitors are devoted to her despite her absolute requirements of sexual abstinence, and contact in small but regular doses.) I have come to accept after many years, that for me to expect this patient to pay a fee as my other psychotherapy patients do would be setting an unrealistic treatment goal; she would simply stop coming to sessions. I have elected to accept this complication of her illness. This patient often brings small gifts, however, which I openly show my pleasure at receiving.

The last situation I wish to discuss is quite different. It raises questions not only about the purpose of the fee in certain therapeutic patient situations, but about the fundamental characteristics of psychotherapy.

TRAVIS

Travis, a white, Catholic, unmarried dishwasher died of metastatic carcinoma last year. He and I were each 46-years old at the time. I had also begun working with Travis during my psychiatric residency. Prior to meeting me, in between hospitalizations, Travis had lived with his parents and intermittently worked at menial jobs. A high school dropout with no skills, Travis had an IQ in the high 80s. His entire social life revolved around the activities of a fundamentalist Christian sect which he had been recruited to join while wandering the streets of New York.

The admission during which I met Travis was occasioned by a sequence of tragic events. He had been involved in a love affair, the only one of his life, with a young schizophrenic woman. She suicided after learning of her mother's accidental death. Travis attended her funeral, following which he hanged himself. A policemen who happened by cut him down and administered resuscitation. Travis was then admitted to the psychiatric hospital where I worked.

Initially severely depressed, after a few weeks Travis appeared brighter, more optimistic. He had discovered that the *spirit* of his lost love lived on, in the bodies of women and men on the hospital ward. After a period of contemplation lasting a few days, Travis formulated a belief system involving the past lives of spirits that presently inhabit living bodies.

Early in our relationship, Travis explained that he had traced his spirit back to the 17th century. He had not yet discovered the terrible crime he must have committed to be sentenced to his present life of suffering. He was confident that it was only a matter of time until this illumination occurred.

I worked with Travis until the end of my residency and then lost touch with him for a few years.

About 1-1/2 years after I returned to New York City from military service, Travis called for an appointment. When he appeared, he looked as he always had: He was 6'2", tall, burly, with red hair cut in a crew cut style - but long, and uncombed. His face was florid and he wore thick eye glasses. His chino pants and green T-shirt were stained. Travis requested hypnosis for what he called "past life age regression therapy." He now wanted to return to a life in which he could be happy.

I told him that this was beyond my power but that I was very pleased to see him, and would work with him (within my limitations), if he wished.

He agreed. Subsequently, we met intermittently, sometimes as often as weekly, sometimes once every few months. Travis simultaneously attended a drug clinic at the hospital where he had been an inpatient. He faithfully took the neuroleptic and thymoleptic medication prescribed, although without improvement in his mental status.

Travis agreed to attempt to be socially appropriate in the lobby of my office building. I insisted that he not scream at strangers or at building staff, and that his clothing be more or less presentable.

Travis and I had many sessions in my office until his death; each precisely like the last and the next to follow. Travis would show me a paperback book on past lives which he kept on his person at all times. He would rail furiously at the incompetence of psychiatrists who in his view "couldn't help anyone." He attempted to get in touch with what he called his "deep feelings." He spoke almost continuously for 45 minutes in a highly stereotyped way and then marched out of the office when his time was up. Much as I wanted to, I could rarely get a word in.

Travis seemed to need the relationship with me. He clearly felt more secure simply to have access to me. In keeping with prevailing practice I initially charged Travis for my time. Given the fact that he was an intermittently employed dishwasher, the amount of the fee was nominal from my point of view. I felt that the responsibility for paying it would help keep Travis organized and might enhance his self regard.

I saw no evidence that either of these goals was accomplished. If I insisted, Travis would bring a money order to sessions. If I did not remind him, he tended to forget. After a while we both let the fee issue fade quietly away.

After a break in our relationship lasting about six months, Travis came to see me – feeling "under the weather." He was being evaluated at a local clinic for anorexia, weakness, fatigue and lower abdominal cramps. He was shortly thereafter admitted to a cancer treatment center, where the diagnosis of metastatic carcinoma of the bowel was made. Because of the advanced stage of the disease, only palliative therapy was offered.

I visited Travis in the hospital and was of some help in explaining the nature of his psychiatric illness to the staff. Six months later Travis died.

This case raises questions about the doctor-patient relationship and the fundamental features of psychotherapy. Thus, it seems to me that Travis and I participated in a doctor-patient relationship. This relationship was clearly meaningful to him (and to me). Nonetheless, there is no reason to think that it was psychotherapeutic. As far as I could tell, I never said or did anything that actually influenced the course of Travis' illness.

It probably would have been ethical for me to charge Travis for my time had I wished to. The charge would not have been for psychotherapy, since as far as I could determine, psychotherapy could not be carried out with Travis. Rather, the charge would simply have been for the use of my time, which might have been spent working with someone who could have used psychotherapy proper, as it were. It was more compatible with my value system not to impose such a charge. I felt enhanced self regard from living according to my inner standards. This helped me not become resentful that Travis did not appear particularly motivated to listen to words of wisdom from my quarter, although he seemed to like the sound of my voice.

DISCUSSION

The situations I have reported on here have arisen infrequently in my clinical experience. Insofar as they illustrate aspects of the financial dimensions of practice that are not often discussed they are important beyond their numbers.

Cases such as this highlight distinctions between private practice and clinic practice. In the culture of private practice, patients can usually count on the fact that their therapist will work with them barring an accident of fate, until termination of treatment. In the public sector it is common for trainees to leave patients after six months or one year in order to rotate to fulfill responsibilities in other areas of their psychiatric educations. Public sector patients, therefore, are frequently exposed to object loss, the loss of the therapist. This is sometimes tolerated and coped with, sometimes not.

The three patients presented in the first part of this chapter came to need a particular person, myself, in addition to a particular technique of therapy. I suspect that requirement for a particular person as therapist occurs with some frequency in private and clinic practice. There are no objective data to support this, however.

In the three cases discussed in the first part of this chapter, I initially had to determine that the patients needed me personally as a therapist in order to make optimal progress. This decision was made after a psychotherapeutic relationship had formed in each case. One could not upon *initially* meeting a patient decide that the only therapist capable of working with the person was oneself. Such naive grandiosity must be distinguished from realistic assessment that a particular therapeutic relationship had become necessary for a particular patient's adaptation. Once I decided that I would be the therapist, the next decision concerned choosing between a nominal fee and no fee. Here, it is helpful to discuss the two nonschizophrenic patients first.

In Timothy's case, had I set a nominal fee the question would have arisen, "For whose sake was the fee set?" This patient lacked funds to the point where even a lowered fee (within usual lowered fee range) was an impractical burden. At a certain point of lowered fee (say 50 cents per session) the financial incentive to the therapist is virtually absent. This is often realized by the patient. The patient on the other hand might well need the money paid for treatment, but nonetheless feel pained by what seems by objective standards to be a terribly small amount. The clinical decision in this situation is whether it is better for the patient to receive a direct gift of therapy from the analyst. It seems to me that the answer to this is most often "no," but that there are patients for whom an affirmative response is appropriate.

From the point of view of countertransference, it should also be kept in mind that the reward to the therapist of being allowed (as it were) to be openly giving, may have a positive impact on morale and buffer against the myriad countertransference problems of extended treatment.

The clinical rationale for no fee was different in the case of the next patient discussed. Timothy had an overriding need for a helping hand. Louise, however, had a rigid need to organize her adaptation around a transference reenactment of an idealized father figure. Here, the treatment decision hinged on the assessment that confrontation and clarification and interpretation would not be helpful because of intrinsic ego limitations of the patient. Description of these exceeds the scope of this article.

Although the third patient described was schizophrenic, one fundamental judgment about her treatment was similar to that discussed for the other two. I decided early on, that she would do best with me personally as her therapist. This decision was made before I had abundant clinical experience, and no doubt, came about as the result of mixed motivations including countertransferential ones. Over the twenty years of our work, I have come to understand many of these. I never saw fit to doubt my initial judgment, however, that the patient had come to need a particular therapist (myself – as well as a particular type of treatment). In this case, however, as a result of schizophrenia, this patient's positive regard for me and commitment to therapy (as she understood it) could not be used to provide leverage to get her to pay a fee. I doubt that she ever will.

I presented the last unusual situation to highlight the fact that collection of a fee is among other things, a matter of a therapist's personal financial value system. My value system is not compatible with the model of simply being paid for my time. Travis seemed to like spending time with me. Indeed, I came to believe that he needed this attachment. Nonetheless, I could never persuade myself that a psychotherapeutic process ever occurred between us. This, despite the fact that an important human relationship was formed and that it fell under the rubric of doctor and patient.

What general principles can be derived from this personal clinical experience? To start with, I am not sure whether I would ever begin extended psychotherapy on a no fee basis. There are two reasons for this. The first is practical, and here I make no distinction between nominal fee and no fee. This distinction is, however, quite important with regard to the second reason. One has to know a patient extremely well in order to dissect out the beneficent versus potentially adverse effects of not charging a fee. Many patients are likely to respond to this with inhibited competitive-assertive striving, guilt about rage towards the therapist, and a sense of burden. As this article illustrates, however, I do not believe that this is always so (even if it often is).

The patients presented here had extremely serious and chronic psychopathology. I think that patients who are more intact would not be likely to respond positively to no fee. I must qualify this, however. I have met many people either from the culture of poverty or with non-bourgeois values, about whom I am not sure.

From the perspective of countertransference, before one attempts treatment without fee, it is of course important that one be as sure as possible that irrational countertransference motives are not motivating this.

Thus, the therapist must proceed with absence of neurotic urges to rescue, and absence of personal hardship imposed by the no fee situation in the particular case involved.

Given these qualifications and constraints, treatment of patients without fee can be an aspect of private practice that is rewarding to therapists and patients.

REFERENCES

Fromm-Reichmann, F. F., (1950), Principles of Intensive Psychotherapy, Chicago and London: University of Chicago Press (Phoenix Books).

Gay, P., (1988), Freud: A Life for Our Time, New York and London: W. W. Norton and Co.

CHAPTER 21

MONEY, ETHICS AND THE PSYCHOANALYST

Joyce A. Lerner, C.S.W

In the early 1960's, Americans were idealistic about what they could achieve through their own efforts. The energies of many were directed toward helping others through the Peace Corps abroad and civil rights activism at home. It was a period of involvement and commitment. There was a sense of possibilities and the feeling that the world could be changed through individual endeavors. Now, after the assassinations of John Kennedy, Robert Kennedy and Martin Luther King, the increase of casual, seemingly irrational, violence in our society, the Vietnam war with its heritage of bitterness and lost innocence, the epidemic proportions of the drug problem, Watergate and the subsequent rash of revelations of wrong-doing for personal and political gain in government with indictments of top public officials and its echoes in the private sector such as in admissions of insider trading, the atmosphere has changed. We've had our scandals in sports, and are familiar with Medicaid fraud in health care. In religion, we have seen evangelists bilking their congregations. We are no longer shocked or even surprised by such disclosures. We adjust at a cost to our morale, with a growing sense of skepticism, and a shift from idealistic, helping pursuits to an age of narcissism (Lasch, 1979).

The psychoanalyst is a product of this milieu which often financially rewards or ignores unethical behavior. As an individual he has a need to maintain his self esteem within his culture. He is also bound to uphold professional ethics. When these sometimes contradictory motives interact with his own dynamics, conflict may ensue. As a consequence he may develop ethical blind spots. At the least, there will be times when he will be subject to opposing pulls that tax his ethics. For example:

A psychoanalyst consulted a senior colleague for supervision. At the end of the hour, the supervisor was asked by the analyst to complete an insurance form so that the latter could be reimbursed. The supervisor expressed surprise and discomfort. Since he had not treated the analyst, to indicate otherwise to the insurance company

Money and Mind, Edited by S. Klebanow and
E.L. Lowenkopf, Plenum Press, New York, 1991

would be fraudulent. The analyst assured the supervisor that his assistance with countertransference certainly was therapeutic. In addition, all of his previous supervisors had agreed to help him this way. One supervisor had even initiated an offer to work on this basis. Without the reimbursement, the analyst could not afford to pay for on-going supervision.

A difficult patient who was being treated at a greatly reduced fee was in a rage and wanted to terminate. She asked the analyst what he thought. Her analyst had two patients waiting for hours to open. Both were able to pay a full fee.

A grateful patient came into a large inheritance, wanted to pay his analyst more, and could easily afford to do so. The analyst had given all of his patients an annual fee increase just the month before.

Three weeks after beginning psychotherapy a patient is fired from her job. She asks the analyst to extend her credit until she can find new employment. The patient is acutely depressed and has a history of accumulating debts and evading her creditors.

These situations pose challenges; all of them call for decisions. All of them involve money; and all of them could constitute ethical dilemmas which force the psychoanalyst to make ethical judgments.

Rothstein (1986) tells of a sixty year old married, childless, wealthy retired patient in psychoanalysis who declared that he was changing his will in order to make his analyst the recipient of a bequest of $250,000. The analyst explored the "fantasy". The patient was irritated but, in the process, uncovered his wish that the analyst would never leave him and would take care of him in his old age. Several months later the patient asked his analyst if he would consider becoming the administrator of a philanthropic foundation to be established by the patient. The work of this foundation would, unbeknownst to the patient, dovetail with the analyst's area of interest. The analyst resisted his countertransference impulse to accept the patient's invitation and continued to analyze. Subsequent analytic productions included a dream with transference referents, followed by the patient's discussion of termination with the accompanying offer to put his analyst on retainer after termination so that his availability could be assured.

This same patient had had a previous psychotherapy. During his current analysis, his former therapist sent him a letter soliciting funds for a psychiatric foundation. The exploration of this material led to further analysis of transference with the current analyst. Rothstein concluded that, "The offer of money in any form and for any reason should be regarded as a transference fantasy. Like any fantasy, it is an overdetermined compromise formation that needs to be analyzed. To do otherwise is to perpetuate a countertransference enactment". "The analyst's attitude toward the future and particularly toward the post-analytic phase is especially important in regard to the issue of money. Because of the analyst's narcissistic investments in his professional endeavors and institutions, he might be tempted to rationalize the feasibility of accepting contributions from an analysand after termination". Rothstein reminds us of the timelessness of the unconscious and that "analyses are all, in a certain sense, interminable". He concludes, "Any other attitude may interfere with the analysis of an analysand's attempts at seduction with money.

I agree with Rothstein's conclusions and I accept the guidelines he endorses. In doing so I reveal my own analytic values. Rothstein recognizes that an analyst who contends that analysis is terminable might come to different conclusions about soliciting funds from a patient when analysis is over. From Rothstein's standpoint and mine, should such behavior with a patient be considered unethical?

Ingram comments that "the clinical and ethical work together and are indistinguishable on close examination" (1988). He refers to the unity of the clinical/ethical and declares, "When we become aware of a technical practice of a clinician from another school, a practice we find objectionable, we don't merely regard it as *clinically* incorrect but enlarge our criticism and find it *ethically* reprehensible" (1988). It can be formidable to draw the line between what's clinically unsound and what's ethically insupportable. Still, it is one thing to call a colleague "non-analytic", and quite another to accuse him of being unethical. We do try to tease the clinical/ethical unity apart when pressed. But we can't escape the fact that we judge our fellow analysts on the basis of our own clinical/ethical values. We also judge ourselves on this basis. When money is a factor, our judgments are further complicated. Money and values are related and can spark ethical dilemmas.

An ethical dilemma is marked by a conflict between contradictory values. Whether a situation is ethically problematic for a psychoanalyst depends upon the structure of his professional and personal values and ideals. Ideals have been given a great deal of attention in psychoanalysis with emphasis on the formation and functioning of the ego ideal and the process of idealization. The analyst's professional ego ideal forms through identification with training analyst, supervisors, teachers and with those who have molded the professional literature. The new analyst wants to be like this reference group, although initially the distance may seem inordinate. They ameliorate what may be the beginning analyst's sense of inadequacy as well and help him to formulate a picture of himself as he might one day be. Similarly, the formation of the professional superego comes about through identification with the values and prohibitions of those invested with authority.

Values express ideals and reflect the shape of the superego and ego ideal. How do we differentiate between values, ideals, and ethics? Ethics are the organization of ideals into an abstract code. An ethical attitude implies conformity with an elaborated code of ideal principles. An ethical psychoanalyst is one whose behavior is congruent with the ethics of the psychoanalytic profession. Ethics have both abstract and behavioral components. The behavioral aspect allows a determination of whether a particular individual is ethical according to his actions. Ideals on the other hand, may exist only in the mind as images; i.e., the ideals of Plato. If an ideal exists in reality, it is in its most perfect form, i.e., an ideal vacation.

What about values? A value is a fair or proper equivalent in money, commodities, etc. for something sold or exchanged (Webster 1955). The fair price is a reflection of intrinsic worth. A value may also mirror the worth of something in money or goods at a certain time. This would be the market price or the relative worth in a given culture at a given moment. Value may also refer to purchasing power or the equivalent of some thing in money. For example, the price of an analytic hour is set at a certain fee which may fluctuate. As the dollar is worth less, fees may increase. Fees may also rise according to fluctuating cultural values. When psychoanalysis is more popular, higher fees may be set. Value is accorded, too, based on the quality of something; the more desirable, useful, estimable, or important, the greater the worth. There are also those things that we prize for their own sake; those qualities or commodities that we imbue with intrinsic worth. Fee setting is influenced both by the value we place on psychoanalytic treatment and by our measure of ourselves as psychoanalysts. Our method of appraisal reveals our process of valuing which discloses the ideals we regard as worthy ones.

Our psychoanalytic values manifest our ongoing sense of who we are in our work. This psychoanalytic identity may be challenged when we face issues of money in practice. For, when we deal with money matters we draw on a deeply etched personal history. Freud (1913) recognized the objective value of money both to sustain living and to provide power. He equated money symbolically in the unconscious with feces, penis, baby and gift (1917). These unconscious equivalents derive from the stages of psychosexual development. Subjectively, money is a part of the fabric of psychosexual development and therefore will be treated by patients as they treat sexual matters. Freud advised the psychoanalyst to handle money matters with the same frankness that he handles sexuality. While the analogy between sex and money holds up to a great extent there is one crucial gap. Analysts are ethically enjoined from participating in sexual intercourse with patients, except in fantasy. Financial intercourse, on the other hand, is a part of the structure of psychoanalytic treatment (Lerner, 1987).

While Freud felt that the analyst could set an example of candor in dealing with money that would help patients to address sexuality in a similar vein, this position fails to consider the possible welter of unconscious influences in the analyst which may be conveyed to the patient beyond the manifest attitude. Similarly, his response to his analyst's presentation of money matters is determined by the patient's psychic structure. Freud referred to an ascetic attitude which lends itself to viewing money as a curse. How would a patient who sees money as the root of all evil react to an analyst who presents the fee forthrightly as his due? Such a question is unanswerable without knowledge of a particular patient in his genetic context. What we do know is that the analyst's attitude cannot transcend the patient's transference. Nor would that be desirable.

Still, the treatment of money matters prescribed by Freud (1913) is to be recommended. It calls for the analyst to recognize his material needs and wishes. He must take responsibility for them with the patient as one of the initial steps in setting up the psychoanalytic situation. Freud states, "It seems to me more respectable and ethically less objectionable to acknowledge one's actual claims and needs rather than, as is still the practice among physicians, to act the part of the disinterested philanthropist – a position which one is not, in fact, able to fill, with the result that one is secretly aggrieved, or complains aloud, at the lack of consideration and the desire for exploitation evinced by one's patients".

As such, Freud's counsel constitutes a standard and a requirement for psychoanalysts and forms part of a financial/ethical code for the profession. What about additional standards? Future psychoanalysts are subject from the start to the ethical imperatives of their respective disciplines. Later, they may become accountable for their ethics to such national organizations as the American Academy of Psychoanalysis or the American Psychoanalytic

Association. While these influences are essential, it is in the crucial years of psychoanalytic training that psychoanalytic/ethical standards develop. And it is at the level of the local institute that an emphasis on an ethical code which is taught as an integral part of the curriculum would be most useful.

Blanck and Blanck (1974) regret that professional societies do not spell out ethics well enough. Where ethical codes exist they are, of necessity, written in generalizations. A typical statement from such a declaration is that, "The treatment of a patient must not be exploited for financial gain or to promote personal advantage" (Principles of Ethics for Psychoanalysts, 1988). Would we all agree on what constitutes exploitation for financial gain or what promotes personal advantage? It is in the discussion of the application of such principles within the psychoanalytic situation that the ethical dimension with its attendant dilemmas come alive. The institute is a natural forum for such exploration. It is an appropriate place to examine what constitutes an ethical breach versus what may be more a matter of theoretical difference. This serious task deserves more attention than it gets.

Agreement on conduct is easier to obtain in other professions. According to Blanck and Blanck, "There is one very delicate aspect of interprofessional relationship which applies more to psychotherapy than to medicine, law, or other professions. In those professions, accepted procedures are more or less firmly established and are taught fundamentally in the same way in all professional schools. Deviations from certain standard practices by a physician, for example, are usually not debatable. Psychotherapy is a field in which there is more diversity than agreement on crucial features of professional practice – on theory and technique. One therapist's conviction may appear as irregular practice to a therapist of another orientation". Blanck and Blanck stress that the theory makes the therapist's stance comprehensible. Its ethical value is in the safeguarding of the patient's welfare. Blanck and Blanck recognize the analyst's ethical obligations and underscore that professional ethics have but one purpose. "Ethics, we repeat, are not for the protection of the therapist, but for that of the patient".

All professions are based on a commonality of ethics. Analysts may recognize that anything can be rationalized and yet may be firmly wedded to an individual/professional ethic which is held above a collective professional ethic. Such a stance may, in fact, better protect the patient if the psychoanalyst's ethical code is more rigorous or encompassing than that of his professional group.

How does the psychoanalyst develop the values that mold his ethical code? While the psychoanalyst works alone and may feel isolated (Cooper,

1986) he does not practice in a vacuum. Even when secluded in his office, he is part of the larger society and has internalized values from it. His values also stem from the psychoanalytic community at large and from his particular psychoanalytic associations, which have socialized him into the profession.

Individual competition is the economic basis of modern culture (Horney, 1937). Each individual is stimulated to strive for financial success which may mean not only being assertive, but may call for aggressively pushing others out of the way. The anal motif of acquiring, accumulating, amassing (Abraham, 1921) comes into interaction here with a cultural imperative. While we strive to win, at the same time, we are "deeply imbued with Christian ideals which declare that it is selfish to want anything for ourselves, that we should be humble, turn the other cheek, be yielding" (Horney, 1937). These culturally derived values clash. Horney (1937) concluded, "For this contradiction, there are only two solutions within the normal range: to take one of these strivings seriously and discard the other; or to take both seriously with the result that the individual is seriously inhibited in both directions".

The relevance for today of the particular contradictions Horney outlined in 1937 may be questioned (Ingram, 1984). Still, it is evident that the psychoanalyst's values may, at times, be at odds with one another. One form this may take is a conflict between the desire for economic success and the wish to help. Helpfulness is a component of the physicianly attitude described by Greenson (1967): The analyst intervenes only for the patient's welfare and is dedicated to healing. The work of psychoanalysis is geared toward helping the patient through self-understanding. The analyst also works to help himself meet his financial needs. Generally these goals are compatible. But should discord arise, how is the analyst to resolve the conflict? Kernberg's work (1976) on the consolidation of superego and ego integration suggests a model for resolution. An on-going reshaping of experiences occurs as external objects influence internal representations, while internal self and object representations color external perception continually adjusting the self concept. "An integrated self, a stable world of integrated, internalized object representations, and a realistic self-knowledge reinforce one another." The resolution of the internalized contradiction would then come about through an integration of apparently contradictory values. In other words, the analyst compromises and creates resolution. The Hegelian model of thesis, antithesis and synthesis (Rendon, 1986) supports the kind of integration Kernberg describes.

Another means of reconciling professional and personal values is proposed by Schafer (1983) through "a second self that integrates the analyst's own biography and personality with the constraints of the analytic method and the needs of each analysand". "In our best work as analysts we are not quite the same as we are in our ordinary social lives or personal relations. In fact, we are often much better people in our work in the sense that we show a greater range of empathizing in an accepting, affirmative, and goal-directed fashion". "This second self is not and cannot be discontinuous with one's ordinary personality; yet, it is a special form of it, a form that integrates one's own personality into the constraints required to develop an analytic situation. It is within this form that one expresses his or her humanity analytically. On this basis a special kind of empathic intimacy, strength, appreciation, and love can develop in relation to an analysand which it would be a mistake to identify with disruptive countertransference". This second self determines the analyst's relation to patients reflective of the analyst's values. Such a composite of personal and professional ideals provides direction for the analyst in the face of financial/ethical dilemmas.

The tension of the analyst's contrary attitudes may lead to another outcome, a lack of resolution. The conflict could simply be kept at bay. This may occur via the analyst's professional character which is viewed by Cooper (1986) as "state-dependent", rather than as "a simple fixed quality". "The analytic situation is so constructed that the analyst's safety is assured - we need not answer embarrassing questions, we need not speak when spoken to, and our quirkiness is hidden behind our technique". Yet what if our needs and values are activated even within that atmosphere of safety? What if our patients become either obstacles to or means to ends that we have for ourselves financially? What happens if a patient's earning power is drastically reduced for the long term and he is no longer able to pay our fee? Or, what if a patient is in a position to offer us financial opportunities that would be beyond our reach otherwise? Our stance may be determined by clinical logic, but our clinical reasoning is influenced by our ethics and vice versa.

Maintaining ethical principles is made more difficult by impediments from within. The danger that comes from the analyst's difficulty in seeing his own character structure is noted by Cooper (1986). The analyst must be able to observe himself in his endeavor, to separate out an observing ego from an experiencing one. His analytic ego must enable him to be aware not just of his patient's behavior but of his own characterologic qualities in interacting with it. However, what the analyst sees depends on the framework of his theory and the values that derive from it. His countertransference is part and parcel of his psychic lens. Horney (1950; Ingram, 1987) found that the character structure is the determinant of values. When a child grows up under favorable conditions, he will find his own set of values through the process of self realization (1950). Yet, such healthy growth is unlikely in our culture. The child is more apt to experience basic conflict, a condition stemming from the incapacity to reconcile rigid, incompatible sets of values (Horney, 1945). There is no satisfactory way of managing such a conflict once it has become neurotic. Horney discarded the concept of the superego in favor of a holistic system (1939) and viewed the idealized image as the outgrowth of neurosis (1939): All idealization was pathological, but values could be either healthy or neurotic.

Horney's holistic approach marked a new psychoanalytical way of conceptualizing the human personality. Its ethics are based on the answer to the question: "is a particular attitude or drive inducive or obstructive to my human growth?" In this model, the analyst's ethics depend upon the degree to which he is self realizing. To the extent to which he is neurotic, he would attempt to actualize neurotic, therefore, non-ethical values.

A picture of development that leads to a different perspective on the construction of ethical principles is offered by Kernberg (1976). In his schema values develop as a consequence of internalization processes. He details the integration of the superego and the ego ideal as independent psychic structures resulting in ego identity, the organization of identifications and introjections brought about via the synthetic function of the ego. Integration, depersonification, and individualization structure internalization of object relations. Kernberg shows how the internal world influences the interpersonal world via the character structure. He discusses the correspondence between the self concept and actual behavior and personality as experienced by others as a function of the character structure which represents the automatized, predominantly behavioral aspects of ego identity.

Kernberg's structure allows for an open feedback system resulting in ongoing conflict resolution, re-assessment of values and continuing reappraisal of an ethical code. But even with such a system temptations arise. Rothstein's article, which I cited earlier, contains counsel for handling those issues of monetary ethics that may entice us to forget the caution of Blanck and Blanck that ethics are for the benefit of the patient. It is when countertransference is stirred that is it easiest to justify an alternative position or to override ethical considerations with narcissistic ones. It is when we need the patient for our own purposes, unrelated to professional standards, that the analysis may be in jeopardy. Horner, (1984) reminds us of the need for the analyst to have a clear sense of boundaries and a sense of self esteem that is not dependent upon the patient for narcissistic supplies. This caveat is particularly relevant where money is at issue. In addition, the analyst must be aware of his values. As Cooper (1986) points out, "We analysts may be blind to our value systems or may be unable to maintain therapeutic neutrality in the face of a challenge to our value system". He recognizes that we may still sustain the illusion that we can be free of values and concludes, "The blend of values and characterological needs may be deep and subtle".

Horney (1939) thought it impossible for the analyst to be free of values. She condemned the analyst's failure to take responsibility for value judgments and doubted that an analyst could tolerate what he secretly deplored. The analyst's values are expressed in everything he does and in every interpretation. What about his ideals? Schafer (1983) sees an exploration of these as appropriate and useful in our work. "But to recognize human limitation and variability is not to conclude that it is useless or foolish to attempt to set forth standards of excellence for analytic work. Nor is it to come to the conclusion that formulating the ideal analytic attitude is equivalent to idealizing, platitudinizing, or being oppressively perfectionistic. For it is on the individual analyst's efforts to approximate this ideal that the beneficial effects of analyzing largely depend, and in the final analysis it is these individual efforts which must concern us". The analyst who has formulated ethical standards and clarified his financial values in relation to them is in a better position to examine whatever conflicts may arise in the clinical encounter.

As individuals in a helping profession, we have an interest in relating in a way that is consistent with what will ultimately be most useful to others and to ourselves. We are also part of a larger society with its values, prominent among which is that money makes the world go around. We have to accommodate, to some degree, to the prevailing norms of our society. Otherwise, we place ourselves in an illusory, impractical world. The question, to what degree, is addressed by our ethics.

In analysis, the interests of self and other are intertwined. When the therapist protects the patient through his ethics, he is also protecting his own analytic values, measuring up to his ego ideal and satisfying the dictates of his superego. To accept financial/narcissistic rewards that come at the expense of the patient, to deny one's own financial needs, or to facilitate or block financial benefits for the patient all affect the treatment situation and the patient. They also reverberate in the analyst. The analyst with a well developed, realistic set of values, ideals and ethics is equipped with built in signals that alert him to the cost in guilt and shame, should he wish to violate his inner convictions. It is the analyst whose guiding internal structure is less developed, regardless of theoretical persuasion, that is a concern for the profession. The support and clarification which might be provided through the establishment of a well defined financial/ethical code that becomes part of psychoanalytic identity through professional socialization and training could make a difference that would benefit analysts, patients and the profession as a whole.

ACKNOWLEDGMENT

I wish to acknowledge Dr. Douglas H. Ingram for the clarification he provided during the development of this paper.

REFERENCES

Abraham, K., (1921), Contributions to the Theory of the Anal Character, Selected Papers on Psycho-analysis. London: Hogarth Press, Limited, 1979.

Blanck, G. and Blanck, R., (1974), Ego Psychology:Theory and Practice. New York: Columbia University Press.

Cooper, A., (1986), Some Limitations on Therapeutic Effectiveness: The "Burnout Syndrome" in Psychoanalysts. Psychoanalytic Quarterly. LV: 576-598.

Freud, S., (1913), On Beginning the Treatment (Further Recommendations on the Technique of Psychoanalysis I), The Standard Edition of the Complete Psychological Works of Sigmund Freud. Vol. XII, London: Hogarth Press, 1958.

Freud, S., (1917), On the Transformation of Instincts with Special Reference to Anal Erotism, The Standard Edition of the Complete Psychological Works of Sigmund Freud. Vol. XVII. London: Hogarth Press, 1958.

Greenson, Ralph, (1967), The Technique and Practice of Psychoanalysis. New York: International Universities Press.

Horner, Althea, Object Relations and the Developing Ego, New York: Jason Aronson, 1979.

Horney, Karen, (1937), The Neurotic Personality of Our Time. New York: Norton.

Horney, Karen, (1939), New Ways in Psychoanalysis, U.S.A.: Norton.

Horney, Karen, (1945), Our Inner Conflicts, U.S.A.: Norton

Horney, Karen, (1950), Neurosis and Human Growth, New York: Norton.

Ingram, D. (1984), Horney Theory: Issues and Directions, corres. in COLLOQUY, pub. by the Assoc. for the Ad. of Psychoan., 1 (1), p. 2.

Ingram, D., Editor, (1987), Karen Horney: The Final Lectures. New York: W. W. Norton & Company.

Ingram, D., (1988), Personal Communication.

Kernberg, Otto, (1976), Object Relations Theory and Clinical Psychoanalysis. New York: Jason Aronson.

Lasch, C., (1979), The Culture of Narcissism:American Life in an Age of Diminishing Expectations. New York: Norton.

Lerner, J., (1987), Limit Setting and the Analyst's Working Through. American Journal of Psychoanalysis. 47 (3). 243-249.

Principles of Ethics for Psychoanalysts. (1988) Academy Forum. American Academy of Psychoanalysis. 32 (2) p. 16.

Rendon, M. (1986), Philosophical Paradigms in Psychoanalysis. Journal of the American Academy of Psychoanalysis. 14 (4), 495-505.

Rothstein, A., (1986), The seduction of money: A brief note on an expression of transference love. Psychoanalytic Quarterly. LV: 296-300.

Schafer, R., (1983), The Analytic Attitude, New York: Basic Books.

Webster's New World Dictionary, (1955), College Edition. New York, The World Publishing Company.

CHAPTER 22

FEE AND EMPATHY: LOGIC AND LOGISTICS
IN PSYCHOANALYSIS

Miltiades L. Zaphiropoulos, M.D.

Money matters are a fertile field for irrationality in our society. In spite of that, and at least from time to time, we manage to make apparently agreed upon arrangements and to participate in transactions on the subject of money. We seem to do so pragmatically, out of necessity, and often by way of stipulation. We do not always do so with equanimity, without resentment or suspiciousness, ambivalence or second thoughts. We may feel righteous or outraged, depending on which side of a bargain we find ourselves. We do not always seek, let alone achieve, consensual validation in the process.

Provisions vary as to the establishment of monetary value for either a product or a service or some other activity or function. There are also differences as to when one pays, for instance before, during or after; what possibilities exist for negotiation; what conditions there may be for refund or credit, based on satisfaction or dissatisfaction, fulfillment or miscarriage of aims; and whether there is room for alternatives to the original understanding or contract. Be there fixed prices or bargaining, specific tender or bartering, individual approaches, attitudes and preferences will account for more or less readily accepted or contested situations.

As a preamble to what may follow in this whimsical and heuristic essay, I wish to bring to the reader's attention two variously pertinent pronouncements. One is from Sigmund Freud: "Money questions will be treated by cultured people in the same manner as sexual matters, with the same inconsistency, prudishness, and hypocrisy". The other is from Ralph Waldo Emerson: "Money which represents the prose of life and which is hardly spoken in parlors without an apology, is, in its effects and laws, as beautiful as roses". Perhaps, some undeniable and unavoidable ambiguity can be gleaned from these statements, and the recognition if not the deeding of it may be taken under advisement.

Psychoanalysis is supposed to be a rational science which takes into account irrational tendencies, that is driven inclinations, subject to elaboration

Money and Mind, Edited by S. Klebanow and
E.L. Lowenkopf, Plenum Press, New York, 1991

leading to fulfillment within socially acceptable limits or constraints. The pleasure principle cannot rule unfettered and the reality principle need prevail in matters of human development, functioning, and entelechy. Where id was, there ego should be, through the mediation of a superego, and the actualization of an ego ideal. Although not alone in its plight, psychoanalysis has had to contend with its deterministic propositions parallel to the problem of the denial or development of a free will. In the matter of values in general psychoanalysis has created its own value laden dilemma. It has done so whenever it has actually tended or was interpreted as tending to the perpetuation of a dichotomy between the individual and the societal, essentially though not exclusively leading to discrepant and disjunctive states of affairs. It has left unresolved or undecided the differences between reasoning and rationalization, reconciliation and resignation, acceptance and submission. It has not been altogether successful in promoting structure as a substratum of action, definitive interpretation as a substitute for continuing inquiry. It has also perpetuated the paradox of its theory or theories being at odds with, if not threatened by their application to and attendant challenge by the therapeutic endeavor and experience.

Psychoanalysis as a healing practicing profession, from its inception and beginning with Freud, has recognized and affirmed the use of a medical model for services as rendered by a specially trained physician to a patient suffering from a particular disease or disorder. It also proceeded with an innovation clearly stated by Freud (1913): "A certain hour of my available working day is appointed to each patient; it is his, and he is liable for it, even if he does not make use of it". As Tulipan (1986) has commented: "He (Freud) cited a threat to the therapist's livelihood if this were not so. In emphasizing the needs of the therapist, Freud courageously advertised that the physician is not only a selfless minister, whose altruism supersedes other more mundane considerations". The reference to the "available working day" suggests the limitation of a particular situation where the rest of the time would be devoted to some other pursuit, probably writing and reading, a practice still applying to some psychoanalysts, though not the majority of practitioners. The Freudian innovation may have constituted a departure from his day's medical practice in terms of the period of time a patient was given each session, and, probably, the absence of free service to a hospital, clinic or the like. In some contrast, Tulipan also refers to Frieda Fromm-Reichmann (1950) who, about one half century later, questioned the therapist's privilege to be exempt from the general cultural standard of being paid only for services actually rendered and mused that a productive personality could make use of time set free through a patient's failure to keep an appointment. The frame of reference regarding making a living essentially through private individual practice was not hers. Be that as it may, altruism and productivity can be related by are not equatable concepts. Also, they are hardly debatable in the abstract.

The dictum "Time is money" may not have been invented by a psychoanalyst but it is evident that it applies rather pointedly and poignantly to our profession. This matter of logistics, presumably based on the reality principle, has been extended to the realm of logic; it has been further enhanced by the argument that once made a part of the contract between analyst and patient it constitutes an incontrovertible acceptance by all concerned. Yet, as realistically and pragmatically, a number of questions may arise. Can it be unequivocally stated that a patient's dependency on an analyst, not only of a conflictual nature but as a therapeutic need, may be logically equated with the analyst's dependence on the patient for the needs of his livelihood? If there are questions in the patient's mind as to the validity or equitability of some aspects of the contract to be entered, are these likely to be brought up or argued at a time when more critical concerns are at stake, with only budding inquiry and virtually no interpretation? Could such questions represent fairly common or usual attitudes or habits, not necessarily characterological or neurotic, in the particular patient's life experience, not challenged by or troublesome to the patient's dealings with the rest of the world, yet put to test and sooner or later thought of as resistances in the domain of psychoanalysis? Need we deem any such doubts in the patient's mind to be essentially, if not exclusively, manifestations of the pleasure principle, duly and eminently analyzable?

No precise, definitive, let alone universal answers can be provided to the above questions. Their value as questions may be of significance whenever they are not kept in mind or when we take for granted our assumptions about freely entered contracts or uniformly explicable adherence to or deviation from their explicit fulfillment. Such questions become of particular interest, and, unfortunately, lead to confusion or conflict at a time when the appropriateness of the medical model for psychoanalysis is questioned, and the medical model of rendering services is criticized. If and when psychoanalysis is not an essentially meliorative enterprise but a therapeutic endeavor dealing with identifiable "disease" or "disorder", it is likely to run into the same quandary as medical care in general does: Is it a right or a privilege? Is it a necessity or an option? Traditionally, the needs of a sufferer, the patient, place such person at a disadvantage; is this to be denied and dismissed, and, if not, does it lend a special hue to any contractual arrangements made in the light of it, or does it accrue to a presumably specious argument?

To the extent that psychoanalytic policies and practices regarding time and money arrangements tend to differ from any other such provisions generally prevailing and followed by prospective patients, we need to keep in mind the degree of persuasion required for the adoption and acceptance of those arrangements by the patient or the person responsible for their fulfillment. That much of a concern with reality must be considered parallel to the awareness of our own realistic needs and to our responsibility for conveying them to those with whom we make a contract. More likely than not, we are toeing a fine line between reality aspects and actual or potential transferential or countertransferential developments.

It would seem that developmental notions within the libido theory, leading to the equation of feces and money with character or neurotic implications, tended to further logicize psychoanalytic policies regarding fees. Hence the belief that no fee or even relatively low or lowered fee would increase the patient's resistances, a notion as much adhered to as questioned in our day. Subsequent theoretical modifications introduced additional interpretations. Instinctual sources of interest in money were supplemented or complemented by social or cultural factors and their significance in stressing the import of money in human transactions. Narcissistic preoccupations, power motives, vicissitudes of identification, authenticity and autonomy have augmented or broadened the sphere in which money matters are considered. Can any of these explain the continuum of interest and irrationality regarding money or reduce it to transferential dimensions and make it the main focus in psychoanalysis as therapy?

Practically speaking, there is merit to making fees and all permutations pertaining to them an integral part of a "frame" within which psychoanalysis is conducted and transferential developments are expected to occur. Langs (1975) has written at length and painstakingly about necessary or unnecessary modifications within the frame. Levenson (1988) has stated pithily: "Paying fees and coming on time does not a patient make. It takes a great deal of mobilization to change the novitiate into a patient, and that mobilization comes from the inquiry". That inquiry applies to vagaries about fees as well as to all matters brought up during an analysis goes without saying. This is different from making out of heeding or deviation a matter of correct and universally valid interpretation. There has been more confusion than clarity, more rationalization than reasoning regarding rigidity or flexibility about fee policies. Suffice it to say that a conflict of interests is likely to arise where financial arrangements are or may become arbitrary, warrantedly so in the view of the therapist but unwarrantedly so in the patient's mind. This may be so either in the setting of a fee or in any modification of it. Rigid adherence to the frame makes it easy for the analyst not to have to gauge what is rational and what is irrational in any deviation by the patient from the prescriptions or conditions of such frame. Flexibility within the frame opens up questions of evaluation or even judgment as to what constitutes valid reasons for deviating, presumably subject to inquiry and possibly leading to consensus between analyst and patient. It is not always clear whether such flexibility will tend to weaken the frame's potential for the occurrence and manifestations of transference in the analysis. Flexibility per se and by definition entails multiple possibilities within the established frame and lends itself to developments both transferential and countertransferential. Paradoxically, adherents to the assumption that flexibility cannot foster transference tend to speak of transference resistances ensuing in the psychoanalytic situation, essentially if not exclusively attributing them to the analyst's countertransference. The disciples of the absolute have always been a source of discomfort and puzzlement to those of the relative and, at times, perhaps vice-versa.

Szasz (1965) has advocated that if psychoanalysis may be viewed as the least coercive of psychiatric or psychological enterprises, it should be both desirable and feasible to obtain and retain an understanding and agreement between analyst and analysand. In such agreement, the obligation of the analyst is to analyze and, in return, the analyst's only expectation is to be financially remunerated. There is a remarkable neatness to this proposition. It leaves somewhat undefined the meaning of analysis at any given time considering ups and downs within it, from hour to hour or even within a particular hour, for which the remuneration remains the same. It is reasonable enough to surmise that the reference is to the adherence to the process in general, which would warrant the agreement. It would certainly be naive and unrealistic to believe that each analytic hour should accrue to the optimal psychoanalytic effect, uniformly and unfailingly. It is not necessarily reasonable to deem altogether unreasonable and exclusively transferential any combination of feeling and thinking that may emerge on the patient's part in reference to the strict adherence to the basic agreement. This is particularly true of instances when there appears to be little or not enough to analyze or when the analyzable fails to be picked up by the analyst for reasons pertaining to the analyst rather than to the patient. Should any of the foregoing seem to be far-fetched or precious, the point being made refers to an occasionally exclusive tendency to logicize the analyst's reality while illogicizing the patient's.

However, the most important question is whether in psychoanalysis there are additional implicit or explicit expectations. It has been variously stated or assumed that where the patient is required to show a certain degree of psychological mindedness, the analyst should possess and demonstrate an ability for empathy. Although empathy has been defined in different ways, basically it refers to an ability to either experience or to be aware of how a patient experiences feelings and their impact. As a process, and in terms of attitudes or actions to which it may contribute, empathy needs to be both respected for what it is and to be given the further respect of seeking some validation of its existence and of its repercussions. Empathy can prove to be rewarding to both patient and analyst. It would be fallacious to conclude that its rewards should preclude any financial claims on the part of the analyst. It would be just as unsound on the part of the patient to claim that no empathy exists if the analyst questions some misconceptions as to the proof of its presence specifically related to the matter of charging a fee. Part of the empathic process may extend to the consideration of conflictual feelings and attendant attitudes that a patient may display in money matters, both within and outside the psychoanalytic situation. As with everything else, the psychoanalyst's empathy need not result in curtailing inquiry, let alone in indiscriminate approval of or capitulation to what the patient does with feelings. Rather, there ought to be some judicious demonstration and use of empathy, with due attention neither to make empathy inoperative by taking recourse to a rigidly constructed frame, nor to foster collusion with the patient's distorting tendencies. Receiving information and pursuing inquiry on a continual basis is different from giving presumably definitive interpretations resulting in premature closure or requiring backtracking and unending repetitiousness. The laborious process of psychoanalysis can do with less belaboring of points or insisting on more compliance instead of consistency.

There is hardly any empathy in the proposition that expenditures for analysis should constitute hardship in order for the process to work. The very idea of it may prove nonviable in instances where usual, reasonable and customary fees are charged to individuals whose financial situation places them beyond the experiencing of such hardship. Thus, a double standard may be in the offing and serious doubts as to the validity of the proposition and its logic or actual merit may be raised. Experience with patients from different socioeconomic levels or those seen in low cost psychoanalytic services, usually connected with training institutes and offering supervision, suggests that the analytic process can be carried out without the once much vaunted notion of necessary financial deprivation (Chodoff, 1972; Goldensohn and Haar, 1974). Specific transferential problems in such situations can be dealt with effectively, and resistances pertaining to them prove analyzable, the outcome often depending on the analyst's theoretical point of view or set of values as these may bear on the process.

Burnside (1986) has reported on studies comparing fee practices of male and female therapists. These have raised disparate questions that range from women's self-esteem to women therapists' economic needs to women patients' lower economic power to women's greater empathic ability in the role of caretaker or healer. There seem to be no data available suggesting any better or worse psychoanalytic aptitude or effectiveness in comparing men and women, related to ascertainable differences in fee policies or practices. Something similar seems to be queried regarding different fees charged by analysts belonging to various professional disciplines and their effect on therapy, namely, does the lower fee charging by such persons affect the analysis even if the analytic training has been the same.

Finally, I would like to touch upon a few points that may be extraneous yet related mainly because they deal with the spirit of our time. Psychoanalysis, at various stages in its development, has been sought by sufferers from neurosis, presumably of the transference variety, and, subsequently, from pathogenic character traits or personality disorders, giving it its legitimate therapeutic claims. Psychoanalysis has also been sought by those who wished for optimal personal growth and for freedom to choose how to best use their assets, productivity and creativity, an essentially meliorative undertaking, occasionally and pejoratively attributed to the worried well. Psychoanalysis has also been thought of as a more or less Western civilization enterprise, usually appealing and available to an upper middle class or an upward mobile segment of the population. It required several sessions a week, first for several months, then for several years. The fiscal policies it developed reflected both the goals of those who came to it and their ability and willingness to pay for it, parallel to the needs of its practitioners. For a long time, psychoanalysis has been an essentially private enterprise in the best sense of the word. Both in terms of vogue or acceptance and in response to prevailing economic conditions, it has flourished or withered, lain fallow or been revived. Peter Gay (1988) cites a letter from Ferenczi to Freud, dated January 20, 1924, poignantly and pithily stating: "People have no money to be sick." Times are changing and, presumably, we should be changing with them. Some changes are welcome and others are unwelcome: Reed and Evans (1987) have deplored the deprofessionalization of medicine, identified the roots of the loss of professional autonomy, called for the reaffirmation of the components of professionalism and its desirability for society. Psychoanalysis has escaped the reverberations of the "new medical-industrial complex" or the "proletarianization of physicians". Elitism is becoming obsolete, at least insofar as to whose claims to it are acceptable or workable. Keeping up with the times, psychoanalysts' basic needs have grown in the direction of the better – more expensive? – things in life. Patients' needs – or wishes – have moved in the direction of rights and challenges. Third parties have come into the picture, ostensibly offering the possibilities for affordable psychotherapy, or even psychoanalysis. Actually, they have dictated limitations to such services and, in the process, have challenged the sacred cows of financial policies and arrangements that had earlier been conceived as reasonable and subsequently maintained as such. Preserving standards we value, be it in services to be rendered or in payment therefore, potentially leads us to ethical impasses or, if we can afford it, moves us into making choices not necessarily compatible with all of our wishes and beliefs. Patients themselves have lost interest in time-consuming and painstaking methods, particularly if they are interfered with by fiscal dicta or constraints. Our logic and logistics, if they ever were halfway plausible, have lost their credibility or no longer generate excitement but only exasperation and mistrust.

   As for ourselves, shall we bow to the limitations that seem to be imposed on us and possibly collude with any demands for misrepresenting reasons for services, ways in which they are rendered, vicissitudes in continuity or efficiency, in order to get paid? Shall we treat only the rich, and will they be willing to value our services and use them accordingly? Shall we extend ourselves to the poor, again if we can afford it, and find out if what we have to offer will be useful in spite of what we thought was unworkable? Shall we manage a judicious mix of the two, and will this not require a modification of some of our views and values? ·

   Perhaps, we must be left to contemplate that on any subject that lends itself to irrationality we can only make personal choices and assume responsibility for them, and extend the same right to others. Otherwise, we can make logical statements about irrationality but cannot necessarily change the nature of it, or explain it or wish it away.

REFERENCES

Burnside, M. A., (1986), Fee practices of male and female therapists, In: The Last Taboo, D. W. Krueger, Ed. Brunner/Mazel, New York, pp. 48-54.

Chodoff, P., (1972), The effect of third-party payment of the practice of psychotherapy, Am. J. Psychiatry, 129:540-545.

Freud, S., (1913), On beginning the treatment (Further recommendations on the technique of psychoanalysis I). In: Standard Edition, Vol. XII, p. 126, London, Hogarth Press, 1962.

Fromm-Reichmann, F., (1950), Principles of intensive psychotherapy, University of Chicago Press, 1950.

Gay, P., (1988), Freud - A Life For Our Time, p. 387, fn. W. W. Norton & Company, Inc., New York, 1988.

Goldensohn, S. S. and Haar, E., (1974), Transference and countertransference in a third-party payment system (HMO). Am. J. Psychiatry, 131:256-260.

Langs, R., (1975), The therapeutic relationship and deviations in technique. I Technique in Transition, Ch. 7, pp. 189-230, Jason Aronson, Inc. 1978.

Levenson, E. A., (1988), The pursuit of the particular. Contemporary Psychoanalysis, 24:1-16.

Reed, R. R. and Evans, D., (1987), The Deprofessionalization of Medicine, JAMA, 258:3279-3282.

Szasz, T. S., (1965), The Ethics of Psychoanalysis, Delta, Dell Publishing Co., Inc. 1969.

Tulipan, A. B., (1986), Fee policy as an extension of the therapist's style and orientation. In: The Last Taboo, D.W. Krueger, Ed. Brunner/Mazel, New York, pp. 79-87, 1986.

CHAPTER 23

THE FISCAL BLINDSPOT IN THERAPY

Josef Weissberg, M.D.

Irrationality and inconsistency in dealing with money represent an almost ubiquitous neurosis in our society. Conflicts of all sorts are reflected in the way in which money is handled. In contrast to other areas, however, money conflicts have been only cursorily examined. Implicit rules limiting the discussion of money led David Krueger(1986) to refer to financial secrets as "The Last Taboo". It seems likely that the money neuroses of therapists themselves result in inadequate attention to money matters in treatments they conduct. We must be alert to avoid perpetuating the fiscal blindspot as we train succeeding generations of therapists.

Freud's insights are not belittled by saying he did not utter the last word on the psychodynamic significance of money, particularly its meaning in the therapeutic relationship. Freud(1908) painstakingly and heuristically used dreams and associations to establish an unconscious link between money and feces and between certain money behavior patterns such as miserliness and parsimony on the one hand and anal libidinal fixation on the other. In recent years, psychoanalytic orientation has to a large extent shifted from a concentration on drive identification and discharge to interest in the overlapping areas of adaptation, defensive maneuvers, and interpersonal transactions, particularly as illustrated in the therapeutic relationship.

While Freud was content to dispose of the non-libidinal aspect of money by defending the analyst's right to charge a fee for his services, it has remained for post-Freudian literary critics like Steven Marcus(1974) and Jane Gallop(1985) to focus on some of these aspects of money in the therapeutic relationship in dynamic psychotherapy. Gallop has reexamined the case of Dora, particularly her termination which, as Freud(1905) learned, she had planned for two weeks before notifying him. Freud inferred she was identifying with a maidservant or governess in giving two weeks' notice. Gallop, however, believes that the master, Dora, was discharging the servant, Freud. The interpretation is consistent with the analyst's economic dependence on his patient. Gallop, along with others claims financial

Money and Mind, Edited by S. Klebanow and
E.L. Lowenkopf, Plenum Press, New York, 1991

dependence is a central feature of the therapeutic relationship, one to which insufficient attention has been paid.

During the past two years, interest in the role of money in the therapeutic process has grown, perhaps in response to significant changes, both actual and projected, in the economics of all helping professions, including psychotherapy. Attention has been focused on the striking fact that, although most patients are able to discuss freely in therapy all details of their sexual and fantasy life, many become distrustful and uncomfortable when asked for details of their financial position. It is easier for them to discuss feces than to talk about the symbol. This inhibition may represent suspicion that such information will be used exploitatively, but seems to go beyond.

Outside of the therapeutic relationship, money data is often treated as taboo even when disclosure is profitable. Even when openness would clearly be beneficial, as when colleagues are preparing to negotiate their compensation, even in such situations disclosure is frequently avoided as representing bad taste or as being connected with poorly defined discomfort. In our money oriented society, where an entire section of the daily newspaper is devoted to finance and where much casual conversation centers on what things cost, disclosure of assets is made only by elected officials or candidates on coercion, and then is accompanied by a great deal of apology if the bottom line is too high, and sanctimony if not. Exploration of money attitudes represents, if not a royal road to the unconscious, at least a serviceable route to conflicts and adaptations that otherwise might remain hidden and untouched by therapy.

Until very recently, psychotherapy training reflected the fiscal blindspot as well as all money discussions between supervisor and therapist, and between therapist and patient which were kept minimal. Attempts by patients to reopen fee negotiations were often treated as resistance and discouraged. Missed hours were frequently a source of intense discomfort to both therapist and patient and were routinely dealt with by formula. Trainees were able to refer their patients to a non-clinical registrar who would set or modify the fee. Therapists brought up with an institutionalized avoidance of money matters had a predictably difficult time dealing with the financial aspect of their new practices and the fiscal blindspot was perpetuated through generations of therapists.

The main financial negotiations between therapist and patient are setting a fee, modifying the fee to reflect changing conditions, collecting the fee, and dealing with missed hours. The first determination one must make is whether these issues will be handled uniformly or flexibly. Thus a therapist may set a fee for his time which will be applied to all patients regardless of their resources, or may set broad limits within which he will respond to an individual's income and obligations. Fee increases may be made across the board, or applied only to those who can easily afford them, or avoided altogether so that long term patients pay a substantially lower fee than new patients, whether or not they are able to support an increase to a full fee. Some therapists do not submit bills but rather have the patient take responsibility for calculating what he owes. Some insist upon payment in seven days, others make credit arrangements, while still others permit debt to pile up without acknowledging it.

Missed hours provide both discomfort and opportunity for rationalization. Some therapists convince themselves, even their patients, that it is necessary to bill for all missed hours in order to maintain mature responsibility, which is essential for a good therapeutic result. Some set a time limit for cancellation to permit filling the hour. Others state they will bill unless they fill the hour, regardless of the time of prior notification. Still others excuse missed hours for "good" reasons, such as illness.

The argument for universal arbitrary rules is that patients inevitably regard insistence on prompt payment, fee raises, and bills for missed hours as punitive. While it may be necessary to take these actions, the therapist must avoid placing himself in a judgmental position, for the judgmental posture augments the punitive aspect of taking the action or the guilt should the action be avoided. The argument against such a rigorous position is, of course, that it gives the therapist no latitude and, more important, it often permits mutual avoidance of discussions of the issues.

The following clinical vignettes are taken from cases in which I have supervised the therapy.

CASE I

A 63-year-old widow with a prolonged grief reaction following her husband's death, was seen in consultation and accepted into therapy. The therapist, influenced perhaps by her presentation of extensive deprivation, set a fee significantly below his usual. After a few sessions, she casually mentioned her collection of impressionist paintings and indicated in various ways that she was quite wealthy. A discussion of her guilt at manipulatively deceiving the therapist was useful to her in terms of defining her fear that she had no value other than the assets her husband had left her, and to the therapist in terms of clarifying the distortion that fueled his rescue fantasies.

This situation could have been handled in a number of ways. (a) The therapist may have chosen to be silent and to stay with her fee setting discussions, contenting himself with periodic fee raises until he reached an appropriate figure consistent with his patient's newly revealed circumstances. Or (b) the therapist might immediately raise the fee to the level appropriate to his updated information. This may be inferred as indicating that the patient was being penalized for her candor by being "fined" a fee increment. A third possibility (c) would be to acknowledge the new information but take no action in terms of adjusting the fee. A fourth more prophylactic course (d) would be to have a set fee rather than a range, which would make the new information irrelevant to the issue of fee adjustment.

Each of these approaches is valid (with the possible exception of (c), which seems to pose some internal inconsistency) and the choice will depend largely on the therapist's personality and money attitudes. The therapist will choose one with which he is comfortable. One hopes that, as he gains experience and understanding of his own conflicts, the therapist will also consider which approaches to billing problems provide most direct access to his patient's core conflicts as they are reflected in the handling of money.

Approach (a) carries the message, "You and I are both aware that you have given me invalid information for fee setting. However, a deal is a deal and I will not greedily punish you by renegotiating your fee. You might assume that I feel cheated but there is nothing you can do about it. This material is too uncomfortable for me to discuss. I might possibly get so angry that my usefulness to you will be impaired".

Approach (d) avoids the whole issue of fee setting and trusting or distrustful disclosure of assets, and may be chosen because of the comfort with which it can be applied. At the same time, the method deprives potential patients with limited funds of therapy. Also, it may waste a valuable early opportunity to enter a patient's core conflicts of trust vs. mistrust, dependence vs. autonomy, and powerlessness vs. omnipotence, as reflected in his handling of money.

Although approach (b) involves admission of error and opens the therapist to criticism of being too interested in money, this would appear to be the route which guarantees his integrity and best protects him from countertransference distortion. The therapist in effect states, "You realize that I have a scale of fees depending on patients' resources. Today I have a different perception of your ability to pay than last time we met. This might be because of a misunderstanding or, possibly, your desire to deceive me. I will adjust your fee on the basis of the latest information. I am interested in our examining fully the way the transaction between us has taken place".

Thus the therapist avoids turning the issue of money into an off-limits area, but rather encourages his patient to respond. This approach has the advantage of being the most heuristic; the patient immediately receives the message that transactions within the therapeutic situation are of great interest and will be handled as openly as possible, that the therapist is willing to consider the patient's possible deviousness without anger, and that he is willing to open himself to charges of greed and inconsistency.

In supervising inexperienced therapists, similar situations have arisen frequently. When approach (a) or (c) has been chosen, there have often been what I assume to represent resultant countertransferential events such as time misunderstandings or episodes of boredom, which appeared directly related to the experience of being "cheated" by the patient.

CASE II

A 40-year-old divorced professional gambler entered psychotherapy because of hypochondriacal preoccupation. Since he had no checking account, he stated he would have to pay his bill in cash. He assumed the therapist would not declare his fee on tax forms and suggested semi-seriously that his fee be lowered in consideration of this bounty. The therapist insisted that payment be made with bank checks. The patient's initial grumbling changed dramatically when a dream at three months featured a wise and trusted teacher. The therapy proceeded uneventfully.

This patient proposed a conspiracy. He may have felt he needed to provide extra ingratiation, a special gratuity, in order to secure the therapist's affection and attention. Variations on this theme include businessmen and brokers who offer investment advice, entertainers who offer hard to get tickets, and patients whose circumstances preclude their claiming fees as tax deductions and offer to pay in cash. Clearly, in all these instances, the therapist's integrity is at issue. Ultimately, there is no reason for the patient to trust a therapist who demonstrates his laxity concerning such issues as the use of insider information and his own tax responsibilities. The classical dictum that a therapist should accept no gratification in the therapeutic situation other than his fee applies here. In the situation described, since the patient did not have a checking account, there was no effective way of convincing him that the fee was being declared as income. Insisting on bank checks or providing receipts were really useless, as it was clear the patient was not about to call attention to himself by claiming any unusual deductions. The man's attitude toward money was marked by extreme ambivalence; his wealth constituted his only asset from his point of view while at the same time large amounts of money meant nothing to him. He demonstrated the common finding of combining extreme generosity with an acute sensitivity to exploitation, frequently testing to convince himself he was not being taken advantage of. Clearly, falling into any of the snares laid by this man might have interfered seriously with the therapy. The only way to work with him seemed to be to treat all financial dealings utterly scrupulously and to assume that the transference was often if not always expressed fiscally. Fortunately, for the treatment if not for this investigation, he gave up his bookmaking operation within several months, entered a legitimate business, and began paying his bills with personal checks. The same dynamics continued to manifest themselves of course, but less graphically and in more familiar ways.

The financial arrangement between therapist and patient is essentially a business agreement, in that the therapist is selling his training and time, thereby supporting himself. Although there are of course dynamic ramifications of every business action in the therapy, the prime motivation remains a business one. The therapist owes it to his patient to recognize, accept, and acknowledge this central fact. Claims that the fee is somehow beneficial to the patient in terms of motivating him, appear to represent attempts to avoid the business realities of the therapeutic situation and encourage perpetuation of the fiscal blindspot. While no systematic studies have been conducted to support or disprove the essential therapeutic benefit of the fee, enough therapies have been successfully conducted while paid for by third parties to cast a great deal of doubt on this allegation. Whatever method the therapist uses, he will probably find it impossible to be fair to both his patient and himself. It is essential that he approach financial dealings openly and willingly, even eagerly.

We must deal with the meanings that money and the reluctance to talk about money take on in the therapeutic relationship, both in the minds of the patient and of the therapist. The power and nurturing aspects of money have a profound effect in determining not only money behavior but the nature of the therapeutic relationship itself. Conversely, as is more widely acknowledged, money behavior reflects conflicts in other areas. Rather than develop a formula approach with patients, it is our obligation to concentrate on examining the merits and meanings of alternate ways of handling fiscal issues, for the greatest heuristic effect and therapeutic value.

REFERENCES

Freud, S., (1905), Fragment of an analysis of a case of hysteria. Standard Edition. Volume VII, pp. 3-122. Hogarth Press, London, 1957.

Freud, S., (1908), Character and anal erotism. Standard Edition. Volume IX, pp. 167-176. Hogarth Press, London, 1957.

Gallop, J., (1985), Keys to Dora. Dora's Case: Freud - Hysteria - Feminism. Bernhiemer, C. and Kahane, C. Editors.Columbia University Press, New York.

Krueger, D., (1986), The Last Taboo-Money as Symbol & Reality in Psychotherapy & Psychoanalysis. Brunner/Mazel, New York.

Marcus, S., (1974), Freud on Dora: story, history, case history. Partisan Review 61:12-23, 89-108. Also in Marcus, S., Freud and the Culture of Psychoanalysis, pp. 42-86. Allen Unwin, Worchester, MA, 1984.

CHAPTER 24

EFFECTS OF THE NEW ECONOMIC CLIMATE ON
PSYCHOTHERAPEUTIC PRACTICE

Paul Chodoff, M.D.

Few would deny that these are not the best of times for
psychoanalysis and medical psychotherapy generally. There is more than one
reason for a decline, or at least a hesitation, in the practice of psychotherapy
by psychiatrists. Certainly the advance of biological methods of treatment
into territories heretofore considered the domain of psychotherapy is a
significant factor. It seems incontrovertible that the changing economics of
medicine and psychiatry are also exacting their toll. In the twentieth century
and especially in recent years, these changes have proceeded so rapidly that
they have had a revolutionary impact on the way medical services are paid
for in this country. In no other specialty has the effect been more profound
than it has been on psychotherapeutic psychiatry, particularly the long-term
intensive variety.

Freud, the originator of psychotherapy as we know it, practiced in a
mode that can be described as individual, entrepreneurial, and unregulated
by outside agencies. Fees were for services rendered and came from the
pocket of the patient or a family member. These conditions appear to have
been very suitable for the development of the new discipline of psychoanalysis
and, subsequently, for its numerous derivatives. Questions about what may
be called the "medicality" of some patients being treated by psychotherapeutic
means did not require resolution or even very much discussion. There was
no requirement to make medical diagnoses, to define medical necessity, to
establish criteria for "cure" or an end point of treatment, or to differentiate
between the qualifications of physicians and other purveyors of psychotherapy.
As long as fees were for service rendered in an ethical and legal manner and

This chapter originally appeared in The American Journal of Psychiatry
144:1293-1297, October 1987.   copyright 1987 American Psychiatric
Association. Reprinted by permission.

came from the pockets of patients, these issues were a matter of agreement between doctor and patient and involved no one else. This kind of individualistic therapeutic relationship continued for several decades after psychotherapy by psychiatrists took hold in the United States, but it has been altered irrevocably by the different conditions under which psychotherapeutic psychiatry now operates.

The first and most important new economic factor has been the widespread introduction of a fiscal third party bearing considerable responsibility for the fee heretofore paid entirely by the patient to the psychiatrist(1). A second, rapidly expanding economic factor is a process that has been called the "industrialization" of psychiatry(2), which is itself the consequence of efforts to curtail the costs of medical care, including psychiatric care. These new forces have subjected psychotherapeutic psychiatry to a grave test of its ability to maintain both viability and integrity.

The record of medical insurance companies in providing third-party payment for psychotherapeutic services can be described as spotty at best. A cautionary example of how reliance on such coverage affected one psychiatric community is afforded by the history of the Federal Employees Health Benefits Program (FEHBP) from 1967 to the present. During its years of full operation, federal employees who chose coverage by Blue Cross and Blue Shield – the largest writer of policies – had the benefit of reimbursement of 80% of a designated fee for each psychotherapy visit within a total lifetime expenditure of $50,000. Under these provisions, psychotherapy of lesser or greater intensity, up to and including psychoanalysis, could be prescribed in accordance with the needs of the patient, with relative freedom from financial constraints. Psychotherapeutic practice flourished. In the late 1970s, the number of psychiatrists per capita in the Washington metropolitan area was second only to that of New York. Psychiatrists who contemplated a career emphasizing psychotherapy or psychoanalysis could be reassured about their economic future; although they were not likely to get rich, they could expect the security of making a satisfactory living by treating patients whose insurance benefits enabled them to afford these services. But storm clouds gathered. After beating off attempts at limitation for some time, Washington psychiatrists were faced with a drastic cutback of outpatient psychiatric benefits, notably for psychotherapy. Since 1984, the Blue Cross and Blue Shield high-option plan, which has the best coverage, has limited mental health benefits to 70% of fees for a maximum of 50 outpatient visits per year.

The effects on practice have been dramatic. Unless they are

personally wealthy, patients obviously have found it more difficult to pay fees out of their own pockets for three to five sessions per week than for sessions only once or twice a week. In effect, there has been a return to preinsurance days, when only the affluent could afford intensive psychotherapy or psychoanalysis. However, even here there is a difference, since middle-class patients, now accustomed to paying medical – including psychiatric – bills with insurance help, are unwilling to adjust to almost full out-of-pocket payment. A survey(3) showed that after the cutback, psychiatrists' hours for psychoanalytic practice decreased by 22%, while the number of patients in psychoanalysis whose treatment was paid for by insurance decreased by 31%, and there was a 38% fall in the number of hours of psychoanalytic practice supported by insurance. In the practices of members of the Washington Psychiatric Society, there was a 7% decrease in the number of patients, there were more open hours than before, and the average fee for psychotherapy was lower. In addition to the negative effect on practice, the curtailment of benefits, with its adverse effects on the economic outlook for psychotherapeutic practice, could be expected to be a deterring factor in the career choices of young psychiatrists. Also, the ambience in which psychotherapy is practiced has become clouded by these uncertain economic prospects and by the amount of time and attention required to deal with them.

Why did the medical insurance companies decrease their coverage for psychotherapy? Spokesmen for these companies deny that the cutback is primarily their responsibility. They maintain that they are trying only to sell contracts to corporations and unions whose memberships clearly seem to prefer "dental" over "mental" benefits. Although there is some truth to this contention, it also appears that most health insurance companies offer coverage of psychotherapy reluctantly and unenthusiastically. However, it has been demonstrated that outpatient psychotherapy takes up only a small percentage of the insurance dollar. Furthermore, there is evidence that a large segment of these psychotherapy costs is compensated for by what has been called the offset effect(4) – a considerable diminution in the utilization, and thus in the cost, of other medical services by the judicious and appropriate use of psychotherapy.

I believe that more covert but very important influences are at work behind the apparently decisive dollars-and-cents judgments advanced by the health insurance industry. These influences constitute what may be called the medical model problem: the extent to which the psychotherapeutic encounter can be considered a medical relationship between a physician and a sick person and thus to fall within the purview of insurance companies that provide protection against medical illness. In its various ramifications, partly including and overlapping the related question of the professional background required to do psychotherapy, the questionable "medicality" of psychotherapy confronts insurance company executives with considerable difficulty in securing the kind of information that they need to assay the risks and project the costs of such benefits-thus their unenthusiastic attitude about covering psychotherapeutic services.

The medical or illness model is an abstract concept, but like a pebble thrown into a pond, it has a ripple effect with far-reaching consequences for the economics of psychotherapeutic practice by psychiatrists. Third-part reimbursement depends on a finding of medical necessity: evidence that the patient is suffering from a diagnosed disorder and that the treatment is appropriate. Under a broad definition of the medical model(5), many-probably most-patients seen in psychotherapy can be given appropriate DSM-III diagnoses. Some patients, however, although they manifest subjective distress and maladaptive behavior justifying psychotherapeutic intervention, do not fall within the purview of an illness model unless, by being equated with the existence of any degree of psychopathology, this model is so extended as to encompass the entire human condition. Yet for patients to be reimbursed, diagnoses must be found for all cases. For this reason (as well as for the very important need to maintain confidentiality), the diagnostic information transmitted to insurance companies is often bland and uninformative or, to put it bluntly, inaccurate. The psychiatrist must also decide whether to share this diagnostic information with the patient and must deal with the consequences of this decision in the therapeutic relationship.

These problems are exemplified particularly in connection with the treatment of the personality disorders (DSM-III axis II disorders). In my own experience(6) and that of others(7), such patients form the bulk of psychoanalytic practices at least, but, as has been recently pointed out, "insurance coverage problems make a third party a most reluctant partner" in their treatment(8). This reluctance is based on an number of factors, including what may be called epidemiological considerations: the difficulty in defining these disorders in terms of expected prevalence and the presence of definable onset and the end of the illness; moral hazard (the encouragement of the use of a service or treatment because it is insured rather than because an illness exists); lack of consumer demand; difficulties in accountability; and problems with provider credentials.

Nevertheless, whatever the merit of these objections, psychotherapy, often intensive, is the only treatment offering considerable hope of remediation for many of the personality disorders. Will such treatment become, in Alan Stone's words(9), "luxury goods" in the third-party era?

Its effect in bringing to the surface hitherto masked medical model problems is not the only way in which third-party involvement has an impact on psychotherapeutic practice. Will the treatment relationship be seriously compromised when responsibility for payment is shared by someone other than the patient? Many conflicting opinions can be heard on this issue, but a recent data-based study(10,11) came to the conclusion that although the payment of a fee by the recipient of psychotherapy is beneficial, it is not essential. Rather than being encased in a rigid theoretical straitjacket, most practitioners have evolved a flexible attitude toward questions of fee setting, and this has not lessened therapeutic efficacy.

Still another consequence of third-party payment has been its influence on the relationships between psychiatrists and their professional colleagues. With regard to the attitudes of many psychoanalytically inclined psychiatrists toward other physicians, there has been a distinct change from the casual indifference of the era before third-party involvement to much closer collaboration as part of the heralded remedicalization of psychiatry. In addition to the upsurge of interest in biological causes and treatments of psychiatric disorders, this rapprochment also can be seen to have economic roots. It is in the interest of psychotherapeutic physicians for the disorders they treat to be dealt with in a nondiscriminatory fashion, just as other medical illnesses are.

Relationships with other mental health professionals, particularly clinical psychologists, however, have become more ambiguous. Certainly collaborative aspects exist, since both psychotherapeutic physicans and psychologists have an interest in combatting prejudices against inclusion of their services in health insurance contracts, but, in a market sense, the two professions are in competition with each other. Psychiatrists are trying to preserve an entrenched position with regard to third-party coverage, whereas psychologists want their services to be reimbursable just as those of physicians are. There is no doubt that psychologists have made great headway in their endeavor. They are now licensed in 50 states and the District of Columbia. So-called freedom of choice laws mandating nondiscriminatory coverage for their services have been passed in an increasing number of states. But will the psychologists' victory have Pyrrhic aspects? Insurance companies have reacted to this competitive situation with an increase in the ambivalence with which they face the whole question of coverage for psychotherapeutic services.

There may be a tendency for them to take the attitude of a "plague on both your houses" by cutting benefits for psychotherapy, or at least by making no great effort to sell these services to corporations and unions. Ironically, the prize in contention between psychiatrists and psychologists-third-party coverage for psychotherapeutic services-may be diminishing in value as the tide turns away from such benefits.

I turn now to the second of the overlapping forces that influence the economic climate in which psychiatrists practice psychotherapy. In order to reduce the runaway inflation affecting the cost of health care in this country (a rise from 5.3% of the gross national product in 1960 to 10.7% in 1985)(12), economies are being imposed on all aspects of the health care industry. Cost-benefit considerations have become paramount and have resulted in a burgeoning of market-based strategies like health maintenance organizations (HMOs), independent practice associations (IPAs), and preferred provider organizations (PPOs), and of regulatory devices like diagnosis-related groups (DRGs). For-profit corporations are taking over an increasing segment of hospital care. While they are being highly touted in some quarters as offering fiscal salvation, there are critics who see in this "social transformation of American medicine"(13) the danger that American physicians may lose their souls, not to the government store but to big business. Although they are still only premonitory for the cottage craft represented by individual practitioners of psychotherapy, we hear warnings(2) that psychiatry is being transformed into an industry where prospective payment, automation, salaried employment, and central control of clinical activity may become the dominant forms of medical practice. These conditions may force both patients and providers toward various alternative provider organizations to shield themselves from economic uncertainties. An atmosphere in which "cost consciousness may supplant compassion"(2) offers little hope for the chronically mentally ill and for others requiring extended treatment. Although not yet affected, patients requiring intensive psychotherapy would fall into the endangered category, especially in view of the difficulty in producing "credible evidence of psychotherapy being both clinically and cost effective(14). As if documenting this prediction, a recent study found an increase in the percentage of practitioners who work part time in a variety of organized care settings rather than independently(15).

The various schemes that have been promulgated to reduce health care costs by introducing competition and, often, prospective payment for services,while at the same time defending high quality care for patients, already pose a challenge to the economic viability of intensive forms of psychotherapy(16). An example of the trend-setting influence of HMO practices is afforded by a recent proposal in Virginia to cut the psychiatric benefits for Virginia state employees in private insurance plans to the lower level supplied by HMOs.

The introduction of DRGs to control hospitalization costs by introducing prospective payment based on predetermined diagnostic categories has been called "the greatest alteration in the economics of American health care since the introduction of Medicare and Medicaid in 1965"(17). It is clear that the overall effect of DRGs is to cut costs by imposing a kind of rationing of care based on economic rather than quality considerations. While this has not yet had an effect on outpatient psychiatric care, it may be only a question of time until even psychotherapists will have to reckon with DRG requirements in order to receive insurance payment and to avoid being divorced even more from mainstream medicine. To construct a diagnostic package for the psychoanalytic treatment of, say, a patient with a compulsive personality disorder certainly would be a formidable task.

If these cost control mechanisms already pose problems for medical psychotherapists, future possibilities are even more troubling. Of course, it is in the nature of crystal balls to be cloudy, and conditions may turn around, especially if, as may be the case with for-profit hospital corporations, supposed cost-saving benefits prove to be illusory. But, to envision a worst-case scenario, it is not impossible that the health care industry and the various cost-control mechanisms, with their acronyms and all their regulations, could gradually take over the bulk of medical care in this country. Would not individual, entrepreneurial, essentially unregulated practice based on fees for service with or without third-party assistance then become exceptional and finally anachronistic? What will be the fate of such a labor-intensive activity as psychotherapy when, in a capital-intensive era, we may all be working for corporations or be banded together in heavily regulated and cost-conscious groups? At the least, the pressure for cost effectiveness would discourage intensive long-term methods and would encourage shorter, time-limited psychotherapy or behavioral methods. There is a serious question whether the removal of the economic conditions underlying practice as Freud knew it would allow psychoanalysis and intensive psychotherapy to continue in anything like their present form.

Faced with the challenges posed by third-party payment and the rise of corporate and regulated medicine, what responses or adaptations do psychiatrists have available? We may rule out as most unlikely in this country a replacement of our present multifaceted system of health care by some form of national health insurance with generous psychotherapeutic benefits, such as exists in Canada. (In any event, Canadian psychiatrists are now complaining that their fees are being increasingly regulated by the government.) I see three possible positions. The first is to attempt to broaden substantially insurance benefits for medical psychotherapy. This involves convincing the insurance carriers and their clients, the corporations and unions, of the necessity, effectiveness, and cost feasibility of these services. The goal here is nondiscriminatory coverage. It requires marketing strategies and efforts to generate and influence relevant legislation. This position, currently maintained by organized psychiatry and psychoanalysis, would be unlikely to alter the present uneasy and ambivalent relationship with psychologists because of its necessary implication that the psychotherapeutic product dispensed by physicians is different and better than that offered by these other professionals.

A second position is to abandon attempts to include within the limits of the medical model all the conditions treated and methods employed by medical psychotherapists and to supplement this model with a broader disability model defined in terms of suffering and interpersonal dysfunction without regard to whether these elements constitute illness. A by-product would be termination of the adversarial relationship with psychologists. The two professions would then band together in promoting society's recognition and approval of their efforts to broaden third-party coverage to include these admittedly nonmedical forms of personal distress. As a corollary, the last barriers to admission of psychologists to psychoanalytic training and full participation in psychoanalytic societies would be dropped.

The third position is to accept a drastic limitation in third-party coverage for psychotherapy. This position amounts to a return to the era before medical insurance, when such treatment was available only to an affluent segment of the population except to the extent that practitioners of psychoanalysis and intensive psychotherapy, out of altruism and interest in their method, would accept lower incomes. Such a retrenchment would have the advantage of disposing of the ambiguities and incongruities attendant upon the need to conform to third-party standards, but it would be at the cost of excluding many persons from necessary treatment. It would also, I believe, discourage medical students from entering psychotherapeutic practice and would have the indirect effect of lessening the humanistic and leavening effect of the psychotherapeutic point of view on medical education and practice.

I believe strongly that psychotherapy, if viewed in realistic perspective(6), is an indispensable tool in the therapeutic armamentarium of physicians. I also believe that skill in exercising it is a defining characteristic of the well-rounded psychiatrist. But, to preserve the viability of medical psychotherapy as a treatment generally available rather than one reserved for the affluent, the economic storm clouds I have described must be heeded. This is a task requiring not only firm conviction in the rightness of the goal but a willingness to be flexible in its accomplishment.

If one accepts, as I do, that individual psychotherapy-at least of the insight-oriented variety that may require a substantial amount of time to accomplish-is not likely to flourish in a corporate atmosphere, it becomes necessary to preserve the ability of psychotherapeutic psychiatrists to function as independent fee-for-service practitioners. To do this without third-party insurance assistance would mandate a restricted socioeconomic range of patients. Even though the goal of nondiscriminatory coverage may be difficult to attain, reasonable third-party benefits for psychotherapy can substantially broaden the spectrum of patients who may be treated without economic hardship.

It has been a theme of this paper that questions about medicality constitute a major, underlying impediment to insurance company coverage for patients treated with psychotherapy. Therefore, these issues need to be addressed in order to provide a firmer basis for third-party financial support and also a useful distinction between medical psychotherapy and psychotherapy dispensed by nonmedical practitioners. The question to be determined is whether an operational distinction can be made between psychopathology, universal among imperfect humankind, and illness. Although this is probably not possible in an absolute sense, approximations of this distinction can be made. For instance, a patient suffering from a bipolar affective disorder certainly is ill, while an otherwise well-functioning individual with interpersonal problems in the marital or career sphere may be found upon investigation not to satisfy illness criteria, even in the broader use of this term. A consequence of such judgments, of course, would be that a minority of patients in some practices could not properly be designated as suffering from a diagnosable disorder, and their cases would fall under the V codes of DSM-III, thus casting into doubt their insurance coverage. The advantages, however, of even a modest use of V code designations would be to strengthen the legitimacy of claims for coverage for the large majority of patients treated by psychotherapeutic psychiatrists. Making this distinction also would protect the ability of psychiatrists to continue to use psychotherapy as well as medication in the treatment of those severely disturbed chronic patients who need care for indefinite periods at flexible intervals. Patients requiring long-term intensive psychotherapeutic care would have to be scrutinized for conformance with illness criteria. I believe that many of them would qualify. In questionable cases, especially those in which the goal of treatment is not always clear, third-party cooperation might be obtained by restricting coverage to some combination of duration of treatment and number of sessions.

In spite of the problems they pose, efforts to establish reasonable criteria for medicality would, it seems to me, be a worthwhile endeavor for preserving the rightful place of psychotherapy within the armamentarium of treatments offered by psychiatrists.

REFERENCES

1   Chodoff, P, Psychiatry and the fiscal third party. Am. J. Psychiatry, 1978; 135:1141-1147.
2   Bittker, T. E., The industrialization of American psychiatry, Am. J. Psychiatry, 1985; 142-149-154.
3   Sharfstein, S. S., Eist, E., Sack, L., et al: The impact of third-party payment cutbacks on the private practice of psychiatry: three surveys. Hosp. Community Psychiatry, 1984;35:478-481.
4   Schlesinger, H. J., Mumford, E., Glass, G. V., et al: Mental health treatment and medical care utilization in a fee-for-service system: outpatient mental health treatment following the onset of a chronic disease. Am. J. Public Health, 1983; 73:422-429.
5   Parson, T., The Social System. New York, Free Press, 1951
6   Chodoff, P., Assessment of psychotherapy: reflections of a practitioner. Arch Gen. Psychiatry, 1982; 39:1097-1103.
7   Gedo, J. E., A psychoanalyst reports at mid-career. Am. J. Psychiatry, 1979; 136:646-649.
8   Sharfstein, S., Gutheil, T., Stoddard, F.: Money and character disorders: on how to get the recalcitrant third party and the impossible patient to pay your bills, in Character Pathology: Theory and Treatment. Edited by Zales M. New York, Brunner/Mazel, 1983.
9   Stone, A. A., Book review, Kernberg, O.F.: Severe Personality Disorders: Psychotherapeutic Strategies. Am. J. Psychiatry, 1986; 143:243-244.
10   el Guebaly, N., Prosen, H., Bebchuk, W.: On direct patient participation in the cost of their psychiatric care, part I: a review of

the empirical and experimental evidence. Can. J. Psychiatry, 1985; 30:178-183.

11 el Guebaly, N., Prosen, H. Bebchuk, W.: On direct patient participation in the cost of their psychiatric care, part II: access to services, impact on practice and training implications. Can. J. Psychiatry 1985; 30:184-189.

12 Culliton, B. J.: Medicine as business: are doctors entrepreneurs? Science 1986; 233:1032-1033.

13 Starr, P.: The Social Transformation of American Medicine. New York, Basic Books, 1982.

14 Eisen, P.: Efficacy and changing trends in the psychotherapy "industry". Aust NZ J. Psychiatry, 1983; 17:9-16.

15 Fenton, W. S., Leaf, P. J., Moran, N. L., et al: Trends in psychiatric practice, 1965-1980. Am. J. Psychiatry 1984; 141:346-351.

16 Sharfstein S., Beigel, A.: Less is more? Today's economics and its challenge to psychiatry. Am. J. Psychiatry 1984; 141:1403-1408.

17 Dolenc, A. A., Dogherty, C. J.: DRGs' the counterrevolution in financing health care. Hastings Cent. Rep. 1985; 15:19-29.

APPENDIX

CORRESPONDENCE

Paul Chodoff, M.D.

1904 R Street, NW
Washington, D.C. 20009

Lawrence Cuzzi, D.S. W.

Department of Social Work
City Hospital Center at Elmhurst
79-01 Broadway
Elmhurst, New York 11373

Marvin G. Drellich, M.D.

123 East 37th Street
New York, New York 10016

Richard C. Friedman, M.D.

225 Central Park West
New York, New York 10024

Robert E. Gould, M.D.

144 East End Avenue
New York, New York 10028

William J. Grace, Jr.

Merrill Lynch
1850 K Street, NW
Washington, D.C. 20006

Edward M. Hallowell, M.D.

7 Linnaean Street
Cambridge, Massachusetts 02138

Althea J. Horner, Ph.D.

1314 Westwood Boulevard
Los Angeles, California 90024

Leonard I. Jacobson, Ph.D.

Department of Psychology
University of Miami
P.O. Box 248185
Coral Gables, Florida 33124-2070

265

Sheila Klebanow, M.D.

2 Chesterfield Road
Scarsdale, New York 10583

Naomi Leiter, M.D.

275 West 96th Street
New York, New York 10025

Joyce A. Lerner, C.S.W.

150 East 37th Street
New York, New York 10016

Eugene L. Lowenkopf, M.D.

150 East 77th Street
New York, New York 10021

Mario Rendon, M.D.

320 East 54th Street
New York, New York 10022

Arnold Rothstein, M.D.

275 Central Park West
New York, New York 10024

Natalie Shainess, M.D.

140 East 83rd Street
New York, New York 10028

Marianne L. Sussman, J.D.

Marcus, Rippa & Gould
4 Cromwell Place
White Plains, New York 10601

Ann Ruth Turkel, M.D.

350 Central Park West
New York, New York 10025

Silas L. Warner, M.D.

24935 Outlook Drive
Carmel, California 93923

Josef Weissberg, M.D.

103 East 86th Street
New York, New York 10028

Miltiades L. Zaphiropoulos, M.D.

28 Yale Road
Hartsdale, New York 10530

INDEX

Abraham, Karl, 155
Acting out
  by borderline patient, 197–198, 201, 204
  by psychoanalyst, 161
Action, money as, 16, 19–20
Adler, Alfred, 139, 140–142, 144
Adolescence, material incentives during,
  27–29, 34–38
Affective disorders, 20, 91
Affluent. *See* Wealthy persons
Alcohol abuse/alcoholism
  affluence-related, 184
  gambling-related, 88
  poverty-related, 42, 47
Alimony, 81, 82
Altruism, 46, 237
Alzheimer's disease, 116–117
American Academy of Psychoanalysis,
  227
American Psychoanalytic Association,
  227–228
Anal character, 136–137
  Freud as, 130–131
Annulment, 77–78
Antisemitism, Freud and, 125–126, 131
Antisocial personality disorder, 88
Anxiety, money-related, 15, 16, 21–22
Autonomy, 51
  development, 35, 37
  fear of, 70–71
  female, 80
  male, 57
  psychological factors affecting, 53
Balzac, Honoré, 77
Behavioral therapy, 92
Berg, Adrian, 70–71
Bergler, Edmund, 90
Bipolar disorder, 91
Blue Cross/Blue Shield, 254
Boesky, Ivan, 17, 55–56
Boleyn, Anne, 78

Borderline personality organization patient,
  197–205
  acting out by, 197–198, 201, 204
  case example, 198–203, 204–205
  clinical features, 197
  depression of, 197
  fee payment by, 200–203
  gambling by, 205
  substance abuse by, 197–198, 199–200,
    202–203
  treatment, 201–205

Breach of contract, 99, 100
Breuer, Joseph, 127, 128, 155
Brucke, Ernst, 122

Capitalism, 138, 139, 143
Career choice, 54–55
Catholic Church, 77, 145
Character Analysis (Reich), 142, 143
Charcot, Jean Martin, 155
Child abuse, 42
Children
  affluent, 183–184, 194
  attitudes towards money, 70
  disadvantaged, 41, 42–44
  identification with parents, 69
  material incentives, 27–34
  nutritional deficiencies, 41–42
  perception of money, 27–28
  value development, 231
Child support, 82
Colleagues, professional relationships with,
  257–258, 260
Commodities, 139–140
Compensation, for damages, 99–108
  calculation of damages, 100, 103, 105
  general damage compensation, 103–104
  legal doctrines regarding, 101–105
  for personal injury, 99, 100, 101–103,
    105